'Once again, Tony Cotton has p̶ ̶ ̶ ̶ ̶ ̶ ̶ ̶ ̶ ̶ ̶ ̶ ̶ ̶ ̶ ̶ ̶ ̶ging book which will be a great support t̶ ̶ ̶ ̶ ̶ ̶ ̶ ̶ ̶ ̶ ̶ ̶ ̶ ̶ ̶ ̶ ̶ ̶ teaching routes, including School Direct and Teach First. The book gives insight into a range of activities and resources which can be used in class, providing comprehensive links to National Curriculum requirements. It supports these with an in-depth analysis of some of the issues related to the teaching of mathematics, such as subject knowledge and pedagogy. Portfolio tasks and self-audits are provided, which will help to develop and enrich practice. This book is altogether a very practical classroom support which will be an invaluable resource for those seeking to enhance their own practice.'

Keith Brentnall, Senior Lecturer in Primary Mathematics,
Northumbria University, UK

'Our students find *Understanding and Teaching Primary Mathematics* accessible and engaging, helping them to understand the "Big Ideas" in primary mathematics. This new edition provides up-to-date links to the new National Curriculum and the latest research which will keep all our students up to date with primary mathematical developments. The content closely supports both the BA and PGCE Primary Education mathematics courses and is referred to throughout the year. This book will continue to be a key text for all our primary BA and PGCE students.'

Brenda Wood, Senior Lecturer in Primary Mathematics,
University of Greenwich, UK

'This is not only an essential handbook for beginning teachers in the primary phase it is also of tremendous value to secondary maths teachers. Many children struggle to make sense of the fundamental concepts in mathematics and carry confusion through their school years. Tony Cotton demonstrates clearly how teachers can work to (re)construct their learners' understanding. This superb handbook connects the findings of research with specific pedagogic approaches and classroom tasks. It will support teachers as they reflect on their classroom practice with their colleagues and mentors. Anyone who is engaged in devising programmes for initial teacher education and for continuing professional development will appreciate the depth of scholarship underpinning this book.'

Corinne Angier, Senior Lecturer in Mathematics Education, Sheffield Hallam
University, and regional mathematics lead for Teach First, UK

'*Understanding and Teaching Primary Mathematics* provides a valuable resource for both in-service and pre-service teachers. It combines both pedagogy and content knowledge to build fundamental mathematical understandings with practical suggestions on how this knowledge is enacted in the classroom. I will definitely be using it in my undergraduate teaching courses and strongly recommend it to other mathematics teacher educators.'

Tracey Muir, Senior Lecturer in Mathematics Education,
University of Tasmania, Australia

'Confidence in the teaching of primary maths is fundamental to successful pupil outcomes and this book provides access to a rich and varied collection of resources to support the novice and experienced teacher at every turn. It combines underpinning theory with relevant and accessible pedagogical approaches which support the development of learners' deep mathematical understanding.'

Sue O'Brien, Principal Lecturer in Primary and Early Years Mathematics, Sheffield Hallam University, UK

'This book should be a core text for all teacher training pathways. It reflects the need for in-depth subject knowledge, pedagogical excellence and an enthusiasm for mathematics. The range of issues and challenges addressed forms a substantial basis for developing an understanding of the complexities and expectations of the modern primary classroom. The style is clear and concise, and the integration of ICT support reflects a modern learning environment in an effective and engaging manner.'

Nick Tinsdeall, Senior Lecturer in Primary Mathematics, University of Cumbria, UK

'This is a comprehensive journey through the key areas of teaching primary mathematics. The inclusion of fundamental big ideas and teaching points, covering mathematical misconceptions, make this a valuable resource for the beginning teacher or more experienced primary practitioners.'

Richard Holme, Lecturer in Primary Mathematics, University of Dundee, UK

'With ongoing education curriculum reviews and political changes at local and national levels, this new edition of a key textbook is both timely and relevant. Cotton continues to remind us of the importance of the methods shaping the teaching and learning of mathematics from teacher trainees through ongoing professional development for all maths teachers in both domestic and international contexts.'

Richard Race, Senior Lecturer in Education, Roehampton University, UK

'Cotton's narrative throughout the book will support teachers and student teachers to make links between mathematical content knowledge and pedagogy. The book weaves theory, content and pedagogy through examples of real-life teaching experiences. Teachers and student teachers alike will find this book and its companion features an informative and useful resource for professional and personal development.'

Karen Major, Professional Teaching Fellow in Primary Mathematics, University of Auckland, New Zealand

Understanding and Teaching
Primary Mathematics

Written by an education consultant with widespread experience of teaching mathematics in the UK and internationally, *Understanding and Teaching Primary Mathematics* seamlessly combines pedagogy and subject knowledge to build confidence and equip you with all the skills and know-how you need to successfully teach mathematics to children of any age.

This third edition has been fully updated to reflect the latest research developments and initiatives in the field, as well as key changes to both the UK National Curriculum and International Baccalaureate, including a brand new chapter on 'Algebra' and a reworked focus on the early years. Extra features also include helpful call-outs to the book's revised and updated companion website, which offers a shared site with a range of resources relevant to both this book and its new companion volume, *Teaching for Mathematical Understanding.*

Stimulating, accessible and well-illustrated, with comprehensive coverage of subject knowledge and pedagogy, *Understanding and Teaching Primary Mathematics* is an essential purchase for trainee and practising teachers alike.

Companion website features new to this edition include:

- video clips in which primary school teachers demonstrate the concepts covered in the book through teaching to a real class
- PowerPoint presentations which provide support for those using the book as part of a teacher training course
- updated weblinks to external sites with useful teaching information and resources.

Tony Cotton was previously Associate Dean and Head of Education at Leeds Metropolitan University, UK. Since 2012, he has been working as a freelance writer and education consultant. Tony has over 15 years' experience teaching maths education and 10 years' experience teaching mathematics in schools.

Routledge
Companion Websites

Enhancing online learning
and teaching.

www.routledge.com/cw/cotton

Understanding and Teaching
Primary Mathematics

THIRD EDITION

Tony Cotton

Routledge
Taylor & Francis Group

LONDON AND NEW YORK

Third edition published 2016
by Routledge
2 Park Square, Milton Park, Abingdon, Oxon OX14 4RN

and by Routledge
711 Third Avenue, New York, NY 10017

Routledge is an imprint of the Taylor & Francis Group, an informa business

© 2016 T. Cotton

First edition published by Pearson Education Limited 2010
Second edition published by Routledge 2013

British Library Cataloguing in Publication Data
A catalogue record for this book is available from the British Library

Library of Congress Cataloging in Publication Data
Names: Cotton, Tony, author.Title: Understanding and teaching primary mathematics.Description: 3rd edition. | London ; New York : Routledge/Taylor & Francis Group, 2016. | Includes bibliographical references and index.Identifiers: LCCN 2015043052| ISBN 9781138906402 (pbk.) | ISBN 9781138906389 (hardback) | ISBN 9781315695525 (ebook)Subjects: LCSH: Mathematics--Study and teaching (Elementary)Classification: LCC QA135.6 .C675 2016 | DDC 372.7--dc23LC record available at http://lccn.loc.gov/2015043052

ISBN: 978-1-138-90638-9 (hbk)
ISBN: 978-1-138-90640-2 (pbk)
ISBN: 978-1-315-69552-5 (ebk)

Typeset in Frutiger
by Fish Books Ltd.

Printed and bound
by Bell & Bain Ltd, Glasgow.

MIX
Paper from
responsible sources
FSC® C007785

CONTENTS

Contents

PREFACE TO THE THIRD EDITION

Introduction

Welcome to the third edition of *Understanding and Teaching Primary Mathematics*. This edition has been updated to reflect the changes that have been made to the English National Curriculum and to ensure it meets the growing international interest in learning and teaching mathematics. I have been lucky enough to work in over 25 countries and it is interesting to see how similar the mathematics curricula are in these countries. Similarly the concerns that early career teachers have around their own confidence in mathematics are shared worldwide. Those of you who teach in schools that follow the International Baccalaureate Primary Years Programme or in international schools following the Cambridge Programmes of Study will find that the mathematical content in these curricula is discussed and explained.

There is a new additional chapter, 'Algebra'. I think you will be pleasantly surprised to discover that algebra can be enjoyable and that it is a fascinating area to work with your learners on. You will also discover that you have been thinking algebraically for as long as you can remember – honestly!

The early years chapter has been reworked and updated to reflect the increased expectations in the new English National Curriculum. Whilst this brings the content into line with some other countries' curricula the emphasis remains on learning through engaging activities and continuous provision to ensure young learners become confident and skilled mathematicians from the earliest stages of their schooling.

There are also additions to the accompanying website. For example there is a new section which provides support for those using the book as part of a teacher training course. I still work on several teacher training courses and I hope that you find the presentations which go alongside each chapter useful. You will see the companion website logo in the margin alongside paragraphs which have accompanying web content available. Some chapters also contain either a clip of learners working on the activities or short interviews with teachers who have been using activities described in the book. You can identify them when you see the video icon appears in the margin. I hope that these short clips allow you to see the ideas I discuss in the book in practice in a range of classrooms. My aim here is that this will give you confidence to try things out for yourself.

As ever my hope is that this book will engage all trainee teachers in developing their mathematical subject knowledge and becoming skilled and confident teachers who enjoy teaching mathematics in primary and early years classrooms. Many beginning teachers I have worked with have told me that when they are confident in their own understandings of a subject they feel much more able to teach that subject creatively and with passion. This confidence stems from what has been called 'deep' mathematical subject knowledge and a clear understanding of the different teaching approaches that can be taken to teach the subject.

The particular approach of this book is to develop your mathematical subject knowledge through exploring the learning and teaching of mathematics. The book will support you in developing your own understanding of mathematics by examining the misconceptions of the learners you will work with and by developing your own repertoire of teaching strategies so you can immediately see the impact of your own learning on your teaching practice.

The English National Curriculum describes 'a high quality mathematics education' as providing

> a foundation for understanding the world, the ability to reason mathematically, an appreciation of the beauty and power of mathematics, and a sense of enjoyment and curiosity about the subject.

The Primary Years Programme followed by learners in over 100 countries around the world is based around cross-curricular themes and 'structured, purposeful inquiry that engages students actively in their own learning'. Teachers are encouraged to draw on learners' prior knowledge, build on this knowledge through new experiences and provide opportunities for reflection and consolidation. (See **www.ibo.org/en/programmes/primary-years-programme** for more information.)

This new edition will support you in becoming a 'high quality' mathematics teacher as defined by the quotation. The expectation that you, the teacher, will learn is also consistent with this educational approach.

The aim of the book

The book aims to support you in developing the three key areas of mathematical subject knowledge. These are

- Mathematical knowledge: The book will support you in developing your own understanding of mathematics through engaging you in activities and investigations.
- Curriculum knowledge: Through reading the book you will come to understand which areas of mathematics are expected to be taught at each stage of learning and understand the progression within learning and teaching mathematics, so you will know which areas of mathematics your learners should have encountered and where they will go next.

- Pedagogical knowledge: The book draws on examples from the classroom so that you can see the best ways to introduce your learners to particular mathematical ideas.

The book is practical and models good primary practice in the way it supports you in developing your own knowledge. In this way you will both develop your own understanding and your teaching repertoire.

Who should use this book?

This book is aimed at all those who wish to develop their own mathematical knowledge in order to improve their confidence in teaching mathematics:

Trainee teachers

Trainee teachers will find this book can be used throughout their course to develop a personal portfolio and to support them on their school placements. They will find it useful for assignments which look at particular areas of mathematics or to give ideas for teaching on placement.

Newly qualified teachers

Newly qualified teachers will be able to draw on the book to support them in areas they have not previously taught or which were not covered specifically during their training.

Experienced teachers

Experienced teachers will find this book useful when visiting areas of mathematics new to them or when working in new year groups. They may also find the book useful to refresh their understanding of areas they have not taught for some time.

Distinctive features

Big ideas

Each section starts with the big ideas which underpin the particular strand of mathematics covered. This allows you to see the big picture immediately and understand how the mathematics you are teaching falls within the overall landscape of the curriculum.

Progression

Each chapter gives you an overview of progression across the early years and throughout the primary years so that you understand which mathematical ideas are appropriate to the children you are teaching. It also helps you understand what knowledge your pupils will bring with them and which mathematical ideas they should progress on to next. This is structured so that you are introduced to the foundations for learning in each area of mathematics and then the ideas which support learners in beginning to understand this area of mathematics are described. The skills and understandings which learners should be taught to become confident mathematicians are outlined and finally suggestions for extending those learners in your classroom who are skilled mathematicians are described.

Links to the classroom and research

Each chapter makes links to key pieces of research and curriculum development. This will support you in writing assignments and in seeing direct links to the classroom. There are also activities that you can try out in your classroom and ideas to support you in developing your own resources.

Audit and portfolio tasks

These tasks allow you to build a portfolio of evidence to show that you have acquired the subject knowledge you need to gain qualified teacher status. There are additional activities for you to consolidate your knowledge available on the companion website.

Teaching points

These draw on common misconceptions in learners and support you in knowing how you can deal with these misconceptions in the classroom. As I mentioned earlier in this preface, it is important that you see your learners' misconceptions as teaching points. By understanding what the most common misconceptions are likely to be you can prepare to overcome learners' common difficulties.

Classroom activities

You will also find boxes in the text which contain activities you can carry out with the learners in your classroom. These are designed to support you in developing your own mathematical knowledge through teaching particular concepts. I always find that I become much more secure in my knowledge if I have to teach something. There is a companion volume to the book called *Teaching for Mathematical Understanding: Practical ideas for outstanding primary lessons*. This book contains all these activities with full lesson plans to help you try them out successfully.

Assessment

Assessing is a key part of learning. It helps you know what your pupils currently understand so that you can plan for the next piece of learning. It also helps you understand how effective your teaching has been and to uncover any areas of difficulty that you need to revisit. Each chapter offers you an assessment activity to use with the pupils you are teaching.

Case studies

Each chapter contains a case study which gives you a lesson plan and an evaluation for each strand of mathematics. This makes a direct link between your own subject knowledge and your teaching. You will also be directed to a video of a lesson which is available on the companion website. This allows you to carry out an observation of a piece of mathematics teaching which links directly to the mathematical area you are exploring.

Drawing on my own teaching of mathematics education in five teacher education institutions over 25 years, as well as 10 years' experience teaching mathematics in secondary and primary schools, I hope I have written a book which will support you in developing your subject knowledge through encouraging you to reflect on your own mathematical understandings and by exploring your teaching of mathematics. My aim would be that through using this book you will develop your subject knowledge and your teaching so that you can confidently and skilfully teach any area of mathematics to learners of all ages.

ACKNOWLEDGEMENTS

This new edition has been particularly influenced by my grandson Felix. He is now nearly three and watching him beginning to see the world in a mathematical way has taught me how we all are mathematicians at heart in terms of the way that we try to order and understand our world. As always I need to thank my children, Holly, Adam and Sam who are my best teachers and my wife, Helen who puts up with me disappearing to the shed and falling silent for too long whilst I think through the work I am engaged in. I also want to thank all the beginning teachers and experienced teachers who allow me into their schools to work with them on mathematics. I am sure they teach me more than I can ever teach them.

Finally, thank you to all my critical readers and reviewers. Your comments are always helpful and result in a much better book.

GUIDED TOUR

Chapter introductions and starting points include a mathematical problem or piece of research to illustrate a concept or theme that is built upon within the chapter.

Each chapter provides an overview of **progression** across the primary years to aid understanding of which mathematical ideas are appropriate to the children you are teaching.

Big ideas deal with the fundamental ideas which underpin each particular strand of mathematics covered. This allows you to see the big picture immediately and understand how the different strands knit together.

They understand the language of 'factors' and 'multiples' and know what 'prime numbers' are. (These terms are all defined in the glossary.) They are also confident in working with equivalent fractions, decimals and percentages, knowing, for example, that 25% = 0.25 = 1/4. They will be able to express one quantity as a percentage of another (e.g. express £400 as a percentage of £1000).

The transition to secondary education will focus on developing children's use of ratio notation. Percentage notation is 30%, ratio notation is 30:100 and decimal notation is 0.3. Here the pupils you wish to extend can learn to reduce a ratio to its simplest form and divide a quantity into two parts in a given ratio. They will be able to use this understanding to solve simple problems involving ratio and direct proportion (e.g. identify the quantities needed to make a fruit drink by mixing water and juice in a given ratio).

The next section of the chapter focuses on the big ideas of 'counting', 'place value', 'fractions, decimals and percentages' and 'proportionality' which are at the heart of counting and understanding number. If you are confident with these big ideas you will be able to teach children successfully across the primary age range and will have a clear understanding of the development of these ideas across the 3–11 age phase.

Big ideas

Counting

Many children will start school able to count – but it is important to be aware of the principles of counting, both to support the children who cannot yet count and to recognise the processes that young children who have already learnt to count have mastered. The key research which supports us in understanding the process of learning to count was undertaken by Rochel Gelman and Randy Gallistel in *The Child's Understanding of Number* published in 1986. Gelman and Gallistel are both psychologists and their book was seen as marking a huge development in our understanding of how children learn to count. Through careful observation of young children undertaking activities that they had planned they described five principles which underpin counting:

1. The one-to-one principle: a child who understands the one-to-one principle knows that we only count each item once.
2. The stable order principle: a child who understands the stable order principle knows that the order of number names always stays the same. We always count by saying one, two, three, four, five … in that order.
3. The cardinal principle: a child who understands the cardinal principle knows that the number they attach to the last object they count gives the answer to the question 'How many …?'.
4. The abstraction principle: a child who understands the abstraction principle knows that we can count anything – they do not all need to be the same

---

Self-audit and portfolio tasks allow you to build a portfolio of evidence to show that you have acquired the subject knowledge you need to gain qualified teacher status.

---

do this by carefully taking you through a series of problem solving activities.

Mason, J., Burton, L. and Stacey, K. (1985) *Thinking Mathematically*. London: Pearson Education.

Self-audit

You should carry out this self-audit and add it to your subject knowledge portfolio. This offers evidence of your own learning and development in the area of 'problem solving using mathematics'. Read through the problem several times before you try to make a start. Also reread the description of rubric writing earlier in the chapter so that you can use this process to describe your thinking.

This task explores number patterns within a 100 square:

1	2	3	4	5	6	7	8	9	10
11	12	13	14	15	16	17	18	19	20
21	22	23	24	25	26	27	28	29	30
31	32	33	34	35	36	37	38	39	40
41	42	43	44	45	46	47	48	49	50
51	52	53	54	55	56	57	58	59	60
61	62	63	64	65	66	67	68	69	70
71	72	73	74	75	76	77	78	79	80
81	82	83	84	85	86	87	88	89	90
91	92	93	94	95	96	97	98	99	100

Look at a block of four numbers, for example:

15	16
25	26

If I add these numbers together I get a total of 82.

This is $(4 \times 15) + 22$, as $4 \times 15 = 60$ and $60 + 22 = 82$.

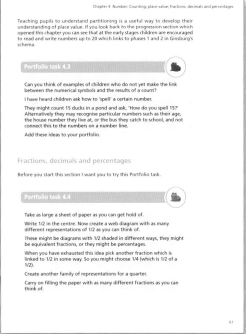

Teaching pupils to understand partitioning is a useful way to develop their understanding of place value. If you look back to the progression section which opened this chapter you can see that at the early stages children are encouraged to read and write numbers up to 20 which links to phases 1 and 2 in Ginsburg's schema.

Portfolio task 4.3

Can you think of examples of children who do not yet make the link between the numerical symbols and the results of a count?

I have heard children ask how to 'spell' a certain number.

They might count 15 ducks in a pond and ask, 'How do you spell 15?' Alternatively they may recognise particular numbers such as their age, the house number they live at, or the bus they catch to school, and not connect this to the numbers on a number line.

Add these ideas to your portfolio.

Fractions, decimals and percentages

Before you start this section I want you to try this Portfolio task.

Portfolio task 4.4

Take as large a sheet of paper as you can get hold of.

Write 1/2 in the centre. Now create a web diagram with as many different representations of 1/2 as you can think of.

These might be diagrams with 1/2 shaded in different ways, they might be equivalent fractions, or they might be percentages.

When you have exhausted this idea pick another fraction which is linked to 1/2 in some way. So you might choose 1/4 (which is 1/2 of a 1/2).

Create another family of representations for a quarter.

Carry on filling the paper with as many different fractions as you can think of.

Teaching points highlight children's common mathematical misconceptions.

Taking it further boxes make links to key pieces of research and curriculum development, to support you in writing assignments and in seeing direct links to the classroom.

The **In practice** section is a case study which gives you a lesson plan and an evaluation for each strand of mathematics. This makes a direct link between your own subject knowledge and your teaching.

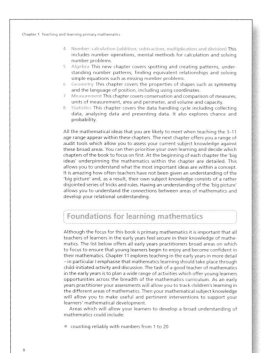

Key terms that are emboldened throughout the text can be found in the glossary at the end of the book.

As well as a chapter focusing specifically on using ICT in your teaching, the accompanying **companion website** provides a range of materials that you can use to develop your own mathematical understanding and in your own teaching.

Wherever you see this icon in the book's margins, you will find related **video** material on the companion website.

Wherever you see this icon, you will find on the website related **further reading** suggestions or web links. On the companion website you will also find PowerPoint presentations for each chapter that will provide support for those of you using the book as part of a teacher training course.

Included in the companion website are a set of **instructional videos** that feature the author demonstrating the concepts covered in the book through teaching a class in a primary school.

CHAPTER 1

TEACHING AND LEARNING PRIMARY MATHEMATICS

Introduction

Learning maths was like a dagger going through my skull – no matter how hard I tried it wasn't good enough. This was really frustrating 'cause I knew there were really important things to discover and when I'm teaching and the kids really get it it's like they've found diamonds. I don't know whether it was my fault or the teacher's.

This is the way a student of mine described the experience of being both a learner and a teacFcuher of mathematics. I had asked my students to describe to me their memories of learning mathematics at primary school. It vividly describes the concerns that some of you may have that you don't have sufficient mathematical understanding to be as effective a teacher as you want to be. It also describes the joys that come with seeing that you have been able to describe a complex mathematical concept well. During the same activity another student described how a feeling of panic can set in if you feel as though you have not got a good grasp of the area that you are teaching.

My problem is being put on the spot – I can't think then, lots of little warnings run through my head the moment I'm asked a question.

Some of you will have had very positive experiences of learning mathematics and some of you may have felt as though you couldn't understand what was being asked of you. Whichever is true for you, working at your own subject knowledge will support you in feeling much more able to find those diamonds that are lurking, and to feel confident that you will be able to answer whatever question a pupil throws at you.

Through working on research projects such as the one I have described above I have become convinced that the best way to develop mathematical subject knowledge is by engaging teachers in actively questioning and reflecting on their learning. Some beginning teachers do not see themselves as 'good' at mathematics because of the way in which they have experienced mathematics as a learner. Through exploring mathematics in a new way they gradually change their view of what being 'good at mathematics' is and can begin to see themselves as mathematicians. Introducing their pupils to a form of mathematics that they have recently experienced themselves allows them to be both tentative in terms of the possible outcomes whilst being secure in the process. They know, or they trust, that interesting things will happen in terms of children learning mathematics. And they notice that through exploring mathematics in an open and investigatory way their learners are themselves developing as young mathematicians. These beginning teachers are moving towards a belief that mathematics is about questioning, exploring and justification.

The beginning of this process is to understand what we might mean by subject knowledge. This chapter offers a definition of subject knowledge for teaching mathematics, as well as setting the scene for the rest of the book. It describes how working with the book will support you in developing your own mathematical subject knowledge. Armed with this understanding you can plan how best you might use the book.

Starting point

Whenever I am asked to describe a teacher with good mathematical subject knowledge I use the following example from my observation of a trainee teacher. The trainee had placed a multiplication grid (you fill in the blanks by multiplying together the numbers at the end of the row and column) on the whiteboard for the pupils in the class to complete as the mental/oral starter to a mathematics lesson.

As the multiplication grid was revealed there were sounds of complaint from the pupils. One of the pupils said to the trainee, 'You don't put fractions in a number grid and we only go up to 10!' The trainee, patiently, persuaded the pupils to accept this 'new' version of what had become an everyday activity for the pupils and then asked them to complete the grid.

After 10 minutes the trainee stopped the class and asked, 'Which column did you fill in first?' One of the pupils put their hand up and said '48'. The trainee paused and said, 'I don't want you to tell me any answers – I want you to tell me which column you filled in first.' At first the pupils did not understand why the answer for the 'first' square wasn't seen as important. Then realisation struck – one pupil said, 'You could do the 2s first – that would be really easy.'

X	8	2	1/2	5	1/4	10	4
6							
3							
7							
9							
4							
5							
12							

Another suggested starting with the 10s for the same reason. By the end of the discussion the class had come to understand that mathematical thinking was about looking carefully at a problem and finding the most effective, or efficient, way of solving it rather than simply following a process which had 'worked' previously. So for this grid, if you complete the '2' column you can then complete the '4' and '8' columns by doubling. Similarly, filling in the '10' column allows you to complete the '5' column by halving. The same process will sort out the '1/2' and '1/4' columns.

I often use this activity with teachers and trainee teachers. Most people will start at the top left corner and work systematically through the grid. This shows how deeply engrained the feeling is that there is a 'right' way to carry out the mathematics. When I suggest the alternative, several people have described how this feels like 'cheating'. It is hard to break away from the image of the mathematical subject that we carry with us from our own experiences at school. However, if you do not feel confident in your own mathematics knowledge this is, in part, due to your experiences as a learner of mathematics. I hope this book will allow you to make such a break.

Why is mathematical subject knowledge important?

You may be training to become a teacher or you may be an experienced teacher who wants to improve their mathematical subject knowledge. I believe that someone with good mathematical subject knowledge is able to be confident in what they are teaching and, more importantly, will be seen as confident by their pupils. We all learn better from someone who we believe is both confident in their own knowledge and who is passionate about sharing that knowledge with us.

That is why the focus of this book is on developing your mathematical subject knowledge by focusing on the types of activities you can use in the classroom. I hope that by engaging you in mathematics that you see as relevant to your

They could anticipate possible misconceptions or misunderstandings and knew how best to support learners at coming to new, more effective conceptions. (Some examples are given below.) This knowledge does not just come through experience – one of the aims of this book is to share common misconceptions with you so that you can plan ahead to support your learners. Knowledge of common misconceptions allows you to respond flexibly and appropriately to the difficulties that children experience.

Examples of such misconceptions might be:

● You can't divide smaller numbers by larger ones.
● Division always makes numbers smaller.
● The more digits a number has, the larger its value.
● All shapes with larger areas have larger **perimeters**.

You may want to take a moment to think of counter-examples to these statements. (For example, $5 \div 10 = 0.5$; $15 \div 0.5 = 30$; 0.000526 is smaller than 2; for the shape example try exploring different **rectangles** with a perimeter of 12cm.)

Teachers with good subject knowledge can also generate probing questions that allow children to articulate their current understandings and through this articulation come to better developed understandings. Often a probing question simply asks how a pupil has worked something out rather than asking for the result of their thinking. So faced with a pupil who has written $28 + 53$ a probing question would be 'how will you work out the answer?' as opposed to 'what is the answer?'. Or, similarly, if a pupil has written $56 - 19 = 43$, a probing question would be 'tell me what you did first to work this out?' rather than asking the pupil to 'check this one again', which signals an error. By asking probing questions you come to understand the pupil's thinking processes rather than simply knowing whether they got an answer 'right' or 'wrong'.

When observing teachers at work, one way in which good subject knowledge is apparent is in the way that they deal with children's unexpected questions. Teachers with good subject knowledge are never thrown by these questions. They deal with them with confidence.

Finally, a teacher with good subject knowledge can support pupils in making the connections between different areas of mathematics so that the pupils see mathematics as a whole rather than a series of separate and often disparate ideas. They can do this because they themselves see mathematics as a whole. This is another example of Richard Skemp's idea of relational understanding.

How will this book develop my subject knowledge?

The three facets of subject knowledge are developed throughout the book. First, your knowledge of the curriculum is developed by beginning each chapter with a clear progression in terms of the mathematical concepts covered.

Each chapter develops your knowledge of the learners and learning processes so that lessons and activities can be structured effectively to meet the needs of all pupils. This is done through the use of case studies and direct reference to how children learn mathematics. A focus on common misconceptions within each chapter also allows you to develop your understanding of how individual learners come to understand mathematics.

The book also focuses directly on developing your knowledge of teaching and learning resources and how they can be used effectively to support learning. There are many ideas for activities that you can use in the classroom. These both allow you to see how mathematics can be taught and give you resources to try out for yourself in your own teaching. They mirror the process you will often go through to plan a session. You may be given a resource with which to teach a particular concept. As a teacher, your role is to plan the most appropriate way to use this resource to develop the children's mathematical understanding. My aim is that this process will support you in becoming skilled designers of your own resources which you can tailor for the children that you teach. This book is accompanied by a companion volume *Teaching for Mathematical Understanding: Practical ideas for outstanding primary lessons*. This book develops the resource ideas into full lessons which you can use. I hope that you find this a complementary resource. I think that by using the resources in your own teaching you will both develop your teaching repertoire and also develop your subject knowledge. I learn best when I am actually teaching pupils.

No book on subject knowledge could teach you everything you need to know across the whole of the curriculum. However this book will ensure that you feel confident in all the key areas of mathematics. Perhaps more importantly it will give you the confidence to develop your own subject knowledge further in a range of curriculum areas through extending and generalising the ideas in the book with a focus on applying them in classroom situations. It will also allow and encourage you to reflect on your own thinking processes in order to develop your own subject knowledge.

A framework for teaching mathematics

You will see that within this book specific attention is paid to progression within specific areas of maths. This is to allow you to plan over the longer term as you gain an understanding of what children's previous experiences will have been and how they will draw on your teaching to support them in the future.

I have split the mathematics curriculum into eight broad areas. These are:

1   **Problem solving using mathematics** This comes first as I think the most important facet of your subject knowledge is your ability to solve problems applying the mathematical understandings that you have.
2   **Number: counting; place value; fractions, decimals and percentages** This includes place value, fractions, decimals, percentages and ratio and proportion.
3   **Number: knowing and using number facts** This chapter will help you understand the underlying rules behind number patterns and number facts including your multiplication facts.

4 **Number: calculation (addition, subtraction, multiplication and division)** This includes number **operations**, mental methods for calculation and solving number problems.

5 **Algebra** This new chapter covers spotting and creating patterns, understanding number patterns, finding equivalent relationships and solving simple equations such as missing number problems.

6 **Geometry** This chapter covers the properties of shapes such as **symmetry** and the language of position, including using **coordinates**.

7 **Measurement** This chapter covers conservation and comparison of measures, units of measurement, **area** and perimeter, and volume and capacity.

8 **Statistics** This chapter covers the data handling cycle including collecting data, analysing data and presenting data. It also explores chance and **probability**.

All the mathematical ideas that you are likely to meet when teaching the 3–11 age range appear within these chapters. The next chapter offers you a range of audit tools which allow you to assess your current subject knowledge against these broad areas. You can then prioritise your own learning and decide which chapters of the book to focus on first. At the beginning of each chapter the 'big ideas' underpinning the mathematics within the chapter are detailed. This allows you to understand what the most important ideas are within a concept. It is amazing how often teachers have not been given an understanding of the 'big picture' and, as a result, their own subject knowledge consists of a rather disjointed series of tricks and rules. Having an understanding of the 'big picture' allows you to understand the connections between areas of mathematics and develop your relational understanding.

Foundations for learning mathematics

Although the focus for this book is primary mathematics it is important that all teachers of learners in the early years feel secure in their knowledge of mathematics. The list below offers all early years practitioners broad areas on which to focus to ensure that young learners begin to enjoy and become confident in their mathematics. Chapter 11 explores teaching in the early years in more detail – in particular I emphasise that mathematics learning should take place through child-initiated activity and discussion. The task of a good teacher of mathematics in the early years is to plan a wide range of activities which offer young learners opportunities across the breadth of the mathematics curriculum. As an early years practitioner your assessments will allow you to track children's learning in the different areas of mathematics. Then your mathematical subject knowledge will allow you to make useful and pertinent interventions to support your learners' mathematical development.

Areas which will allow your learners to develop a broad understanding of mathematics could include:

● counting reliably with numbers from 1 to 20

- placing numbers in order and saying which number is one more or one less than a given number
- using practical materials to add and subtract two single-digit numbers by **counting on** or back to find the answer.
- using practical materials to solve problems, including doubling, halving and sharing
- using everyday language to talk about size, weight, capacity, position, distance, time and money
- comparing quantities and objects by their properties
- recognising, creating and describing patterns
- exploring characteristics of everyday objects and shapes and using mathematical language to describe them.

Practical activities to develop these areas of mathematical understanding are described in more detail in Chapter 11.

Using this book will ensure that all early years practitioners have the knowledge and understanding to teach these concepts well. It is not the case that early years practitioners need a less well-developed mathematical subject knowledge than their colleagues who teach older children. On the contrary it is vital that early years practitioners have solid subject knowledge across the mathematics curriculum so that they can see how these early mathematical concepts develop. In order to plan for mathematics to be developed in a broad range of contexts, and to plan for children to gain confidence and competence across the very broad range of standards, teachers need to have a secure subject knowledge themselves.

Organisation of the book

The second chapter of the book allows you to audit your subject knowledge in three ways. You can use these initial audits to create an action plan that will personalise your study to develop your subject knowledge in a way that suits your own individual needs.

Chapters 3–10 are structured in the same way so that you can easily manoeuvre your way around the book and so that you can see your subject knowledge developing across the whole mathematics curriculum. Each chapter is introduced using a starting point. Here you will be asked to engage in an activity which illustrates the main mathematical ideas underpinning the theme of the chapter. This is followed by a detailed breakdown of the progression within the mathematical ideas which are covered in the chapter. This supports the development of your curricular subject knowledge and allows you to plan appropriately for all of your learners, whatever age or stage they have reached.

The subject knowledge which underpins the strand is then discussed in more detail, explaining the 'Big Ideas', with particular care taken to highlight key terms, which are highlighted in the text when they first appear. These key terms are gathered together as a glossary at the end of the book. Careful explanations of the key areas of mathematics are also given so that you are able to understand how to explain important areas of mathematics to pupils. The main bulk of each chapter is constructed around key teaching points. These teaching points often use a common misconception as a starting point for the discussion of a mathematical idea together with suggestions of how best you may introduce this idea to your pupils. The chapters also offer examples of activities which you can use in your classroom. This allows you to develop your own bank of teaching activities whilst developing an understanding of how best to use these examples. If you buy the companion volume you will find these teaching activities developed into full lesson ideas.

Each chapter also includes an In practice section. Here you are given an exemplar lesson plan focusing on a key concept from the mathematics covered in the chapter. The In practice section also includes a commentary by the teacher on the effectiveness of the lesson when they taught it. The final part of this section refers you to a video of a mathematics lesson which you can watch on the companion website. This supports you in developing your mathematical subject knowledge by watching skilled teachers at work.

Each chapter contains Portfolio tasks which can be used to help you reflect on your learning and can be included in any portfolio you need for your assessment on a teacher training or professional development course. In addition each chapter contains sections which direct you to the most important research exploring the learning and teaching of this particular area of mathematics. These 'Taking it further' sections are contained in boxes labelled From the research for articles which take a research focus and From the classroom for articles written with a classroom focus. These features will be of specific interest to those of you who are studying at Masters or a more advanced level.

At the end of each chapter you are offered ideas for assessment in the particular area you have been studying. This section consists of a range of tasks and activities you can use in your classroom to assess your learners' understanding of the areas you have been teaching. There are also ideas for 'cross-curricular projects' which will allow you to explore the ideas introduced in the chapter in an extended project which draws on other areas of the curriculum.

Finally there is a Self-audit and you are also invited to construct a lesson plan focusing on one facet of the subject knowledge covered in the chapter. Your response to these two activities could form part of your portfolio.

Chapters 11–13 further develop your expertise in teaching mathematics – your pedagogical subject knowledge – through exploring subject knowledge in terms of early years practice, inclusive teaching and learning, the use of calculators and using ICT to support the learning and teaching of mathematics.

The companion website

Everyone who purchases the book is given access to the companion website. It contains the initial audit activities and the proforma for your personal action plan, as well as templates for lesson plans. You will also find a summary presentation of each chapter which can be used by teacher trainers using the book to support their teaching. Some chapters are also supported by a video clip of learners working on the mathematical activities in the classroom or short interviews with classroom teachers discussing how they have used these activities in their classrooms. In addition to this, academic papers which are discussed in the book are available on the site together with additional suggested reading.

Summary

This chapter has two aims. To describe to you what is meant by subject knowledge and to outline to you how the book will support you in developing your mathematical subject knowledge in order to become a confident teacher of mathematics. You have seen how subject knowledge can be described as having knowledge in three areas:

- mathematical subject matter knowledge (you understand the maths)
- curriculum subject knowledge (you know the requirements of the curriculum)
- pedagogical subject knowledge (you can make good choices to help you teach the maths).

And you have been introduced to the key features in the book which will allow you to develop across these areas. Your next task is to complete the audit in Chapter 2 – and then enjoy yourself as you draw on the appropriate chapters to complete your personal portfolio.

Going further

Diamonds in a skull: Unpacking pedagogy with beginning teachers

TONY COTTON

This research paper is based on the opening of this chapter. It describes a piece of research which involved 20 trainee teachers in describing and exploring how they developed their subject knowledge in mathematics. These trainees had described themselves as lacking confidence in teaching mathematics and the research tracks their development in becoming skilled teachers of mathematics.

Cotton, T. (2010) 'Diamonds in a skull: Unpacking pedagogy with beginning teachers', in Walshaw, M. (ed.) *Unpacking pedagogy: New perspectives in mathematics classrooms.* Charlotte, NC: Information Age Publishing.

Relational understanding and instrumental understanding

RICHARD SKEMP

This book is seen as one of the most important pieces of writing about mathematics teaching and learning of the last 50 years. Skemp uses a metaphor which describes mathematics as a landscape to be explored rather than seeing mathematics as a ladder to be climbed. Through gaining an understanding of how different points in a landscape are connected and the different paths we may take to navigate this landscape, we come to a much better understanding than if we have to blindly follow paths without any sense of where they might lead. The full text of the article is available at **http://math.coe.uga.edu/ olive/EMAT3500f08/instrumental-relational.pdf** and is well worth reading.

Skemp, R. (1976) 'Relational understanding and instrumental understanding'. *Mathematics Teaching*, 77(3), 20-26.

CHAPTER 2

WHAT SHOULD I KNOW?
WHAT DO I KNOW?

Introduction

Very often at the end of an explanation, which in my mind was very clear, one of the children I am working with will put their hand up. When I ask them what they want they will tell me 'I'm stuck'. Sometimes I reply, 'What are you stuck on?' 'Just everything' they say! Developing your subject knowledge in mathematics can feel a bit like this – it is hard to focus on the particulars when at first you are not sure what you understand and what you need to work on. Similarly, I have often told people that my dad was my best teacher. I remember him being able to explain things to me really clearly, especially mathematics that I was 'stuck' on. It was only recently that he told me he did not always understand the ideas himself but that he just encouraged me to explain things to him until I was able to discover myself what it was that I was 'stuck' on. If you find yourself struggling on any of the questions here try to see this as a positive. You have found an area that you need to work on. Then carefully reflect on what you do understand, and ask yourself exactly what questions you have. If you can identify your questions carefully you may well be able to move forwards yourself. Indeed, try to accept 'stuckness' as a natural part of learning. In some senses we cannot learn anything without being stuck. If we never have to stop and think, if we are not challenged then we are simply completing exercises that we already know how to do. And what is the point of that?

Chapter 1 described what I mean by subject knowledge. This chapter expands on this by offering you audit tasks so that by the end of the chapter you have a clearer understanding of what knowledge you already have and the steps you might take to build on your previous experiences.

Starting point

Two groups of trainee teachers I was working with were discussing the ways that their courses assessed their subject knowledge to ensure that they could teach mathematics effectively. Neither group were happy. One institution asked its trainees to take examinations at the end of each year. This group asked me,

How does an exam show that we can teach mathematics well – if we've got GCSE mathematics why should we have to do more exams?

The other group were equally unhappy. They had to complete subject knowledge files and felt that gathering 'evidence' showing that they had 'revised' all the mathematics necessary didn't support them in their teaching either. They felt that although this file contained evidence that they had covered all the areas of mathematics it didn't necessarily show that they could use this knowledge to teach others. In England those who wish to apply for teacher training courses have to pass a numeracy skills test. As a result of this it has been argued that all those I now work with on teacher training courses have the necessary mathematical knowledge to develop as great teachers of mathematics. This is not the case. We still have to spend a great deal of time unpicking mathematical ideas in detail. Being able to answer a question in an exam is not the same as having the deep understanding of a mathematical concept that allows us to teach it.

It is clearly important that trainee teachers are confident in their mathematical subject knowledge before embarking on teaching particular mathematical ideas. However, what the stories above show is that it is also important that you can see, and make explicit, the connections between your own subject knowledge and your teaching.

During an inspection an inspector asked these two questions of the students I was teaching:

- How do you know what mathematics you should know?
- How do you know if you know it?

I thought at the time that these were very helpful questions in terms of assessing our own subject knowledge. So answering these questions and making connections between your answers and your teaching is my aim for this chapter.

Auditing your current knowledge

This chapter will ask you to consider your subject knowledge in three ways. First, you will reflect on your previous experiences of learning mathematics and think about your current levels of confidence in teaching mathematics. It is important to explore this area in an initial audit as confidence is a key facet of good subject knowledge. The audit will allow you to recognise your developing confidence as one measure of your improving subject knowledge.

The second part of the audit explores your personal beliefs about what makes up effective mathematics teaching. Your own beliefs play a central role in the way in which you teach mathematics, and this again links back to how confident you feel when teaching mathematics. As I have already suggested, feeling confident in the classroom is a large part of demonstrating good subject knowledge. This section of the audit allows you to illustrate how you will develop in order to plan appropriate activities in order to ensure effective learning of mathematics.

Finally, you will audit your current understandings of mathematics in the areas of:

- problem solving using mathematics
- number: counting; place value; fractions, decimals and percentages
- number: knowing and using number facts
- number: calculation (addition, subtraction, multiplication and division)
- algebra
- geometry: properties of shapes; position and direction
- measurement
- statistics and handling data.

These areas correspond to the chapters which follow in the book. This section of the audit takes the form of presenting you with common misconceptions for you to analyse in the areas listed above. Using the proformas available on the companion website you will be able to complete these audits online and they will form the introductory section of your personal e-portfolio of mathematical subject knowledge.

Audit: Section 1 – Previous experience in learning mathematics and confidence in teaching mathematics

This section of the audit documents your previous experience in learning mathematics and allows you to document your developing confidence both in teaching mathematics and in planning for teaching and researching your own subject knowledge.

Visit the companion website to complete the audit online. You will see that the audit is in two columns. Complete the first column before using the book to develop your subject knowledge and then return to this section and complete the second column after using the book. This allows you to document any changes in the way you view your previous experience of learning mathematics as well as any changes in your confidence levels as a result of your studies.

The comments do not have to be detailed – you may not have many memories of your primary school in order to make comments, for example. The aim of this section is to allow you to take some time to think through your prior experiences and achievements and to reflect on how this makes you feel at the moment as a learner and teacher of mathematics. The second part of this opening section allows you to record statements about how you feel about teaching, planning and working on mathematics. The aim here is that you can 'take note' of how your feelings develop as a result of your studies.

The final part of this section explores your initial confidence levels across the mathematics curriculum and then allows you to reflect back to these initial thoughts after you have worked through the activities in the book. If you are uncertain as to the content of any of these areas of mathematics turn to the appropriate chapter and skim through the 'progression' section. This will remind you of the mathematical content contained within each of these areas.

An example of a completed audit is shown below. If you wish, print off this initial audit and place it in a file as the opening piece of evidence of your developing mathematical knowledge.

Mathematics Subject Knowledge – Personal Profile		
Name	Tony Cotton	
Previous experience and qualifications	Comment on your learning and achievement at the following stages	
Age 11:	*Felt very confident in learning maths – was always placed on the high achieving table*	*I realise that I was often not challenged in my primary classroom. I simply spent a lot of time completing exercises that I could already do. I did not really develop my mathematical thinking skills*
Age 14:	*Achieved an 'average' level in my SATs. I was not really enjoying maths and it seemed like we were repeating a lot of the work that we had already covered*	
GCSE or equivalent:	*I got my grade 'C' – I was still not enjoying maths as a subject*	*I realise that I feel a bit frustrated that my secondary teachers did not make the subject enjoyable or interesting. I'm determined to make sure my pupils enjoy maths*
Post-16 experience and qualifications	*I have avoided maths ever since I got my GCSE!*	

Mathematics Subject Knowledge – Personal Profile (continued)		
My confidence in teaching mathematics	Complete the sentences below Before using *Understanding and Teaching Primary Mathematics*	After using *Understanding and Teaching Primary Mathematics*
When teaching mathematics in school I feel...	*OK. I do seem to just follow the school's plans or use ideas from the web rather than thinking up ideas for myself*	*That it is important for me to have a really good grasp of the maths rather than simply read through the maths at the same level as the children – it helps me see where the maths is leading in the future*
When planning for teaching mathematics I feel...	*See above*	*That I need to ensure the activities are challenging and interesting – not simply find something that will cover the curriculum*
When researching mathematics in order to develop my own subject knowledge I feel...	*That I can find activities that will help the pupils. I find it hard to find exciting activities, though*	*See above*

Audit of confidence in mathematical subject knowledge

The second audit available on the companion website supports you in thinking about your current confidence across all the areas of mathematics that are covered in the book. Think about each of the areas – if you are not sure what mathematical ideas are contained in an area flick to the chapter and look at the 'Progression' section. This outlines the content covered in a particular area in detail.

   Please complete this audit using the following key:

1   I feel very comfortable with this area of mathematics and could answer questions from children with confidence.
2   I feel fairly comfortable with this area of mathematics and would be happy to teach it with some preparation.
3   I am a little uncertain with this area of mathematics and would need to spend a lot of time preparing before I could teach it.
4   I do not understand this area of mathematics at all.

An example of a completed audit is given on the following page.

Area of mathematics	Before reading book		After reading book	
	Confidence level	Comment or evidence	Confidence level	Comment or evidence
Using mathematics	3	*I'm not really sure what is meant by 'using and applying' as it is an area I feel I did not learn in school*	2	*I feel much more confident that I understand what I need to teach – I still find it a challenge to find appropriate activities, though. I have included my response to the initial audit task here as well as my notes from reading the chapter to show how my understanding has developed*
Counting; place value; fractions, decimals and percentage; ratio and proportion	2	*This is an area I feel OK about – it has been an area I have previously focused on. My successful response to the initial audit tasks supports me in this comment*	2	*I did not focus on this area*
Knowing and using number facts	2	*As above*	1	*I read the chapter and found the In practice section interesting. I have included a lesson plan in my portfolio which I have used in school. I am now very confident in teaching this area of mathematics*
Calculating	2	*As above*	1	*I also completed the tasks at the end of the chapter and was very pleased with the results. I have included these as evidence of my growing confidence in this area*

Area of mathematics	Before reading book		After reading book	
	Confidence level	Comment or evidence	Confidence level	Comment or evidence
Algebra	3	*I only remember doing algebra at secondary school so was surprised to see it included. I thought it would be too difficult for the children I teach*	2	*After reading the chapter and trying the tasks I realise that I did not really realise that algebra starts very early. In fact a lot of what I already taught was algebra. I feel much better about this area now*
Geometry	2	*This is another area I feel comfortable with. I have a good memory for the names and properties of shapes. I have included my successful initial audit as evidence of this*	2	*After working on the chapter I realise that there is a lot more to 'shape' than simply remembering the names. I really enjoyed working through this chapter and have included all my notes in my portfolio*
Measurement	3	*I am uncertain about areas and volumes and need to study this in some detail*	2	*I feel much more confident with my knowledge in this area. I have included my response to the tasks in the chapter and an exemplar lesson plan in my portfolio*
Statistics and handling data	3	*This is not an area that I feel confident in at all as it is something that I avoided at school and have not had to teach at all*	2	*After working on the chapter I realise that this area is not as complex as I thought. I have included my notes from working through the chapter as evidence of my improvement*

Audit: Section 2 – Beliefs about learning and teaching mathematics

For this section of the audit you are asked to reflect on your beliefs about learning and teaching mathematics and comment on any changes to your thinking after working through the book. You do this through completing a questionnaire based on important research into effective teaching of mathematics carried out by Mike Askew and others at King's College in London (for full details see Going further, page 23. They carried out a wide range of observations across many primary schools exploring the impact of teachers' beliefs on learning mathematics and divided these beliefs into three categories: 'connectionist', 'transmission' and 'discovery'.

To summarise these beliefs, connectionist teachers think it is important to make connections between all the different areas of mathematics. They are likely to draw on a wide range of mathematical ideas to solve problems themselves and will make these links for their learners. These teachers will favour open-ended, investigative approaches to learning and teaching mathematics. Teachers who feel comfortable with a transmission model take the view that mathematics is a fixed body of knowledge that their learners should be introduced to by a teacher who can 'transmit' this knowledge effectively. A model here would be that the teacher works through examples with their learners who then practise similar examples on their own. Finally a teacher who believes in a discovery approach will plan activities that allow their learners to explore mathematics at their own level, coming to their own understanding of how mathematics operates.

Your own beliefs are likely to have been influenced to a large extent by your prior experiences of learning mathematics and how this makes you feel as a learner of mathematics. They will also have been influenced by your experiences in the classroom as a trainee teacher and the beliefs of teachers you have worked with in schools.

Once you have completed the initial questionnaire you may like to explore the differences between your own beliefs and those that you would ascribe to your own teachers and to teachers that you have worked with in schools. Differences in beliefs may account for personal feelings of inadequacy as both a teacher and a learner.

Visit the companion website containing the questionnaire and highlight the statements that most closely mirror your current beliefs using the highlighter tool. You can select statements from different columns – in fact it is very likely that you will want to select statements from across the spectrum of beliefs. You may even want to choose more than one statement per row. The idea is to engage you in thinking about your beliefs before you embark on working with the ideas in this book. When you feel as though you have completed working through the book revisit the questionnaire and underline those statements you now agree with. Of course, many of these may be the same. Then complete the comment box to reflect on the impact of your working at your mathematical subject knowledge on your beliefs about learning and teaching mathematics.

Look at the completed table as an example before completing the questionnaire.

	Connectionist	Transmission	Discovery
Beliefs about what it is to be a numerate pupil	Being numerate involves:	Being numerate involves:	Being numerate involves:
	The use of methods of calculation which are both efficient and effective	Primarily the ability to perform standard procedures or routines	Finding the answer to a calculation by any method
	Confidence and ability in mental methods	A heavy reliance on paper and pencil methods	A heavy reliance on practical methods
	Selecting a method of calculation on the basis of both the operation and the numbers involved	Selecting a method of calculation primarily on the basis of the operation involved	Selecting a method of calculation primarily on the basis of the operation involved
	Awareness of the links between different aspects of the mathematics curriculum	Confidence in separate aspects of the mathematics curriculum	Confidence in separate aspects of the mathematics curriculum
	Reasoning, justifying and eventually proving results about number	**An ability to 'decode' contextual problems to identify the particular routine or technique required**	Being able to use and apply mathematics using practical apparatus
Beliefs about pupils and how they learn to become numerate	Pupils become numerate through purposeful interpersonal activity based on interactions with others	**Pupils become numerate through individual activity based on following instructions**	Pupils become numerate through individual activity based on actions on objects
	Pupils learn through being challenged and struggling to overcome difficulties	Pupils learn through being introduced to one mathematical routine at a time and remembering it	Pupils need to be ready before they can learn certain mathematical ideas
	Most pupils are able to become numerate	Pupils vary in their ability to become numerate	Pupils vary in the rate at which their numeracy develops
	Pupils have strategies for calculating but the teacher has responsibility for helping them to refine their methods	Pupils' strategies for calculating are of little importance – they need to be taught standard procedures	Pupils' own strategies are the most important: understanding is based on working things out yourself

	Connectionist	Transmission	Discovery
	Pupil misunderstandings need to be recognised, made explicit and worked on	Pupils' misunderstandings are the result of a failure to 'grasp' what was being taught and need to be remedied by further reinforcement of the 'correct' method	Pupils' misunderstandings are the results of pupils not being ready to learn the ideas
Beliefs about how best to teach pupils to become numerate	Teaching and learning are complementary	Teaching is separate from and has priority over learning	Learning is separate from and has priority over teaching
	Numeracy teaching is based on dialogue between teacher and pupils to explore understandings	Numeracy teaching is based on verbal explanations so that pupils understand teachers' methods	Numeracy teaching is based on practical activities so that pupils discover methods for themselves
	Learning about mathematical concepts and the ability to apply these concepts are learnt alongside each other	Learning about mathematical concepts precedes the ability to apply these concepts	Learning about mathematical concepts precedes the ability to apply these concepts
	The connections between mathematical ideas need to be acknowledged in teaching	Mathematical ideas need to be introduced in discrete packages	Mathematical ideas need to be introduced in discrete packages
	Application is best approached through challenges that need to be reasoned about	Application is best approached through word problems which offer contexts for calculating routines	Application is best approached through using practical equipment
Comment on impact of self-study on personal beliefs	*I think I have moved more towards the 'connectionist' viewpoint. This was quite a difficult move for me as I have never been taught by a 'connectionist' teacher and most of the teachers I have observed have focused on 'transmission'. However, I am now much more able to see the links between different areas of mathematics and think it is important for pupils to be able to make this link too*		
	I have also realised that using children's misconceptions as a starting point for teaching is really useful. I think my own growing understanding of where misconceptions come from has helped me		

Audit: Section 3 – Exploring subject knowledge

The final section of the audit asks you to work with a range of questions across the strands of mathematical subject knowledge covered in the books. This allows you to decide which areas of mathematics you already feel comfortable with and those areas you need to concentrate on for further study. Again visit the companion website to carry out this section of the audit. The questions and worked answers are available on the companion website.

Don't worry at all if you find yourself thinking 'I don't know what to do in this question' or if you become 'stuck'. This is a signal for you that it will be worth working through the appropriate chapter in the book. This is an initial audit of your subject knowledge so that you can focus on the areas you most need to develop. Once you have worked through all the questions you can complete a personal action plan on the companion website which will help you to prioritise your use of the book. You should make your first priority those areas that you have assessed as 3 or 4.

Summary

This chapter has asked you to reflect on your own starting point in terms of your subject knowledge of mathematics. I hope that you are now able to answer the questions for yourself:

- What do I need to know?
- What do I already know?
- Which areas should I focus on to develop my own knowledge?

The audits have provided you with the opening sections for your personal portfolio. You will develop this portfolio as you complete the portfolio tasks throughout the chapters you focus on and the audit sections at the end of these chapters.

Going further

Effective teachers of numeracy in primary schools: Teachers' beliefs, practices and pupils' learning

MIKE ASKEW, MARGARET BROWN AND COLLEAGUES

Mike Askew, Margaret Brown and a team of researchers from King's College observed and interviewed a large number of teachers to try to find out what beliefs correlated with effective teaching of mathematics. They explored teachers' beliefs about the nature of mathematics; their beliefs about the way that mathematics should be taught; and finally their beliefs about how mathematical achievement should be assessed. The final report makes fascinating reading.

Askew, M., Brown, M., Rhodes, V., Wiliam, D. and Johnson, D. (1997) 'Effective teachers of numeracy in primary schools: Teachers' beliefs, practices and pupils' learning' (paper presented at the British Educational Research Association annual conference in 1997). London: King's College, London.

What makes great teaching?

The Sutton Trust have published a review of the research called 'What makes great teaching?' Although this is an overview of research related to teaching in general there is a lot we can learn as teachers of mathematics. There is particular attention paid to subject knowledge and teacher beliefs.

Coe, R., Aloisi, C., Higgins, S. and Major, L.E. (2014) 'What makes great teaching? Review of the underpinning research'. The Sutton Trust, **www.suttontrust.com**.

CHAPTER 3

PROBLEM SOLVING USING MATHEMATICS

Introduction

Whenever I share the story that follows with students they tell me that they don't believe it really happened. However when I suggest that I also used to sit reading a book to myself in the reading corner and that very quickly my class would start to gather round to share the book they can see that this might have happened. And it did, honestly – children can find mathematics as fascinating as reading. It is important that we show the learners we work with that we enjoy doing mathematics for its own sake. The story suggests one way of doing this.

I had been experiencing difficulty in engaging a group of nine- and ten-year-olds in a problem-solving activity. They seemed happy simply completing exercises that I gave them but would not investigate mathematics in a more open way. So I decided on a new tactic. Whilst the group were out at playtime I surrounded myself with large sheets of flip chart paper and began to explore a particular number chain. (The rule was that if the number is divisible by 5 I divided by 5 otherwise I added 4 – the aim was to see how long the chains were depending on which number I started with). As the group came back into the classroom they started to gather round and asked me what I was doing. They then started to ask me other questions – how long do you think this chain will be? What happens if you start with a number bigger than 10? They made suggestions about how they could help me in finding the answers. Before I knew it the whole class was engaged in exploring number chains. Sometimes exploring mathematics alongside our pupils engages more effectively than always working at something which we already know the answer to.

The aim of this chapter is to support you in becoming confident in teaching how to problem solve using mathematics. To do this you need to explore your own learning of mathematics, so I would like to ask you to work on a piece of mathematics as an initial step. This will give you some insight into how your learners may feel when you ask them to carry out a mathematical activity they have not met before. By reflecting on your learning process you will be better able to see the support you might offer to your learners.

Starting point

Portfolio task 3.1

Look at this number square.

Imagine you can extend it as far as you like both horizontally and vertically.

You may want to sketch your own enlarged version in a notebook.

1	3	5	7	...
2	6	10	14	...
4	12	20	28	...
8	24	40	56	...
...	...	...	...	...

What patterns do you see in the number square?

Jot down anything you notice.

Spend some time on this before you read on.

Now let us focus your thinking a little.

- Do you think every number will appear if you extend the square far enough?
- If you think every number will appear, write down why you think this is the case.
- If you don't know what to write, talk to somebody about it and then hone your ideas so that you can write something down.
- Will every number appear once, or more than once? Again, try to make notes describing your reasoning.

Now, to focus even more, do you think 1000 will appear in an extended version of the square? If you think it will, describe its position. If you think it won't, explain why this is the case.

I often use this activity with my students and many tell me that they find the first question too open. They say, 'I don't notice anything!' or even 'What am I supposed to notice?' Usually one group of students will make a suggestion like:

| 1 | 3 |
| 2 | 6 |

'If you look at a block of four numbers from the grid, by adding the two numbers in the first column you get the number at the top of the next column.' Once someone has noticed a pattern, any pattern, this seems to give others permission to look for other patterns. I think perhaps at this stage my students realise that I am not asking them to find a particular pattern that will give the 'right' answer but genuinely asking for any patterns.

Unlike the other chapters in this book the ideas which underpin 'problem solving' cannot be summarised as a set of content to be taught, rather it is a structure which you can use to solve and investigate problems across all areas of mathematics. Later in the chapter you will see that ideas of communication, reasoning, and enquiry are at the heart of this mathematical problem solving. It is for this reason that I have chosen to open the book with this chapter. I think that these ideas are at the heart of all mathematical activity. If you become confident and skilled in the areas of mathematical communication; if you are able to use your mathematical knowledge to investigate and solve problems through applying mathematical reasoning you will have become a mathematician.

If you tried to share your insights into the previous number square task with friends or children you would start to see the centrality of communication. Sometimes our own thoughts and ideas become much clearer when we try to share them with others – or we gain new insights through asking questions as other people try to explain their thinking. You may have realised that the prompt questions asked you why you thought your solutions were correct – this is to enable you to begin to articulate your 'reasoning'. It is only when we ask 'why' that we begin to explore mathematical reasoning. Finally, the process of enquiry and problem solving encourages learners to engage with open questions. I asked, 'What patterns can you see?' This may have felt too open for you at first. How would you know when you had finished? Were there particular patterns I wanted you to spot? This unease perhaps comes from your prior experience of mathematics, which may have been presented through a series of closed questions and answers supplied by the teacher, followed up by a series of exercises to practise a particular skill. When developing problem-solving skills we often start with a fairly open question so that we can investigate the mathematics in a number of different ways.

Before moving on to explore problem solving in more detail I want to outline how the ideas above can be developed throughout a learner's time in primary school. This allows you to see how the activities you design for the children you are working with build on ideas which they will have met already.

The English National Curriculum has as one of its aims that all pupils should be able to:

> solve problems by applying their mathematics to a variety of routine and non-routine problems with increasing sophistication, including breaking down problems into a series of simpler steps and persevering in seeking solutions.

Perhaps you can see how the task above began to model this process. In this sense it was teaching how to break problems down into simpler steps. It was also encouraging you to persevere. In fact it was expecting you to become resilient – to not jump to the first answer you thought of but to explore different routes through the problem.

The International Baccalaureate Programme for Primary Schools expects learners to be:

- exploring, wondering and questioning
- taking and defending a position
- using critical thinking skills to understand a concept
- making and testing theories
- experimenting and playing with possibilities
- solving problems in a variety of ways.

Looking back at the portfolio task I hope that you can see your thinking developing along these lines.

The statements in the details of progression below show how you can gradually 'teach' these skills to the learners that you work with. It also shows you how your own skills should develop. The statements are taken from the English National Curriculum but are applicable generally. There is a direct match to the Cambridge Primary Mathematics Curriculum

Progression in problem solving using mathematics

Foundations for problem solving using mathematics

Initially, young learners should be asked to recognise and recreate simple patterns and talk about what they see. Early skills include matching similar objects and sorting objects into categories they can describe. Children will also start to talk about the decisions they are making, for example they may arrange blocks in colours and tell you that the blocks 'go red, blue, red, blue'.

Beginning to problem solve using mathematics

At this stage children will use diagrams and numbers to represent problems and to organise their thinking. For example, they may choose to use cubes if you ask them to carry out calculations they cannot work out mentally. They will be able to describe more complex patterns to you and complete patterns that you start off. They will also be able to explain the reason for their choice of calculation. They will identify, describe and explain simple patterns involving numbers and shapes. They might notice that answers all end in 2, or that answers are all odd or all even. Children will also start to use ICT both to explore problems and to present their solutions using simple word processing programs and software which allows them to sort and categorise. They will be able to create word problems to go with a calculation or a picture.

Becoming confident in problem solving using mathematics

By this stage children are coming to an understanding of the way in which mathematics can be used to communicate and explain ideas from a range of curriculum areas. For example, a geography unit that the children will study explores 'Our school and local area'. The children will draw on their mathematical skills to undertake this learning. When you offer them an open-ended investigation they will also be able to follow a specific line of enquiry, explaining the choices they are making. For example, in the number square at the beginning of this chapter they may choose to look at patterns in specific rows or columns. If appropriate they will relate their solutions back to a real-life context to check the reasonableness of their solution. If, for example, they are working on a series of word problems based around shopping they will be checking to see that the prices are reasonable. They will be making well-informed decisions about the most appropriate way to represent and report their thinking. They will suggest a range of possible lines of enquiry given a starting point and discuss a range of approaches to the problem offering a clear rationale for the approach they take. By the end of their time in primary school children will enjoy using mathematics as a problem-solving tool across the curriculum and will be able to explain their thinking clearly.

Extending learning in problem solving using mathematics

Children operating at this level will be able to break down two- and three-step problems into simple steps and prioritise the information they are offered in order to make sense of a problem. They will continue to describe and explain their methods using a wide range of appropriate pictures and diagrams and increasingly sophisticated mathematical vocabulary.

The next section of the chapter focuses on the 'big ideas' of communication, reasoning, and enquiry and problem solving. These 'big ideas' are the starting point for all the mathematical problem solving we will carry out with our learners. You will explore ways in which you can become a confident mathematical thinker and in this way you will be able to model mathematical thinking successfully with the learners with whom you work.

Big ideas

One of the most influential texts exploring this area of our subject is *Thinking Mathematically* by John Mason with Leone Burton and Kaye Stacey. John Mason is the Professor of Mathematics Education at the Open University (OU). He has written for 25 years about the processes of mathematical thinking and was the Director of the influential Centre for Mathematics Education at the OU for 15 years. He has a particular interest in the ways in which we search for generality as a way of thinking and making sense of the world.

In *Thinking Mathematically* we are offered five key assumptions to support our teaching of mathematical thinking:

1   Everyone can think mathematically.
2   Mathematical thinking can be improved by 'practising reflection'.
3   Mathematical thinking is provoked by contradiction, tension and surprise.
4   Mathematical thinking is supported by an atmosphere of questioning, challenging and reflecting.
5   Mathematical thinking helps in understanding oneself and the world.

You may realise that these assumptions underpin the approach I have taken to developing your subject knowledge in this book – and that they offer a classroom ethos rather than a series of skills to be taught. However, there are 'skills' which underpin the process of problem solving using mathematics which will be outlined in this chapter.

Two other ideas which are important when working with children on their mathematical thinking are **specialising** and generalising. Specialising is the process you use when you look at specific examples in order to get started on a problem. So, for example, if you suggested that the 'numbers doubled as they move down the rows' you will have started by noticing that 2 is double 1 and that 4 is double 2. You may even have checked that this was always the case by extending the number square to look at further examples. You will have used this to come to a generalisation – this is when you make a statement about all numbers in the square. So generalising is making a statement that is true about a wide range of cases. An example might be 'if you add two odd numbers together you get an even number'.

The ideas of specialising and generalising appear throughout mathematics. A common confusion you will see with children is that they will take a 'special' case as true for all cases. If you were to ask your learners to draw you a triangle I am almost certain that they would draw an equilateral triangle. We see the special case – a triangle with all sides and angles the same size – rather than the bigger picture. In general, any three-sided shape is a triangle.

TAKING IT FURTHER: **FROM THE RESEARCH**

In *Mathematics Teaching* 182 (on the companion website), Laurinda Brown, a mathematics education lecturer and researcher, reports on a research project where she worked with four teachers on problem-solving activities in the classroom. She suggests that the approaches they took which we discuss in this chapter will encourage children to become mathematicians rather than simply 'learn' mathematics. Her criteria for mathematical thinking will be very useful if you are devising activities or trying to analyse the mathematical thinking that is taking place in your classroom.

She suggests that thinking mathematically involves:

- being systematic and organised
- being able to analyse situations and make generalisations
- predicting and testing predictions
- being precise in our definitions
- developing precise mathematical vocabulary to describe situations
- being aware of the big picture whilst working in a particular direction
- being able to pose our own questions
- being able to share ideas and work independently
- challenging other people's ideas by asking 'what if?' questions.

Next time you engage in some investigational work, ask yourself which of these criteria you have met. Similarly, the next time you work with children on developing their mathematical thinking skills, use the list to evaluate your own practice.

Enquiry and problem solving

I think it may be useful at this point to explore a mathematical problem to exemplify what I mean by 'enquiry and problem solving'.

Reflect on how you approached this problem. I used the Primary Years Programme aims earlier to argue that learners should be 'exploring, wondering and questioning' and 'experimenting and playing with possibilities'. This suggests that it is not sufficient to teach children how to solve problems but that we should teach them to want to solve problems. Is this how you felt when faced with the problem above – did you want to extend the problem and find out why certain results were happening, or did you feel rather confused by the apparent openness of the problem? Many of my students when faced with this problem will ask me how they will know when they have 'done enough' or 'finished'. I would suggest that this attitude to problem solving is learnt – many of you will remember having to submit coursework as a part of your examinations.

Many of you will have been given very clear guidelines as to the approach you should take and the way you should present the problem in order to maximise your mark. However, this places a reliance on the teacher to give you answers and to keep you on the right track, rather than an inclination to solve problems through following your own lines of enquiry.

An important way to develop your own subject knowledge is to explore mathematical problems for yourself, if possible with the children you teach, and model how problem solving can be open ended. Show your learners that you explore, wonder and question when faced with a mathematical problem. If your approach is to experiment and play with possibilities, they will follow your model. I offered a view of how this can be effective as a teaching approach at the beginning of the chapter.

Portfolio task 3.2

Look at the number line below:

1	2	3	4	5	6	7	8	9	10	11	12	13	14	15

Look at chunks of the number line which consist of two consecutive numbers, such as 1, 2 or 6, 7 or 13, 14.

Add these pairs of numbers together.

What do you notice?

Do you think this result is true for any two consecutive numbers?

Why do you think this happens?

Now try adding together three consecutive numbers, or four.

What are you noticing?

What do you think is the reason for these results?

You may still feel a little insecure with the openness of this task.

You may not be sure if you have 'answered the question'.

This isn't unusual. There is in fact no 'question to answer' – the point is to 'plan and follow lines of enquiry', which is one of Laurinda Brown's themes.

Hopefully, by trying to answer the 'why' questions you are beginning to 'communicate your mathematical thinking'.

Similarly, the last task modelled a line of enquiry in the following way:

1   Start with a question – what do we notice about consecutive numbers?
2   Find a starting point to examine this question – in this case look at pairs of numbers.
3   Specialise – that is, look at specific pairs of numbers to see what you notice. You may have noticed that adding together pairs of numbers gave you an odd number as an answer.
4   Try a range of similar cases to see if the result can be generalised – does the result always happen whichever pairs you choose?
5   Try to 'prove' the result – why does this happen? Proving is being able to convince someone that your explanation is correct.

Time for another task.

Portfolio task 3.3

I have used this problem with young children and they proved the result for me by building towers from cubes.

Try to prove the statement

'The sum of two consecutive numbers is always an odd number'

through a drawing.

Here is a drawing that may get you started:

Representing

In the book *Assessing Children's Mathematical Knowledge: Social class, sex and problem solving*, Barry Cooper and Mairead Dunne showed that many children fail to demonstrate their skills in problem solving as they find it difficult to decode representations of mathematical problems. For example, if children are asked the question 'if there are 77 children in a year group and the coaches to take them swimming hold 35 children, how many coaches are needed?', some children responded 'two'. When asked for the reason for their answer they said it would be silly and too expensive to hire three and that seven children could have lifts in parents' cars. They did not realise that the answer expected was three, as in a sense the 'real' context was a mathematical context and not a genuine problem to solve. The children who are most successful in solving problems which appear on high-stakes tests are those who can make the link between a realistic mathematical problem and the mathematical processes they will need to carry out to solve the problem. In the example above these children would realise that the question was asking for a repeated addition to be carried out until an answer greater than 77 was reached. The best way to support children in developing their skills in decoding different representations of problems – in words, in tables, in graphs, in pictures – is to allow them to explore a range of problems which are represented in a variety of ways. This range of representations can then be shared with the class so that your learners begin to understand the range of representations that are possible. Whilst children are exploring the range of ways in which they may represent problems, they also need to be developing their skills in communicating their mathematical thinking, which is discussed below.

Reasoning and communication

Reasoning is the process of being able to plan an enquiry, that is decide how you will tackle a problem, and then being able to draw on the range of mathematical skills that you have available to work at the enquiry. You can teach reasoning by asking children questions that allow them to draw on the knowledge they already have to solve a problem, and most importantly by encouraging them to articulate their thinking processes. Think back to the portfolio task that opened this section – could you explain the thought processes you went through? In his book *Thinking Mathematically*, John Mason describes a process of rubric writing to help develop mathematical reasoning and communication. Rubric writing is following a routine every time you notice you are 'stuck'. The key processes in rubric writing are noticing when you are 'stuck' and writing down how you know you are stuck – what is it that you don't know? When you have a new idea, described as an 'aha' moment, you write down 'aha' and describe the discovery you have made. Finally, at regular intervals you pause to 'check' your calculation or reasoning and make note of this. Then, at the end of a process of problem solving you take time to 'reflect' and notice what you have discovered and what you have learnt.

Portfolio task 3.4

Take a sheet of A3 paper and fold it in half – use a 'portrait' orientation.

On the left-hand side of the paper revisit the consecutive numbers problem.

Try to re-create in as much detail as you can the thinking process you went through when you explored the problem.

Now on the right-hand side of the paper use the method of rubric writing to annotate your thinking.

When were you stuck?

Why were you stuck?

Jot down your 'aha' moments.

What did you do immediately following these thoughts?

At what stages did you check back over your calculations?

What did you discover?

Finally, take time to reflect.

What did you learn from working at the problem?

How might you approach a similar problem in the future?

How might you explore this problem further?

Try to develop your skills of 'rubric writing' as you work on the tasks in the rest of the chapter.

If you can try this problem with a class you are teaching, encourage them to tell you when they are stuck, or have 'aha' moments.

Support them in checking back over their solutions and most importantly give them time to reflect on the process.

Teaching points

When you introduce your class to mathematical problem-solving activities you will notice misconceptions and misunderstandings. It is important that you don't treat these as mistakes or errors but that you use them as prompts to intervene and to support the pupils in coming to a better understanding of the mathematics they are working on. The following teaching points are based on my own experience of teaching problem solving. You may recognise some of the areas as ones which you have difficulty with yourself. You will also see how they link to the big ideas described above.

Teaching point 1: Not carrying out appropriate steps in multi-step word problems

This can take two forms. Some children will scan a problem to see if they can quickly spot the operation that is being asked for – these children might put their hands up and ask a question such as 'Miss, is this one a divide?' Other children may carry out the first operation within a problem and then stop. They have become used to problems having a single answer each.

I was working with a group of Year 6 children on solving word problems. They were given a table of information which told them a serving of cereal contained 350 calories per 100g. They were asked to calculate how many 30g bowls of cereal they would need to eat to meet the daily requirement of 2000 calories.

Many of the children realised that the operation they needed to carry out was to divide but did not take care when they were deciding what to divide. Some also were looking for an answer that was exactly 2000, not realising that it would be OK to eat more than 2000 calories.

So for example they answered:

5.714285714 (the answer on a calculator if you divide 2000 by 350).

It would be difficult to eat such a precise amount of cereal and five bowls of cereal would not really satisfy a growing child over a whole day.

67 (the answer if you divide 2000 by 30 and then round up to a 'whole' number of bowls).

This is quite a lot of cereal!

There are three ways to support children in not just jumping to the first operation they see. First, always ask if they think the answer is sensible and lead them back to the context – this does of course mean that you need to make sure the contexts are mathematically accurate. So, for example if you are using prices try to be accurate. Children will have an understanding of the real costs of certain items and will be able to spot when you are just making things simple.

Secondly, I often give children the answer to a multi-step problem and ask them to explain why this is correct. So in this case I would give them the same information but tell them that:

19 bowls of cereal provide you with 1995 calories, which is very close to the daily requirement

and ask them to explain why this is correct. Another useful method is to present children with mathematical data and ask them to set each other multi-step problems, together with a solution. Getting children to pose their own questions is a very good way of teaching them to solve problems. This helps them to get inside the process of problem posing and once they begin to understand how you set multi-step problems, they become more adept at solving them.

Teaching point 2: Not using a systematic approach to solve a problem

This area of difficulty is directly linked to the first one and I think it often arises from children thinking that the result of a problem-solving activity is a simple answer which the teacher knows and the child has to find out, as quickly as possible. For example, I set the following problem to a group of Year 4 children:

How many different ways can you arrange four different coloured cubes?

Say we are using red (**R**), blue (**B**), green (G) and yellow ( ) cubes.

One way would be:

Another would be:

The group started to guess: '12' one group said, 'because it's 4 × 3'.

Another group suggested 24, although they had no reason – they were just taking my non-committal response to mean that '12' was incorrect.

So I gave the group boxes of different-coloured cubes and asked them to find all the different arrangements.

I asked my students recently to explore how many ways they could arrange four different coloured cubes in a line so that each arrangement is different.

I asked them to use sketches to make sure they can convince each other that they had them all.

One group came up with this solution:

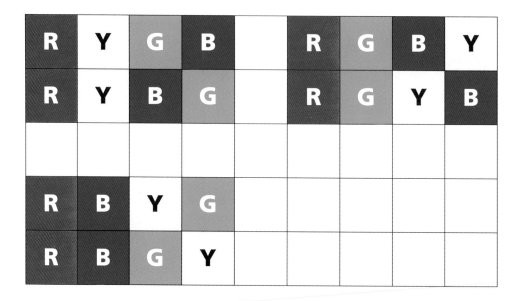

The students' description was as follows:

> *Here I have made sure that I have found all the arrangements that 'start' with a red cube. I also began by realising that if I place red, then yellow, there are two ways to arrange the blue and green cubes, and that this pattern repeats.*

This is a good example of articulating mathematical reasoning, and it can be seen as a proof because it is convincing.

An effective way to encourage children to work systematically is to make sure the problem is complex enough that a system will be needed to keep track of all the possibilities. The problem we have been working on here demands a system as it is then easy to see the patterns.

The most important question you can ask children to encourage them to work systematically is 'Are you sure you have found all the arrangements?'

Teaching point 3: Difficulty explaining the thinking process ('I just did it')

One of the big ideas that I introduced at the beginning of the chapter was the ability to communicate mathematical reasoning. By the time pupils are leaving primary school we would hope they will be using sophisticated mathematical language to describe mathematical reasoning as I mentioned in the progression section.

However, this is not something that comes naturally. When I first ask a learner of any age how they have worked something out they often tell me 'I just did it'. This is not through an inability to describe their thought process. Until we start to try to remember how we are thinking mathematically it really does feel as though we 'just did it'.

One way to get children to describe their thinking is to present a mental calculation – for example, working out how many children are in school today.

Say the numbers in school were:

Year 1	28	Year 4	22
Year 2	31	Year 5	25
Year 3	25	Year 6	30

Quickly calculate the total number in school. Now write down how you carried out the calculation. Two Year 6 children who worked on this told me:

I added all the tens, so 20 + 30 + 20 + 20 + 20 + 30 and that gave me 140, then I added on 21 because that is what the units came to.

I noticed that 28 and 22 made 50, and that 25 and 25 made 50 so that was 100, then I added on 31 and 30.

I got them to think more carefully about how they had worked it out by asking the first learner how they added the 'tens'. When they thought about it, they realised they had added all the '20s' together first and then added 60 to get to 140.

The best way to 'teach' children how to explain their thinking is through your questioning. Look at this example overleaf.

DOMINO TOTALS

Play a game of dominoes.

Can you make a total of 6 each time?

Can you use all the dominoes?

Play again.

Try to make totals of 5.

Can you use all the dominoes?

Try for other totals.

What do you notice?

You will see that the text offers open questions,

Can you use all the dominoes?

and asks the children to write about what they notice. A question invites the children to try other totals.

You might want to support children in getting started on this by thinking about which totals are possible and which aren't possible.

Always respond to an answer from one of your learners with a question.

For example, if they say 13 isn't possible ask why, even though it seems obvious.

You might want to encourage different pairs to try different totals too – some will be easier than others and the pairs will then have an outcome to talk about.

Teaching point 4: Unwillingness to try to prove an assertion ('It just works')

A group of Year 2 children are making patterns with hexagons and equilateral triangles.

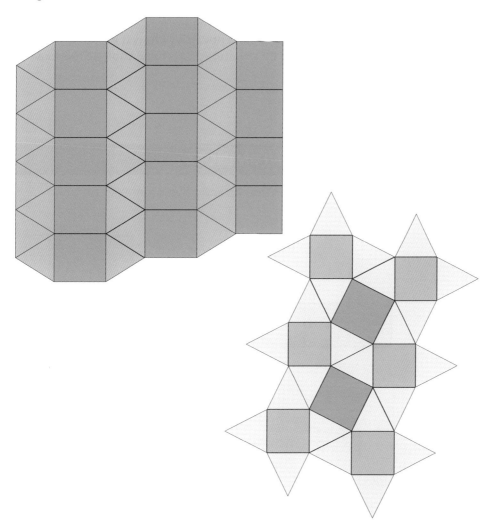

Their teacher is trying to work with them to get them to 'prove' some of their findings:

Teacher: What if you made two rows of squares around your design, how many triangles will you need at the corner?

Child: Two, I think. Oh no, look, it takes three.

Teacher: And what if you made three rows of squares?

Child: I don't want another row of squares.

Earlier in this chapter I commented that many children did not immediately develop an 'inclination to solve problems'. It is often our younger learners who make this clearest to us. We can only work to develop the willingness of our learners to 'prove' their assertions by modelling this expectation as the norm in our classrooms. Again, this comes down to questioning. Several learners in classes I have taught have ended up frustrated with me as my usual response to an assertion they offer me is 'Why?' or 'Are you sure?' However, they quickly realise that 'being sure' of an answer is my measure of success and they stop telling me the answer and begin to explain how they know it is the right answer.

Developing ideas of proof can be structured carefully. Look at this example in the following box:

PENTOMINOES

- How many different ways can you arrange five squares so that two sides touch exactly?

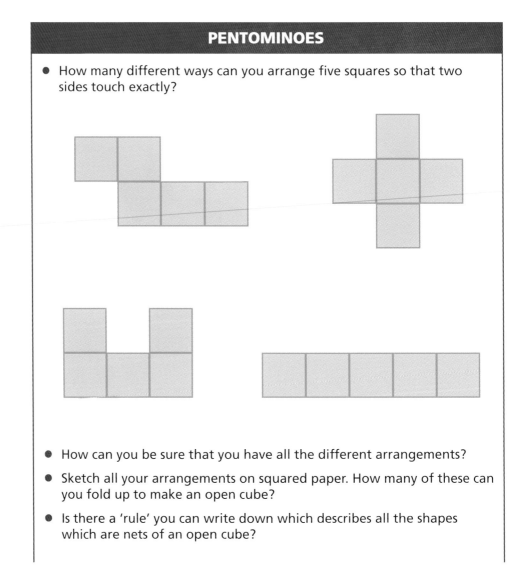

- How can you be sure that you have all the different arrangements?
- Sketch all your arrangements on squared paper. How many of these can you fold up to make an open cube?
- Is there a 'rule' you can write down which describes all the shapes which are nets of an open cube?

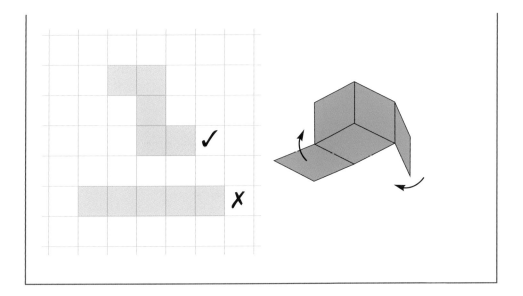

Try the activity for yourself. The activity is open at first but by asking you to check that you have all possibilities I move you towards proof. You have to introduce some system to your recording so that you can check that you have all possibilities. Giving a convincing reason why something is the case is the beginning of 'proof'. I then ask you to think about the shapes you have drawn in a different context. This is one way of asking you to make connections between different areas of mathematics. This time you can check your conjectures by cutting out the shapes and seeing if they will make an open cube. Then we move to trying to come up with a rule, or an '**algorithm**' which allows you to '**generalise**' from these special cases.

Teaching point 5: Not applying logical thinking

I will often find pupils looking back over correct answers they have written down and calling me over to ask me if they are correct. If I ask them what they think they will say – 'well I think it's right but it seemed too obvious'. It is almost as if they expect mathematics to trick them. If something seems obvious, or logical, they must have got it wrong. Maths can't be that easy. This may be because they have just been taught a series of 'tricks' or routines rather than having been shown that mathematics is inherently logical and follows very predictable patterns. If I can add 7 to 15, I can follow exactly the same process to add 7 to anything. And any time I add 7 to a number with 5 'ones' my answer will have a '2' in the 'ones' column.

One of my favourite problems to work on with young learners to help them see the importance of logical thinking and careful recording is the chessboard problem. I would ask you to work on this too. The question is very simple:

How many squares are there on a chess board?

At first you will think the answer is straightforward – there are 64 squares on a chessboard. But if you look carefully there are many 2 × 2 squares, many 3 × 3 squares and so on. Right the way up to an 8 × 8 square which forms the whole board. The next task is to find a way of counting these different squares.

I will leave you to work on this.

Portfolio task 3.5

How many squares are there on a chessboard?

The answer is not 64!

The answer is not 65!

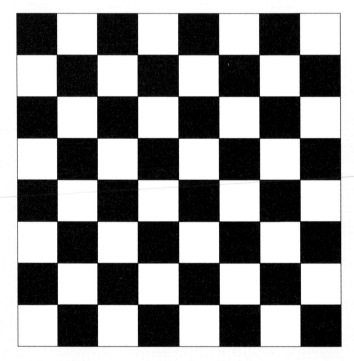

When you have an answer can you use this answer to work out how many squares there would be on a 10 × 10 board?

Many schools now use logical thinking activities, which do not necessarily draw on mathematics, to develop their pupils' problem-solving capacities. You can download many logic puzzles from the web from sites such as **logic-puzzles.org**. Some of these are lateral-thinking-type problems and some come with down-loadable grids which your pupils can use to solve these puzzles. This gets you into the habit of reasoning things out logically. This is a very useful habit when it comes to working at more complex mathematical investigations.

In practice

The following lesson plan was used to support a group of pupils beginning to develop their skills in problem solving using mathematics. I used this with pupils in lower primary. It would be suitable for Stages 1 or 2 in international schools and explores number patterns when using odd and even numbers.

Following the plan is an evaluation of the lesson which explores how successful the plan was in supporting the children to develop their knowledge, skills and understanding.

Objectives:	• To introduce the terms 'odd' and 'even' numbers • To describe number patterns orally or using pictures	
Key vocabulary: Even, odd, pair	**Context:** This is the fifth lesson in a series exploring counting on number lines and number tracks. Most of the children can count to 100 and can count backwards in 1s from 20. The previous lesson worked with the class on counting in 2s. All the groups could count in 2s from 0 but some found it difficult to start from any number other than 0. The higher attaining group could count backwards in 2s from any number	
	For this series of lessons I have grouped children according to their prior experience to provide support and challenge	
Resources: Washing line and pegs, white socks (real!), 0–20 grid on the whiteboard, hoops, odd and even labels, multilink, 0–30 number cards	**Starter activity:** I will ask the whole class to stand in a circle. We will start by counting in ones around the circle. Then I will ask every other child to clap rather than say their number, e.g. 1, clap, 3, clap. … We will then swap round: clap, 2, clap, 4. … We will repeat this counting backwards starting at 28, which is the number of children in the class	
	Next we will count feet around the circle – first counting everybody's feet, then counting in 2s. At this stage I will introduce the term 'even'	
Main activity:	Ask the children to work in groups and give them all some socks (these should have been counted earlier and organised so that some groups have an even number of socks and some have an odd number)	
	Each group has to calculate how many pegs it will need if they peg the socks on the washing line in pairs.	
	Ask each group to come and peg their socks on the lines. I will ask each group if there is an odd sock, or an even number of socks which make 'pairs'. As each group pegs up the socks I will circle the even numbers in green and the odd numbers in red on the number square on the whiteboard	
Group activity: Children operating above expected levels	These children will work with the 0–30 set of cards. They will pick a card at random and have to decide if it is even or odd. I will focus on this group to encourage them to discuss how they know it is even or odd	**Assessment:** I will ask the children to convince me how they know it is even or odd. They can draw pictures or use diagrams to convince me
Group activity: Children operating at expected levels	These children will be using the multilink towers. They need to make some odd towers and some even towers and place these in the correct hoop. I will ask the children how they are deciding which are even numbers and which are odd numbers	I will split this group into two so that they can check each other's towers at the end

45

| Group activity: Children operating below expected levels | This group will continue working with socks on the washing line. This time they will work with ten pairs of different coloured socks | I will ask the teaching assistant (TA) to support this group. She will ask them to peg up a number of pairs of socks and then count all the socks |

Plenary: All the groups will come back together on the carpet area. I will use a set of 1–30 number cards. I will ask the children to come to the front and pick a number to uncover

When they uncover it they will have to say if it is even or odd. The class will decide whether they are correct. All even numbers will be moved to the top left of the board and odds to the bottom right

Finally I will ask pupils to work with talk partners to explain how they can decide if a number is odd or even

Rationale and evaluation

The counting activity involved all the children. They were all successful too, which I was pleased about, although I could see Claire and Hannah mouthing the numbers when they were clapping. Rupa got a bit lost at one point so I asked him to use the number line on the classroom wall to count. He tapped the numbers as the rest of the group said them. This seemed to help as he could match his tapping to the rhythm of the clapping. Counting in 2s was a bit more difficult – I supported those who were having difficulty by circling all the even numbers on our number line. This allowed them to join in the activity, but I think they were simply reading the numbers off the line rather than coming to an understanding of their 'evenness'.

The children using the number cards really got into the idea of describing odd and even. Nasreen drew each number as a series of dots and circled pairs, so whenever there was an 'odd' dot outside her circles she knew it was odd. This showed that she was drawing on her learning in the socks activity.

The multilink towers worked well too. Both groups realised fairly quickly that by making towers that were two cubes wide they could very quickly decide which ones were odd and which were even. They finished this activity very quickly so I gave them number cards and asked them to label all the towers so they could see the odd and even numbers.

I was pleased that I continued with the washing line with the lower attaining group. They labelled the numbers of socks on the line and this reinforced the idea of counting in 2s for them.

During the plenary the rest of the children found Nasreen's suggestion about how to find out if a number was odd or even by using dots very helpful; they also liked the idea of odd and even towers. Both these images will help them consolidate the idea of odd and even. Finally, I asked if they could tell me how many socks there would be if I had 20 pairs of socks. They thought for a bit and then Michael told me, 'It's easy. They're all just doubles, so it's 40.' I was impressed – generalisation at age six!

Audit task

For every chapter you will be asked to write your own lesson plan exploring an area covered in the chapter. You should focus on learning which is appropriate for a group of learners that you are working with and select an area of mathematics that has been discussed in this chapter. Construct a lesson plan using the proforma on the companion website or any planning proforma that is used by your course or by the school in which you work. Teach the lesson and then evaluate it carefully with a focus on children's learning and misconceptions.

Add this lesson plan and evaluation to your subject knowledge portfolio. This is a very important piece of evidence to show your developing subject knowledge.

Observing problem solving using mathematics

You can access an example of a problem-solving activity on the companion website.

The activity uses the idea of a party and starts off with a table that seats six children, two at each side and one at each end. As more people arrive tables are added to the end of the previous table. Watch the piece of video and work out for yourself what the pattern will be. Once you have a pattern that will allow you to predict the number of people seated at any number of tables try to generalise the formula using an algebraic expression. Now explore other possible arrangements of tables. What would happen if you formed 'L' shapes with the tables? What would happen with tables which are different shapes?

Think carefully about how you would introduce this to a class you are working with. What questions would you ask to scaffold the activity? How would you leave the activity open enough so that your children move beyond simply filling in tables of results; and how would you encourage them to generalise?

Assessing problem solving using mathematics

When you wish to assess your learners to ascertain their skills in problem solving using mathematics you need to make sure you give your learners the opportunity to evidence: how they are approaching the problem that you have set them; the extent to which they are being systematic; their abilities in predicting possible outcomes and testing these; the effectiveness of the recording systems that they adopt; and finally the effectiveness of their communication of their reasoning process to others. As an example reflect back on Portfolio task 3.1 and answer the following questions as honestly as you can.

1   How persistent were you at looking for a range of patterns? Did you explore a range of patterns or stop after you had found two or three?
2   Were you able to explain why the pattern appeared or did you just describe the pattern?

3   Did you use 'increasingly complex' mathematical vocabulary to describe these patterns?

4   How systematic were you in exploring whether every number appeared and in your search for 1000?

5   Did you have a convincing explanation for your answer to whether or where 1000 appeared?

Try this activity with the group you are currently teaching, or any of the other activities in this chapter, and use the questions above to assess your pupils. Be open with them about the criteria you are using to assess them so that they are clear about your expectations. It is important that your pupils become aware of what counts as 'success' in problem solving as this may be slightly different to previous success criteria.

Cross-curricular teaching of problem solving

Learners respond very well to solving problems in their real world. This can also help them see the 'point' of learning new skills and motivate them to come to new understandings. A cross-curricular project offers you the possibility of working with mathematics over extended periods of time rather than in small chunks, often only an hour. Of course, when we problem solve outside school we don't limit ourselves to a single hour a day in order to solve our problem.

   A project focusing on developing a more sustainable school will both engage your learners and allow you to engage in a wide range of problem-solving activities. The most effective way to begin such a project is to ask your learners how they could explore this issue. Do some research for yourself first. How much waste paper is thrown away each day? How much does the school spend on paper and photocopying? What are the annual fuel bills? What are the implications for pollution for the ways that pupils travel to school? Some of the areas which learners have explored with me on this extended project over the years have included the following.

• Car parking: What is the most effective way of redesigning the car park so that it uses a minimum of space and so that it can incorporate a bike shed to encourage cycling to school. This involves measurements of cars, the construction of scale models and trying out different arrangements for parking spaces. The issue of ensuring there are sufficient parking spaces for those needing accessible parking is also important

• Travel to school: My pupils have always enjoyed surveying the whole school to find out how teachers and pupils get to school. They can then calculate the current carbon footprint. This has led to pupils exploring ways of lift sharing, of walking buses, and of cycling schemes where pupils meet up and cycle to school together. The mathematics involves exploring shortest routes to school, and possible 'pick-up' points.

- **Recycling paper:** Again, a brief survey can ascertain which classes use most paper; which classes are best at recycling paper; and the money that can be saved through recycling paper internally as scrap paper, or in home-made exercise books. A trip to the recycling plant is always popular.

- **Energy bills:** Sharing the energy costs within a school has always led to pupils becoming incredibly vigilant about turning off lights and thinking carefully about energy usage. In two schools I have worked in they have offered the school council a share of any money saved through cutting energy costs and the school council has been able to make the decision about how they will spend this money.

Summary

The focus of this chapter has been 'problem solving using mathematics'. This chapter is deliberately placed early in the book as the whole approach of the book in developing your subject knowledge is through a problem-solving or investigative approach. I hope that the chapter has given you insight into how you can learn mathematics through problem solving and that this in turn will enable you to teach children to problem solve and investigate effectively. The key ideas of 'communication', 'reasoning' and 'enquiry and problem solving' were outlined early in the chapter as a set of key skills in this area. The big ideas section also introduced you to ways in which 'specialising' and 'generalising' underpin any mathematical problem solving. The portfolio tasks throughout the chapter and the exemplar activities within the teaching points will also give you a wide range of starting points with which you can explore mathematical problem solving with the children you teach.

Reflections on this chapter

There are several key points to take from this chapter. First, you should now feel able to make a start on an investigation that is open – and you should be able to support your learners in 'attacking' an investigation through questioning rather than through directing them too closely. Perhaps you will be able to work with the children you teach to explore mathematical problems with them so that you model being a mathematician.

You should also have an understanding of how important it is to work with very young children on describing their thinking processes and realise that you can teach children to articulate their thoughts. You will have become more aware of the way you think mathematically when working at problem-solving activities. You can then share your thinking processes with the children you are teaching as a way of helping them understand their own thinking processes.

You have been introduced to key concepts such as specialising and generalising. Just a reminder: specialising means to look at specific examples to look for patterns; generalising means being able to make a statement about all cases. The most important thing that you should take away from this chapter is that a problem-solving approach means teaching your children to act like mathematicians rather than to simply follow rules that you have given them. If the children you are teaching are reflecting on their thinking, asking interesting questions about the problems they are working on and most importantly 'having an inclination' to solve problems, you will be succeeding.

Going further

The following books will help you explore the area of problem solving using mathematics in much more detail. The books also offer a wide range of activities both for you and your pupils.

Transforming Primary Mathematics

MIKE ASKEW

Mike draws on a huge body of research conducted in UK primary schools to argue that mathematics teaching in primary schools should be transformed to be based on problem solving and mathematical enquiry. He is clear that children should not be allocated to sets or groups to learn maths but should work together, collaboratively, on problem-solving activities, and that this will prepare them best for their futures.

Askew, M. (2011) *Transforming Primary Mathematics*. London: Routledge.

The Elephant in the Classroom: Helping children learn and love maths

JO BOALER

This book draws on Jo's research in both the UK and the USA exploring how children best learn maths. She has followed thousands of learners over several years and argues convincingly that problem solving through mathematics should be at the centre of the curriculum. The book includes examples of problem-solving activities that she has used or observed. You should also visit her 'youcubed' website **www.youcubed.org** which offers lots of activities you can use in your classroom. There are also several papers describing Jo's research in this area. The tagline is 'depth not speed'.

Boaler, J. (2009) *The Elephant in the Classroom: Helping children learn and love.* London: Souvenir Press.

Thinking Mathematically

JOHN MASON, LEONE BURTON and KAYE STACEY

In *Thinking Mathematically* the authors carefully describe the 'art' of problem solving which lies at the heart of mathematics. They demonstrate how you can encourage, develop and foster this process both in your own thinking and in the children that you teach. They do this by carefully taking you through a series of problem solving-activities.

Mason, J., Burton, L. and Stacey, K. (1985) *Thinking Mathematically*. London: Pearson Education.

Self-audit

You should carry out this self-audit and add it to your subject knowledge portfolio. This offers evidence of your own learning and development in the area of 'problem solving using mathematics'. Read through the problem several times before you try to make a start. Also reread the description of rubric writing earlier in the chapter so that you can use this process to describe your thinking.

This task explores number patterns within a 100 square:

1	2	3	4	5	6	7	8	9	10
11	12	13	14	15	16	17	18	19	20
21	22	23	24	25	26	27	28	29	30
31	32	33	34	35	36	37	38	39	40
41	42	43	44	45	46	47	48	49	50
51	52	53	54	55	56	57	58	59	60
61	62	63	64	65	66	67	68	69	70
71	72	73	74	75	76	77	78	79	80
81	82	83	84	85	86	87	88	89	90
91	92	93	94	95	96	97	98	99	100

Look at a block of four numbers, for example:

15	16
25	26

If I add these numbers together I get a total of 82.

This is $(4 \times 15) + 22$, as $4 \times 15 = 60$ and $60 + 22 = 82$.

Picking another block and looking at the number in the top left box

18	19
28	29

I notice that $(4 \times 18) + 22 = 72 + 22 = 94$ and $18 + 19 + 28 + 29 = 94$ too.

This is an example of specialising – I have looked at two different blocks of four squares and explored the patterns in them. In order to generalise I can write down

n	$n + 1$
$n + 10$	$n + 11$

or

n	One more than the number to its left
10 more than the number above	11 more than the number in the top left square

So, adding these 'numbers' together:

$$n + (n + 1) + (n + 10) \ 1 \ (n + 11) = 4n + 22$$

This shows that if I take any section of four numbers from the grid and add them together I will always get a total which is four times the number in the top left corner + 22.

Now look at other blocks of numbers in the 100 square on page 51, for example:

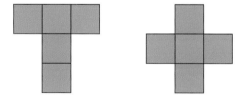

As you work at these problems jot down your thinking process at the side of the page. Use the rubric writing mentioned in the chapter. How do you get started on the problem? When are you stuck? What questions do you ask yourself to move forward? When are you specialising and when are you generalising? What 'aha' moments do you have? And finally, what have you learnt about this problem and yourself as a mathematical thinker?

CHAPTER 4

NUMBER
Counting; place value; fractions, decimals and percentages

Introduction

It is very difficult trying to remember how we learnt to count. It is one of those things many of us learnt before we had clear memories. However you have probably either worked with or been with young children beginning to make sense of 'counting'. I am currently enjoying watching my grandson – age two as I write this chapter – making his first steps in learning about numbers and the numbers system. Recently I was sitting with a three-year-old child of a good friend who had 'learnt' to count to 20. He did not have a sense of what 'counting to 10' meant but he had heard the pattern repeated many times. He counted carefully, saying each word accurately, 'one, two, three…' and so on. I wondered what would happen if I deliberately miscounted and so I jumped from 6 to 8 missing out 7. For some reason he thought this was hilarious. 'No' – he shouted at me, so of course I repeated the 'joke'. He did not yet know that 8 was two more than 6, but he did know that you should always say 7 immediately after 6. This chapter will unpick the big ideas in learning to count and in understanding number. It will also engage you in activities which will allow you to reflect on how you learn counting and understanding number and will draw on research to illustrate how best to support children in their learning.

This opening activity helps you reflect on the skills you bring to counting without really thinking about it.

Starting point

Portfolio task 4.1

You will need to work with a small group of friends or colleagues.

Take it in turns to pick up a number of small cubes, between five and twelve. Drop them onto a flat surface and cover them with a piece of cloth. Remove the cloth so that your friends can see the cubes but replace it before they have chance to 'count' the cubes.

Ask them how many cubes they saw.

Then ask how they calculated. It is likely that the group will have counted in 2s, or 3s, or even larger groups depending on the arrangement of the cubes.

Try this several times with increasing numbers of cubes to see how many cubes they can 'count' in this way.

This activity illustrates the basic principles of counting which will be explored in more detail later in the chapter. Indeed, those children who can quickly see the number of cubes are likely to have a well-developed 'number sense'. They are able to see the cubes in a range of ways to help them count quickly and understand that the total of the count is the same as the total of the groups they are counting. They probably have a range of mental images attached to particular numbers. For example, they might see '5' as an arrangement of dots on a dice, as two dots next to three dots, or as a line of five dots. This means that when they see the number '5' they also see:

$$5 = 2 + 1 + 2 \qquad 5 = 3 + 2$$

It can be argued that counting and understanding place value is at the heart of mathematics: the essence of numeracy. There are many counting games and traditional rhymes which show that counting is a skill that is often developed outside the traditional classroom. There are also different traditions for finger counting – some cultures count each finger separately, some use knuckles so that each finger can represent a count of three, others use the thumb as a symbol for five or ten.

The big ideas that are explored in this chapter are 'counting', 'place value', 'fractions, decimals and percentages' and 'proportionality'. The next section shows the progression in counting and understanding number in terms of the key objectives within the framework.

Progression in counting; place value; fractions, decimals, percentages and proportionality

Don't worry if you don't understand all of the ideas in this section at the moment. You will have been introduced to the key vocabulary by the time you have finished working through this chapter. All of the ideas are discussed in detail as you work through the chapter.

- **Foundations for counting and understanding place value** Initially, young learners will learn to say and use number names in order in contexts that are familiar to them. They will start to understand that numbers identify how many objects are in a set and use this understanding to count reliably up to 20 everyday objects. They will be able to estimate how many objects they can see and check this by counting (the activity that opened this chapter would be a useful assessment activity to see how well this skill has been developed).

  At this early stage they will always use concrete objects to explore problems and will have begun to solve problems involving doubling and halving.

- **Beginning to count and understand place value** The next stage is for pupils to read and write numerals from 0 to 20 and beyond (up to 100 by the end of this stage), and to use their knowledge of place value to place these numbers on a number track and number line. (Number tracks and number lines are used to support children in developing their counting skills. Number tracks have the numerals in the spaces. They can only represent positive whole numbers and must not include zero. Number lines have numerals on the lines and can therefore represent fractions and zero and even negative numbers at a later stage.) They will become used to counting aloud in 1s, 2s, 5s and 10s and will have heard and developed language such as 'more' or 'less' to compare two numbers. They will also understand what makes a number 'odd' or 'even' and know the even and odd numbers up to 20.

  They will use **ordinal numbers** (these numbers indicate position – first, second, third and so on) in different contexts and will be able to recognise the **cardinal numbers** 1 to 9. They will also be able to find one more or less than a given number and ten more or less than a given number.

  Once pupils can count up to 100 objects they can learn to group them and count in 10s, 5s or 2s. They will also learn to explain what each digit in a two-digit number represents, including numbers where zero is a place holder; ('0' is often described as a 'place holder' as it has no value. So, for example, in the number 4026 there are no 'hundreds' but we need to use the '0' as otherwise we would confuse 4026 with 426.) When they understand the meaning of the digits in two-digit numbers they can be taught about **partitioning** two-digit numbers in different ways, including into multiples of 10 and 1. Partitioning is a very useful skill to develop in order to support the development of mental methods.

For example, we can partition 47 into 40 + 7.
So if we are to try to add 47 + 15
we can see it as 40 + 7 + 10 + 5
or 40 + 10 + 7 + 5 = 62.

Pupils will be beginning to understand the idea of halves and quarters of shapes and quantities, knowing that there are two halves in a whole and four quarters in a whole.

- **Becoming confident in counting and place value and developing an understanding of fractions, decimals and percentages** Pupils can now develop their understanding of partitioning so that they can partition four-digit numbers into multiples of 1000, 100, 10 and 1 in different ways. They can count from 0 in multiples of 4, 8, 50 and 100 moving on to counting in multiples of 6, 7, 9, 25 and 100. They can find 1000 more or less than a given number through ordering and comparing numbers up to 10 000. They can use this knowledge to round numbers to the nearest 10 or 100. They are also introduced to negative numbers in context at this stage.

  They are also ready to be introduced to fractions. They should use diagrams to identify **equivalent fractions**. Examples of equivalent fractions are 6/8 and 3/4, or 70/100 and 7/10. Equivalent fractions have the same value. Children can also learn how to interpret **mixed numbers** and position them on a number line. An example of a mixed number is 3 3/4. It is a fraction which contains a whole number as well as a fraction. They will learn the decimal equivalents to 1/4, 1/2 and 3/4.

  They can also begin to explain what each digit represents in whole numbers and decimals with up to two places, and partition, round and order these numbers. The rule to remember with **rounding** numbers to a particular decimal place is that if the next number to the right of that decimal place is 5 or more, you round the figure up to the next highest number, and if it is 4 or less it remains the same. For instance, if I were to round 4.72 to one decimal place I would write 4.7. If I were to round to the nearest whole number I would write 5. They will understand **decimal notation** in contexts such as length and money.

- **Extending learning in counting and place value and developing an understanding of fractions, decimals and percentages** Towards the end of their time in primary school learners will have developed their understanding of number and place value to work up to 10 000 000 (ten million). They can round any number and use negative numbers in a context confidently. They can count on and back in fractions and decimals through 0 in both directions and understand the effect of multiplying and dividing by all multiples of 10.

They understand the language of **'factors'** and **'multiples'** and know what 'prime numbers' are. (These terms are all defined in the glossary.) They are also confident in working with equivalent fractions, decimals and percentages, knowing, for example, that 25% = 0.25 = 1/4. They will be able to express one quantity as a percentage of another (e.g. express £400 as a percentage of £1000).

The transition to secondary education will focus on developing children's use of **ratio notation**. Percentage notation is 30%, ratio notation is 30:100 and decimal notation is 0.3. Here the pupils you wish to extend can learn to reduce a ratio to its simplest form and divide a quantity into two parts in a given ratio. They will be able to use this understanding to solve simple problems involving ratio and direct proportion (e.g. identify the quantities needed to make a fruit drink by mixing water and juice in a given ratio).

The next section of the chapter focuses on the big ideas of 'counting', 'place value', 'fractions, decimals and percentages' and 'proportionality' which are at the heart of counting and understanding number. If you are confident with these ideas you will be able to teach children successfully across the primary age range and will have a clear understanding of the development of these ideas across the 3–11 age phase.

Big ideas

Counting

Many children will start school able to count – but it is important to be aware of the principles of counting, both to support the children who cannot yet count and to recognise the processes that young children who have already learnt to count have mastered. The key research which supports us in understanding the process of learning to count was undertaken by Rochel Gelman and Randy Gallistel in *The Child's Understanding of Number* published in 1986. Gelman and Gallistel are both psychologists and their book was seen as marking a huge development in our understanding of how children learn to count. Through careful observation of young children undertaking activities that they had planned they described five principles which underpin counting:

1   The one-to-one principle: a child who understands the one-to-one principle knows that we only count each item once.
2   The stable order principle: a child who understands the stable order principle knows that the order of number names always stays the same. We always count by saying one, two, three, four, five … in that order.
3   The cardinal principle: a child who understands the cardinal principle knows that the number they attach to the last object they count gives the answer to the question 'How many …?'.
4   The abstraction principle: a child who understands the abstraction principle knows that we can count anything – they do not all need to be the same

type of object. So we can count apples, we can count oranges, or we could count them all together and count fruit.

5   The order irrelevance principle: a child who understands the order irrelevance principle knows that we can count a group of objects in any order and in any arrangement and we will still get the same number.

Portfolio task 4.2

Can you think of examples of children who do not yet understand these principles?

For example, a child who is asked to count seven multilink cubes laid out in a row and then count them again when you put them into a different arrangement to 'check' there are still seven would not yet understand the order irrelevance principle.

Write your examples and enter this reflection in your personal portfolio.

The mathematics curriculum in New Zealand has recently been developed and they have published a series of progression guides which support teachers in planning for progression at the early stages of children's learning. They break down teaching to count into the following steps.

1   Pre-counting: The focus here is on the ideas of more than, less than and the same as. Children will often make these comparisons by lining up objects rather than counting.

2   One-to-one counting: This is the ability to say the number words in order and to match each number to one object as described above.

3   Counting sets: This links to the cardinal principle and the stable order principle.

4   Counting from 1 to solve number problems: These may be addition problems involving combining sets and counting all the objects in both sets, or they may just be questions like 'how many...?' Children can also count from 1 to solve subtraction problems. They count from 1 to see how many objects to remove from a set and then count how many are left.

5   Counting on to solve number problems: By this stage children understand the cardinality principle and can count forwards and backwards and so can add 7 and 2 by starting counting at 7.

Place value

Place value refers to the value of a digit which is dependent on its location within a number, such as units, tens, hundreds. So in 352, the place value of the 5 is 'tens' and the 5 is worth 50.

The system of place value consistently used across Europe and in much of the Western world is described as the Hindu–Arabic method. It is based on the following key principles:

There are 10 digits (0, 1, 2, 3, 4, 5, 6, 7, 8, 9).

The column that a digit is placed in determines its value. A digit one place to left of another digit is worth ten times its value. Zero is used as a place holder to represent an empty column.

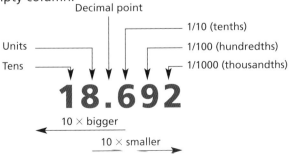

This place value system developed from the use of counting boards by traders. Beans or counters would be placed in each column on the board to represent a number. If ten beans were placed in a column they would be replaced by a single counter in the column to the left.

Teachers often ask me at what stage they should introduce 'zero'. The word zero derives from the Arabic word *sifr* meaning 'empty' and that is why we need the symbol '0' or zero. We use zero to represent an empty column in place value so the number

Hundreds	Tens	Ones	.	Tenths	Hundredths
3	0	7	.	6	

has 3 hundreds, 0 tens, 7 ones and 6 tenths. It also has 0 hundredths and even 0 millions but we do not write the zeroes if they are at either end of the place value grid otherwise every number would contain an infinite number of digits!

So – to answer the question 'When should we introduce zero to young children?' my answer would be that we use the word zero from the very beginning. Children will see zeroes around them as soon as they start noticing numbers. If we say 'Can you see a zero?' in the same way that we would ask 'Can you see a nine?' as we walk past number nine in the street children will come to see that zero is not the same as the letter 'O'. They even look slightly different – '0' and 'O'. That is why there are two separate keys for the symbols on the keyboard that I am using to type this sentence.

I would not use them when counting – so start counting at 1. We don't spend our time looking for things that there aren't any of do we? But whenever you have a number line rather than a number track include a zero. And as soon as you begin to explore place value with your learners you can introduce the idea of zero as a place holder.

As we saw in the previous section, many children begin their formal school able to count. However, it is not always the case that they link the counting to the symbols which represent numbers. In the book *Children and Number*, which we referred to earlier, Martin Hughes suggested that children move through three stages when beginning to represent numbers. At first they will represent their counting pictorially, so they will record five sweets by drawing five sweets, then they move on to an iconic form of recording so they might represent five sweets by drawing five sticks. Finally they use the symbol 5 to represent the count.

In 1989 Herbert Ginsburg, from Columbia University in New York, developed some of Piaget's ideas to suggest that there are three facets to understanding place value:

1   A child can write numbers but does not make the link between the symbol and the number they are counting.
2   A child can recognise when a number is written incorrectly.
3   A child understands the value of each digit in a number.

Teaching pupils to understand partitioning is a useful way to develop their understanding of place value. If you look back to the progression section which opened this chapter you can see that at the early stages children are encouraged to read and write numbers up to 20 which links to phases 1 and 2 in Ginsburg's schema.

Portfolio task 4.3

Can you think of examples of children who do not yet make the link between the numerical symbols and the results of a count?

I have heard children ask how to 'spell' a certain number.

They might count 15 ducks in a pond and ask, 'How do you spell 15?' Alternatively they may recognise particular numbers such as their age, the house number they live at, or the bus they catch to school, and not connect this to the numbers on a number line.

Add these ideas to your portfolio.

Fractions, decimals and percentages

Before you start this section I want you to try this Portfolio task.

Portfolio task 4.4

Take as large a sheet of paper as you can get hold of.

Write 1/2 in the centre. Now create a web diagram with as many different representations of 1/2 as you can think of.

These might be diagrams with 1/2 shaded in different ways, they might be equivalent fractions, or they might be percentages.

When you have exhausted this idea pick another fraction which is linked to 1/2 in some way. So you might choose 1/4 (which is 1/2 of a 1/2).

Create another family of representations for a quarter.

Carry on filling the paper with as many different fractions as you can think of.

This task shows how closely related fractions, decimals and percentages are. They are usually taught separately, which leads to children not making the link between the three ideas. In fact, they are just three different ways of representing numbers. It is very useful to move between the three representations as this allows us to see mathematics as connected rather than separate. It also allows us to draw on our understanding of one area of mathematics to solve problems in another area.

Fractions are 'parts' of whole numbers. We need to be able to describe 'parts' of whole numbers for two reasons. First, when measuring we can't be sure that a length or weight will also be a whole number. Second, when we 'share' or divide numbers there are many occasions when the result of the division is not an **integer**, so we need a way of writing an answer that is not an integer. We call this a fraction.

Terezinha Nunes and Peter Bryant have explored for many years the ways in which children understand fractions. In 1996 Blackwell published their book called *Children Doing Mathematics* and in this they suggest that understanding fractions is not simply a case of extending the knowledge we have of whole numbers. There are key differences. For example, a whole number can only be represented in one way: if we count three objects we will write 3. However, there are classes of fractions – 1/4 is the same as 2/8, 4/16 or even 25% or 0.25. Fractions are also used for different purposes, and appear to mean different things in different cases. So, if a fraction represents part of a whole, the **denominator** represents the number of parts into which the whole has been 'cut' and the **numerator** represents the number of parts taken. So in the fraction 5/7, 5 is the numerator and 7 is the denominator.

Nunes and Bryant suggest that children have to come to an understanding of two key ideas:

- First, that for the same denominator, the larger the numerator, the larger the fraction. So

    1/7 < 4/7 < 6/7.

- Second, that for the same numerator, the larger the denominator, the smaller the fraction. So

    3/5 < 3/7 < 3/10.

Learning fractions is something we associate with 'rules'. For example:

- You must multiply the numerator and denominator by the same number when making equivalent fractions.
- You must divide the numerator and denominator by the same number when making equivalent fractions.
- When dividing fractions you turn the second fraction 'upside down' and multiply.

Ratio and proportion

Many of my students have come to me very worried when they have been asked to teach ratio and proportion. This has always interested me as it is an area of mathematics that we all have intuitive understandings about. In the book *Street Mathematics and School Mathematics*, Terezinha Nunes and her colleagues showed that street children in Brazil had well-developed ideas and strategies to work with ratio and proportion when they worked in the street markets, but that they could not transfer the methods they employed out of school to contexts that were introduced to them in school. For example, try to complete the conversion table below (this activity is most effective if you carry it out with some colleagues):

Pounds sterling	1	2	3	4	5	10	20	50	100
Euros	1.25								

When you have completed the table talk to your colleagues about the strategies that you used. Many people find that using 'doubles' is effective, so they will complete the 2 and 4 columns first. You can than find 3 euros by adding 2 + 1 pounds, or multiplying by 3. If you know 3 and 2 you can find 5. Once you have 5, doubling can allow you to complete the table. Try this sort of strategy to complete this table:

Euros	1	2	3	4	5	10	20	50	100
Pounds	0.8								

It is important to use the language of ratio and proportion from the early stages so that when the ideas are introduced more formally, later in primary school, children have the linguistic base on which they can build their understanding when they are introduced formally to ratio and proportion. A formal learning objective may be phrased as: Pupils should use the vocabulary of ratio and proportion to describe the relationship between two quantities (for example: 'There are two red beads to every three blue beads, or two beads in every five beads are red').

You can see how this vocabulary can be introduced at a day-to-day level across the school – perhaps at the beginning and the end of school days looking at things like school dinners and sandwiches, numbers of boys and girls, people who walk to school or come in the car, and so on.

The big ideas above have introduced you to the mathematical content that you need to come to understand in order to teach young children to count; to support children in coming to understand place value, without which no calculations are possible; to introduce them to ideas of fractions, decimals and percentages and finally to make sense of ratio and proportion. The following teaching point offers you support in teaching these ideas in your classroom.

Teaching points

Teaching point 1: Inconsistent counting

Tony asks Holly how many ducks there are in the pond:

Holly says it's easy and counts 1, 2, 3, 4, 5, 5, 7, 8, 9.

Here Holly has not grasped either the one-to-one principle as she counts the big duck twice – perhaps in her mind she sees the size as important and so counts twice. She also misses 6 out of the count. This shows she does not yet realise that you always have to use the number names in order.

The best way to support children in overcoming this misconception is by giving them plenty of experience in counting. Try to use everyday objects that can be arranged in many possible ways for the children to count. Asking them to check each other's counting is a useful way of their supporting each other. Counting with the children is also important as you can model touching each object as you count it. Ask the children to count the same set of objects several times, arranging the objects differently each time. This will help them come to an understanding of the order irrelevance principle. It is also important to teach the children lots of counting rhymes and songs. This supports the development of the stable order principle.

Teaching point 2: Miscounting on a number track

Sam is playing a game and he sometimes starts counting from the square that his counter is sitting on. This will cause a problem for him later when he uses a number line to support his mental calculations. This may be the reason that some children give incorrect answers for addition calculations. For example, they may write

$$5 + 3 = 7$$

1	2	3	4	5	6	7	8	9	10

This is because they counted 1, 2, 3, 4, 5 and then start on the 5 and count 5, 6, 7.

Again the best way to support children through this is to use number lines regularly in many different contexts – frogs on lily pads; house numbers. It is particularly useful to ask young children to move on number tracks that you create in the classroom or the playground. Playing games is also important. The children very quickly correct each other if they are counting incorrectly!

Teaching point 3: Directed numbers

A **directed number** is one which has a plus or minus sign attached. This tells us whether it is a 'positive' or 'negative' number. So +7 means 'positive' 7 and –3 means 'negative' 3. A student of mine was researching directed numbers before planning a lesson for her Year 6 group. She remembered being told by a teacher in her secondary school that 'two negatives make a positive'. She had written – 4 + –2 = +6 and said to me, 'that can't be right'.

I illustrated the calculation using a number line – moving to the right on a number line represents addition and to the left subtraction. So I start with the arrow at –4. I am adding so I expect to move to the right; however, I am not adding 2, I am adding –2, so in this case the minus sign reverses the direction and the arrow moves to –6. So –4 + –2 = –6.

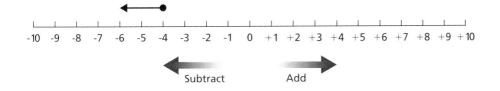

Primary age pupils should be using directed numbers to find the difference between positive and negative integers in context, or to count down in whole number and decimal steps extending beyond zero. An integer is a number which has no decimal or fractional part. We sometimes call them whole numbers. An integer can be either positive or negative. Integers should not be confused with 'natural' numbers. The **natural numbers** are all the positive integers, that is 0, 1, 2, 3, 4 and so on. Pupils may also be expected to position positive and negative numbers on a number line and to be able to use the < and > symbols to state inequalities. (An **inequality** is a statement showing which number is greater or less than another: < means 'less than' and > 'greater than'. So –2 < +7 and –4 > –9.) This is helpful when pupils come to explore more complex equations at later stages of their learning.

The most appropriate way to support pupils with all of these ideas is to use a number line which extends beyond 0. I would suggest that it is appropriate that the number lines used for display, or used to support children's calculations in the later stages of primary school, should always extend above and below 0 by the same number. This develops the pupil's visual representation of the number system to include negative numbers. One useful context to use in support of the pupils' understanding of negative numbers is temperature.

Measuring temperature

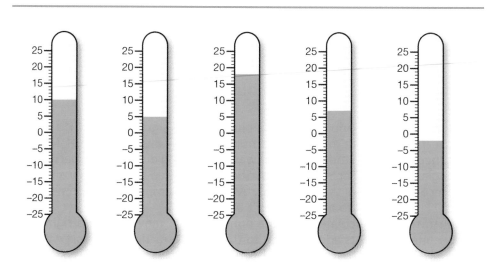

Jan	Feb	Mar	Apr	May	Jun	Jul	Aug	Sep	Oct	Nov	Dec
–2	–5	3	5	8	10	13	18	12	17	7	–8

This table shows the average temperature for each month in Otley. Which months do the thermometers represent? Shade in the blank thermometers to show the average temperatures in other months.

This example shows how directed numbers can be illustrated using temperature. It is even better if you use temperatures for the local area in which you teach. To provide a wider range of temperatures use other contexts that are meaningful for the pupils. If your school is twinned with a school in Africa or another area with a different climate this is ideal.

The thermometer provides an image of a number line for the learner and the children are asked to draw their own number lines/thermometers to support them in developing their own use of number lines to model calculating using directed numbers. It is helpful to describe 'getting warmer' as addition and 'getting colder' as subtraction. The following activity shows how this activity can be developed to support children in developing their own use of a number line to come to understand directed numbers.

Properties of numbers and number sequences

You will need:

- cards with numbers 1–20
- cards with numbers 10–20

You will be creating number sequences with seven numbers.

- Pick a card between 1 and 20 to get the size of the steps.
- Pick a card between 10 and 20 to get the starting number.

The teaching points so far have focused on counting. The next series of teaching points move into the area of place value.

Teaching point 4: Errors in writing numbers

Zeynab counts 19 sweets in the play shop. She writes down 91. Her friend Jasbir looks at the date written on the shopping list – she says, 'I can read that number, 2008, it is two hundred and eight.'

This is a common misconception and comes from children literally 'reading' the number. Zeynab sees the '9' digit first and knows she should say nine – teen. So she writes '9' and then adds the '1' to signal 'teen'. Similarly Jasbir notices the '200' and then the '8' so she sees 200 and 8.

Counting activities which involve children grouping objects in 10s and then finding the appropriate numeral on a number line will help these children. So for example you could give children 18, 23, 47 kidney beans – ask them to count them and then find the appropriate place on a number line and write a card which shows how many beans there are. As children get older the use of place value cards to support the children in partitioning numbers helps them understand the value of each digit in a number.

Teaching point 5: Confusion about the use of 0 as a place holder

Some children become confused about the use of 0, particularly in decimals. For example, a child may think that 1.5 and 1.50 are different numbers. This can happen in particular when a child is using a calculator to work out money problems as often calculators will 'remove' the 0 in £1.50 when it is entered. Many calculators will 'remove' the 0 if you type in 1.50 when you press the 'operation' key. It is worth deliberately doing this with pupils so that they notice it happening. Using a resource such as arrow cards can support your pupils in coming to an understanding of place value as they show the 'value' of each digit in a number when you remove the arrow cards. The best form of the activity is to let your pupils have a set of arrow cards (you can download these from the companion website) and set each other challenges to make numbers. Once they have 'made' the number they have to be able to say the number. It is also helpful to make a series of numbers and ask the pupils to order them in order of size.

Place value

You will need:

- a partner
- place value cards
- mini-whiteboards

Read the numbers below to each other. Then make them with your place value cards. Read aloud the number from your cards to make sure it is the same as the one written in words.

The first one has been done for you.

1 twenty-four thousand three hundred and sixty-one

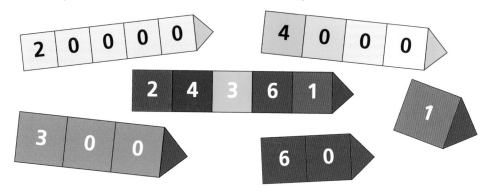

2 eighteen thousand five hundred and nineteen
3 thirty thousand seven hundred and eighty-two
4 seventy-two thousand and forty-seven
5 forty-five thousand eight hundred and twenty
6 eleven thousand two hundred and fifteen
7 fifty-six thousand and seven

Teaching point 6: Multiplication and division by powers of 10

A friend of mine questioned me when I suggested that teachers who told young children to 'add a zero' when multiplying by 10 were contributing to developing a misconception. I gave her the example of 1.7 × 10 and asked her what she thought the answer was. She came up with 10.7. The rule 'add a nought' was fixed in her mind from her time in school, but she realised that 1.70 was the same as 1.7 so couldn't be correct. However, 10.7 is approximately correct as 1 × 10 is 10. So 10.7 seemed a sensible answer.

A focus on moving the digits one place to the left when multiplying by 10 and moving to the right when dividing will overcome this misconception. Use place value mats when carrying out activities which involve multiplying and dividing by multiples of 10.

Thousands	Hundreds	Tens	Ones

or

Thousands	Hundreds	Tens	Units	Tenths	Hundredths	Thousandths	Ten Thousandths	Hundred Thousandths	Millionths

You can also model multiplication and division by multiples of 10 using pupils and large number cards. The only rule is that the person holding the decimal point can never move!

The example below shows how you can introduce the idea of moving 'digits' and not adding a zero to your pupils.

Multiplying and dividing by 10

1   Write a single digit in the middle of a page.
2   Multiply this number by 10 and write this number above the first number. Repeat working up the page, until you have five numbers.
3   (a)   Now divide your original number by 10. Write the new number below your original number.
    (b)   Repeat, working down the page. What patterns can you see?

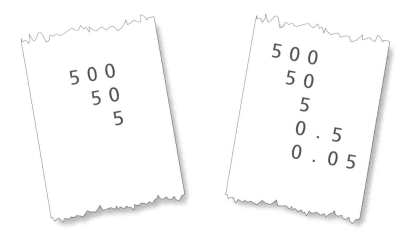

4   What happens when you divide a whole number with up to four digits by 10 and then multiply the answer by 100?

Teaching point 7: Ordering decimals

Kev asks a group of children to order the following decimals:

1.7, 2.52, 1.65, 2.435, 0.812

One of the children writes:

1.7, 1.65, 2.52, 0.812, 2.435

The child has ignored the decimal point to order the numbers. So the child sees seventeen for 1.7 and two thousand, four hundred and thirty-five for 2.435.

If children have this difficulty give them a place value grid to place the numbers on. For example:

Units	Decimal point	1/10	1/100	1/1000
0	.	8	1	2
1	.	6	5	0
1	.	7	0	0
2	.	4	3	5
2	.	5	2	0

Encourage the children to use the 0s as place holders and look for the patterns. When they write the numbers in ascending order outside the grid they can remove the 0s which are not needed and discuss when we need to write a 0 and when it can be omitted.

Teaching point 8: Rounding numbers

A pupil I was working with recently was asked to round 795 to the nearest 10. The pupil had written 800 and crossed it out and written 790. I asked why they had crossed it out and they told me it couldn't be right as they had been asked to the nearest 10 and not the nearest 100; they also knew that 810 was 'too many' so they had gone back to 790. Not recognising multiples of 100 as possibilities for multiples of 10 is an error that many pupils show.

A similar error with decimals would be a pupil who rounded 0.3 to 1.0 when asked to round to the nearest whole number. Here the pupil does not see zero as a whole number and so ignores the convention of rounding up from 5. So 0.3 to the nearest whole number is 0 as it is nearer 0 than 1.

An empty number line is a very useful resource to use when working with pupils on rounding numbers. The most effective strategy is to ask pupils to set each other challenges. They can write numbers down for each other to place on the number line and then round to an accuracy either you decide or the pupils themselves decide. The activity below gives another example of an activity you could try with your pupils. This can be adapted for rounding to any degree of accuracy.

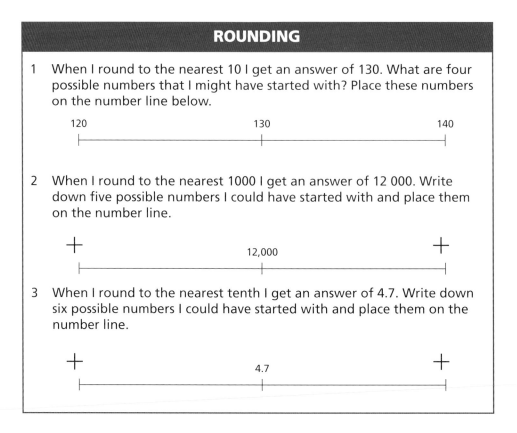

ROUNDING

1   When I round to the nearest 10 I get an answer of 130. What are four possible numbers that I might have started with? Place these numbers on the number line below.

    120   130   140

2   When I round to the nearest 1000 I get an answer of 12 000. Write down five possible numbers I could have started with and place them on the number line.

    +   12,000   +

3   When I round to the nearest tenth I get an answer of 4.7. Write down six possible numbers I could have started with and place them on the number line.

    +   4.7   +

Teaching point 9: Fraction names and writing fractions

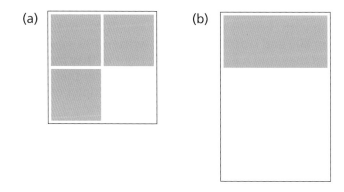

(a)

(b)

When faced with naming or writing the examples of fractions above, children may say many things. For example, a response to naming the fraction represented by (a) might be 'three-fourths'. Here the learner has remembered the convention for the denominator (number of parts in total) and the numerator (number of shaded parts), but has applied the convention of naming numbers that they are used to. Similarly I recently heard fraction (b) called 'a threeth'. It is important to listen carefully to the names that children give to fractions. In the examples above the children had an understanding of the ways in which the names are formed and so have understood the underpinning idea – they simply need help in selecting the appropriate language. This can best be done through the use of display, flash cards and the repetition of key words.

Sometimes, however, the naming and writing of fractions may point to a deeper misconception. Another child looking at fraction (b) wrote 1/2. They also wrote 3/1 and then crossed it out to write 1/3 for fraction (a). Here they are noticing shaded and unshaded parts of the diagrams but are not seeing a fraction as a division of 'a whole'. So, in shape (b) they saw one shaded part and two unshaded parts. They knew that 1/2 is a common fraction and so wrote the fraction as shaded parts:unshaded parts. The same thinking led to their response for fraction (a). In this case, however, they saw the answer 3/1, coming from shaded parts:unshaded parts, but told me that this 'didn't look right', so they inverted the fraction to a fraction which they had seen before.

An understanding of naming and writing fractions is key to successful calculation. It is probably worth repeating that a fraction is made up of:

Numerator	The number of parts of the 'whole'
Denominator	The number of fractional parts the 'whole' has been divided into

It is often helpful to remind children that the line separating the numerator from the denominator refers to division. So in the examples above, (b) can be seen as 'one out of three' or 'one divided by/into three'. Similarly for (a) we can say 'three out of four' or 'three divided by four'.

Portfolio task 4.5

Write down all the errors that you can remember children making when they have named or written down fractions.

For each example decide whether the children's misconception was based on a misunderstanding of the language of naming and writing fractions or a lack of clarity around what defines the numerator and denominator of a fraction.

Add these notes to your portfolio.

Teaching point 10: Fractions as equal areas

I was observing a student teacher who had asked her learners to draw as many examples of 1/2 as they could by shading in a square.

There were many imaginative and correct answers such as:

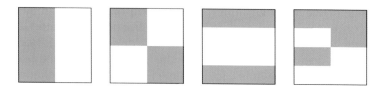

This showed me that both the student and the young learner understood that 1/2 could be represented by any four parts out of the eight that made up the whole; 1/2 does not have to be symmetrical, or obey a particular pattern.

Other children had used diagonal lines which allowed them to show many more views of 1/2.

However, one boy had drawn the following:

At first he was adamant that this was 1/2 as there were 'two out of four shaded in'. He was persuaded that this wasn't a half when I asked him if he would be happy to have the 'smaller half' if this was a bar of chocolate.

This misconception often arises as informally we may call any sharing into two 'halving' – if we are splitting a cake, for example, we will ask our friend, 'do you want half?', without thinking the two parts have to be exactly the same size. So when introducing fractions to children it is important to focus on the importance of equal areas.

The following activity focuses on this idea as well as making the link between fractions and decimals. This activity can only be carried out practically as the pupils will take great care to make sure things are fair!

CHOCOLATE FRACTIONS

Place three chairs at the front of the class.

Place one bar of chocolate on one chair, two bars on the next and three bars on the next.

Ask ten pupils to take it in turns to stand behind one chair making their choice of chair one after the other.

When all the pupils are standing behind the chairs they can divide the chocolate on the chair equally between the children at that chair.

This activity leads to a great deal of discussion about fractions as equal areas.

It can even make quite a good party game!

Teaching point 11: Fractions must be less than one

Before exploring this teaching point in more detail try this task.

Portfolio task 4.6

Can you write down 2.75 as a fraction and a percentage?

Can you do the same for 1.5 and 4.9?

When I ask my students to carry out this activity some find it difficult. Although they are used to seeing decimals greater than 1 they feel different about **improper fractions** (an improper fraction has a numerator larger than or equal to the denominator such as 7/4 or 4/3) or percentages larger than 100%. This is probably because we are so used to thinking of fractions as simply a 'part' of a single whole rather than as a way of representing any part of a number between two whole numbers. So we can write 2.75 as 2¾ or even 275%. It is important to use fractional number lines with children, and very important that these number lines extend beyond 1, and that you represent fractions and decimals together so that children begin to see how they can move between decimals and fractions in order to carry out comparisons and calculations.

Teaching point 12: Ordering fractions and decimals

Children often have difficulty ordering fractions. For example, they may think that 2/5 is larger than 2/3 as they notice that 5 is larger than 3 and they do not have mental images of the two fractions to fall back on. The most effective method I have found to support children in their ability to order fractions and decimals is to use an approach which uses multiple representations of fractions and decimals. This image shows you how you can represent fractions and decimals as areas and on a number line.

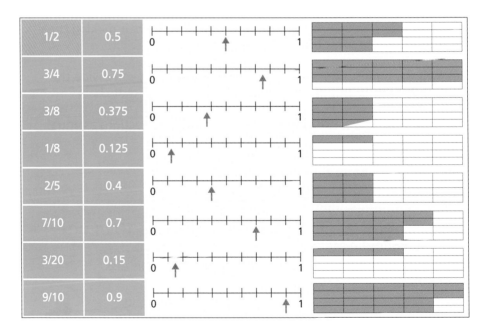

The following activity will help you to support pupils in coming to an understanding of fractions, their decimal equivalents and how to order them. Here children are encouraged to draw on their mental images of fractions and decimals to place them on an empty number line and draw on their current knowledge of fraction/decimal equivalents to calculate new equivalents. It would be even better to carry out this activity practically using a physical washing line in the classroom.

FRACTIONS AND DECIMALS

1. Look carefully at the pegs on the washing line. Estimate which fractions they could represent. Copy the numbers onto a large sheet of paper. Label the points A to H with their fractions and equivalent decimals.
2. Working with your partner, look at the gap between peg B and peg C. Think of a fraction that will hang on the line in the gap. Predict where it will hang. Calculate the decimal fraction to check it will fit before you hang it on the line.
3. Find a fraction to hang in each gap between the pairs of letters. Remember to calculate the decimal equivalent before you add it to your line.
4. Look at the gaps between the pegs. Now find a space to add three more fractions that have a different denominator to any that are already on the line.

Teaching point 13: The meaning of percentage

I began my career teaching in secondary schools and I still clearly remember the following comment from one of my 15-year-old boys. He had arrived at my maths lesson fresh from a French test – he was beaming and said, 'We've just got the results of our French exam. I did really well, the teachers said. I got 85% – the only trouble is that I don't know how many it was out of.' Like fractions, children have intuitive understandings of percentages. More specifically they will have seen 50% and may know that this is equivalent to a half. They may well have come across 10% in sales as well. A good starting point for working with fractions is to explore children's current understandings of percentages. Look through the papers and magazines that they read – ask them to bring in examples of percentages so that you can set a real context for the exploration of percentages. By the time that percentages are introduced the children should have an understanding of the equivalence between fractions and decimals, so it is important immediately to make this link as well. Of course, a percentage is always 'out of 100', per meaning 'for every' and cent meaning '100'.

Another example of the misconceptions that can arise with percentages is confusing a percentage 'of' (e.g. 20% of 60 = 12; 20% is the same as 2/10 so we can write 2/10 × 60, a calculation I would carry out mentally: 1/10 of 60 is 6 so 2/10 is 12) with the idea of 'out of'. For example, if I get 15/20 in a test I have achieved a mark of 75% (15/20 can be cancelled down to 3/4 which is equivalent to 75%). A good friend once telephoned me. He is a police officer and was having to submit a report on crime figures. He told me that he knew the old figures for burglary and knew the increase but 'couldn't remember which one to divide by 100'. This is a good example of trying to remember a rule or an algorithm that we were taught at school but being unable to see how this applies to a real context. In this case the following calculation was appropriate.

Last year's burglary figures 124,000

This year's figures 142,000

This gives an increase of 142,000 – 124,000 = 18,000. So the percentage increase is (18,000 / 124,000) × 100 = 14.5%. First you find the fractional increase by dividing the increase by last year's total, and then you find the percentage by multiplying by 100.

In order to change a fraction into a percentage you carry out the division to form a decimal from the fraction and then multiply by 100. You need to multiply by 100 to express the fraction as 'out of 100'.

Teaching point 14: Recurring decimals

As your pupils use calculators to carry out conversions between fractions and decimals or to carry out complex calculations they will discover recurring decimals. The most common recurring decimals are thirds, sixths and ninths. When we write recurring decimals we write enough digits after the decimal point to show the recurring pattern and insert a dot on the last decimal place to show it is a recurring pattern. For example,

1.3333 would be written as $1.\dot{3}$

or

$$1.214214214 \text{ would be written } 1.21\dot{4}$$

Portfolio task 4.7

Use a calculator to explore the following fractions in their decimal forms.

What do you notice about the patterns that are formed?

a)   1/3, 2/3, 3/3

b)   1/6, 2/6, 3/6, 4/6, 5/6, 6/6

c)   1/9, 2/9, 3/9, 4/9, 5/9, 6/9, 7/9, 8/9, 9/9

What other fraction families give you recurring decimals?

Teaching point 15: Confusing ratio and proportion

One of my students asked this question at the end of the day: 'What proportion of the class are boys?' In her class of 25, only 10 were boys. One of the children replied 10/15. This response showed some understanding of the idea of ratio and proportion – the learner knew the answer should contain the numbers of boys and girls, and knew there was a link to fractions, but had confused ratio and proportion. Many adults find the difference between ratio and proportion difficult to remember. The definitions are given below.

> **Ratio:** A ratio compares part to part. We use a phrase like 'to every' or 'for every'. So in the above example there are 10 boys to 15 girls, so the ratio is 10:15.

As with fractions we can cancel this down by dividing each number by 5. This give us a ratio of 2:3. We might also say that for every two boys there are three girls.

> **Proportion:** Proportion compares a part to the whole. In the above example there are 10 boys in a class of 25, so 10/25 or, by cancelling, 2/5 of the class are boys. We would say that 2 out of 5 of the people on the trip were boys.

Similarly, 15 out of 25 are girls which is the same as 3 out of 5.

Teaching point 16: Adding rather than multiplying when increasing ratios and proportions

Another error you may come across when teaching ratio and proportion is children reverting to adding rather than multiplying when increasing ratios and proportions.

For example when given a recipe for soup which contains 2 onions in a recipe for 3 people and asked to work out how many onions would be needed for a recipe for 12 they add 9 onions, giving an answer of 11.

The answer is of course 8 onions. We are cooking for 12 people – we must multiply 3 by 4 to get to 12 (the original recipe was for 3 people).

So we need '4 times' as many onions giving us $4 \times 2 = 8$ onions.

Carrying out practical cooking activities is a great way to 'practise' calculations involving ratio and proportion.

Portfolio task 4.8

Look back over the misconceptions you have explored in this chapter.

Which of the misconceptions did you share?

How do you think you developed this misconception?

What might a teacher have done to support you in overcoming the misconception?

Before moving on to the 'In practice' section, try to write a convincing explanation to support a colleague in understanding why this misconception is incorrect.

Add this to your portfolio.

In practice

The lesson plan which follows was used to support a group of children early in their understanding of place value. Following the plan is an evaluation of the lesson which explores how successful the plan was in supporting the children to develop their knowledge, skills and understanding.

Objectives:	• Explain what each digit represents in whole numbers and decimals up to two places and partition, round and order these numbers • Relate numbers to their position on a number line
Key vocabulary: Equal to, ascending, descending, < , >	**Context:** This is the second lesson in a series of five looking at place value, ordering and rounding. In the last lesson the pupils used digit cards to create numbers up to seven digits and named the numbers and wrote them down. All the group could recognise numbers up to four digits but found it difficult to name the numbers with five digits and above. One group worked with the TA naming the numbers and she acted as a scribe for them. A particular difficulty was numbers containing zeros, such as 10,007 The children often work with numeracy partners – that is, one child achieving at expected levels or above paired with a child achieving below expected levels
Resources: Ten-sided dice, digit cards	**Starter activity:** I will use a counting stick. Initially, we will count in 10s, starting at 0. Then we will count in 100s, then 1000s up to counting in 100 000s. I will then throw the ten-sided dice once to generate a number and we will count up in 10s from this number. I will repeat this with a two-digit number counting in 100s and then a three-digit number counting in 1000s and then 10 000s. I will use 'numeracy partners' for this activity. They will take it in turn to count on

Main activity:	**Teacher:** On the whiteboard draw _ _ _ _ _ < _ _ _ _ _ _ _ _ _ _ > _ _ _ _ _ Use a single set of 0–9 digit cards to generate a digit, one digit at a time. The pupils sit with their numeracy partners and have to place each digit to try to make the expression correct	**Pupil activity:** Discuss placing each digit in pairs – understand the importance of placing the digits appropriately showing an understanding of place value Recognise the 10,000 column in order to name the numbers Respond to my prompts in order to name the numbers
Group activity: Children operating above expected levels	Children generate six-digit numbers using ten-sided dice. They place these in ascending order and write the numbers also in ascending order	**Assessment:** I will point to digits and ask the children what the value of the digit is. I will write down numbers such as 120,002 and ask what the zeros represent. I will ask them to think what the values of some seven-digit numbers might be
Group activity: Children operating at expected levels	I will give these children the digit cards 0, 2, 5, 6, 9 and ask them to make as many different five-digit numbers as they can. They should then place them in ascending order	I will ask the children how they make 'big' and 'small' numbers. What is their strategy for making the largest possible number?
Group activity: Children operating below expected levels	These children will use the digits 0, 3, 5, 8 to generate four-digit numbers and then order these numbers	I will ask the TA to support this group. She will pay particular attention to the naming of the numbers and the effect of zero in a column

Plenary: I will use the ten-sided dice to generate two different five-digit numbers. I will select pupils to write these on the whiteboard saying the numbers as they write them. Pupils will say the numbers to their 'talk partners'. They will then decide with their partners which number is the largest. I will select a pupil to come to the front and use the > or < symbol correctly. We will repeat this several times.

Rationale and evaluation

The counting stick activity allowed most of the children to see the patterns although I did notice Helen and Rhupal watching rather than joining in. I made sure that I sat with them later. I repeated the activity and realised that they can count on in 10s and 100s but lose the pattern after that. The numeracy partners are effective I think. I heard very useful discussion. Martin said to Kerry, 'It's easy – you just put the biggest numbers on that end to make a big number.' When I asked Martin he knew that 'that end' was the 10,000 column.

The children operating at or above expected levels all found the ordering of the numbers relatively straightforward. It was important that I intervened, however, as they were more challenged when I asked about the values of the columns. I was pleased that Rob realised that 'all seven-digit numbers are millions'.

The group working with four digits still find the zero problematic – the TA told me that they all described 3058 as either thirty, fifty-eight or three hundred and fifty-eight. I will devise more activities with a number line for this group. For homework I asked them to write down the names of these numbers 358, 308, 3055, 3158, 3508, 3580. I gave them a place value board to take home to support them with the activity.

The plenary supported the children in saying the numbers. I drew a place value grid on the whiteboard to help and this certainly supported the pupils in realising the importance of zero as a place holder. I realised that I should have used place value charts throughout and will use them in future lessons.

Audit task

Devise a lesson plan which is appropriate for a group of learners you are working with. The focus should be 'counting and understanding number'. Construct a lesson plan using the proforma on the companion website. Teach the lesson and then evaluate it carefully with a focus on children's learning and misconceptions. If you can, use ICT to support the children's learning but only do this if the ICT enhances the children's learning. Give evidence for the effectiveness of the ICT in the evaluation. Add this lesson plan and evaluation to your subject knowledge portfolio.

Observing counting and understanding number

On the companion website you can watch a session called 'Decimals forever' taught by Jonny Heeley who won a teaching award. Although the session is put together especially for TV and described as a 'master class' there are lots of ideas that are directly transferable to most classrooms. The opening activity for example is a practical version of the activity suggested earlier in the chapter and helps pupils match decimals to their equivalent fractions and percentages. When you have watched this piece of the lesson think carefully about how you might organise this in your classroom. The key things to think about are which fractions you would choose and how you could differentiate the activity so that all your pupils could take part.

Focus on the opening five minutes of the session rather than watching all the way through and think how you could expand this for a full session. The first thing that I would do is work with the 'number families' so that they arrange themselves in ascending order. It would also be useful to ask your pupils to place themselves on a number line which you could place on the classroom floor or in the playground.

I was also very surprised at the decision to ask the pupils to explore recurring fractions by carrying out long division rather than using a calculator. If the purpose of a calculation is to explore the patterns which the results make it is much more sensible to use a calculator to carry out the calculation.

Assessing counting and understanding number

For early learners it is most appropriate to assess their understanding of counting and understanding number through practical activity. For example you can give 20 pupils in your class cards each with a separate number between 1 and 20 on it. Pick children in the class to give them instructions so that they are sorted into the correct order. Similarly, you could ask children to stick numbers onto a picture of a street with house numbers, if you want to include odd and even numbers, or a block of flats if you simply want to order whole numbers. Ask the children to stick the numbers on the doors so that the post(wo)man can find the correct houses to deliver to.

Estimation games are great for assessing learners' understanding of number and place value. Fairground games such as guess the number of sweets in a jar can be used to assess the pupils' 'sense' of number. You can also observe how they count the sweets – do they count in 2s, 5s or 10s? They can then round to the nearest 10.

Real-life data such as heights of tallest buildings or lengths of rivers can be used to explore larger numbers and assess pupils' skills of rounding. Similarly use very small measurements of micro-organisms to round to a given number of decimal places.

Matching equivalent representations of fractions, decimals and percentages is an excellent assessment activity too. To assess pupils' understanding of finding equivalents leave some of the equivalence cards blank so that the pupils have to fill them in for themselves. It is important to ask learners to order these numbers as a part of this activity so that they come to see how useful it is to move between different representations. Many pupils will find it difficult to order fractions but much easier to order decimals or percentages. Having this understanding can also help if your pupils still have difficulty in ordering fractions by looking at the numerator and denominator.

A cross-curricular project involving counting and understanding number

Almost any planning for a class or school event will involve the pupils in counting and applying their understanding of number. Children of any age can be involved in planning and organising events in the classroom or for the wider school community.

If you are working in an early years setting there will be many occasions when you wish to invite parents and carers to events in the classroom. The children can be involved in making sure there are enough seats, enough hangers for their parents' coats and if you are serving food making sure that there are enough places set so that everyone has a knife, fork and plate. You can even involve the children in making refreshments. Making buns with a cherry on top leads to lots of counting activities – particularly if you cut each cherry in half to make the buns look even better.

As the pupils get older they can get much more involved in making the refreshments. You can use recipes for smaller numbers of people and use ratio and proportion to ensure that you have enough ingredients to make sure everyone has enough to eat. If you are buying pizzas the pupils will need to think about what fraction of each pizza everyone will want and then use this to calculate how many pizzas to buy.

You may want to divide your class up into separate groups each with different responsibilities. One group can organise the invitations and make sure the class knows how many guests to expect. Another group can be in charge of refreshments; both buying and providing sufficient food and drinks for all the guests. A third group will need to organise hospitality during the event and make sure there is enough space for the event to take place. Finally, one group will need to be in charge of the budget for the event.

Summary

The aim of this chapter was twofold: to support you in understanding how children learn to count – something it is hard to recall from our own experience – and to offer a range of activities which will support you in teaching young learners this most basic of skills. I would also hope that these activities will allow you to observe young learners coming to an understanding of counting. The big ideas of 'counting', 'place value', 'fractions, decimals and percentages' and 'ratio and proportion' have also been explored with teaching points to accompany each of these big ideas. I hope that by exploring each of them holistically you are able to make the connections between and within them. That is, you can see how fractions, decimals and percentages are all simply different ways of writing numbers and that choosing the most appropriate representation can make calculating simpler.

Reflections on this chapter

I opened the chapter by suggesting that 'counting and understanding number' is an area you may find difficult to teach as it is something we cannot remember learning ourselves. If I had to pick a key idea from this chapter it would be the five principles underpinning counting. These principles are observable when we watch learners beginning their journey to counting confidently and support us in deciding how to structure the learning experience. The more you observe children at these early stages, the more you will be able to see these principles in practice. This area is also one in which we may bring our own misconceptions from our own experiences.

How many of us were told to 'add a 0' when multiplying by 10, or that 'two minuses make a plus' when we were introduced to directed numbers? Our teachers who used these stock phrases were showing that they were not confident in their own mathematical understanding. I would hope that the teaching points within the chapter have offered you alternative ways to describe these processes – explanations that won't lead to misconceptions.

Going further

The following books have been referred to in this chapter. Here is a brief overview in case you want to explore these areas in more detail. I have also included the full reference for each book.

Children and Number: Difficulties in learning mathematics

MARTIN HUGHES

Reading this will give you a new perspective on young children leaning number, and in particular the skills of counting and understanding number. Martin Hughes shows how young learners bring a wealth of knowledge about counting and understanding number with them when they start school. He argues that it is important for teachers to support children in making links between their own informal understandings and the more formal language of school mathematics. He includes lots of ideas for activities which teachers can draw on to make this possible.

Hughes, M. (1986) *Children and Number: Difficulties in learning mathematics.* Oxford: Blackwell Publishers.

Mathematics with Reason: The emergent approach to primary maths

EDITED BY SUE ATKINSON

This is a very practical book which aims to support teachers in connecting their teaching with the ways that children learn mathematics outside the classroom. As with the Martin Hughes book, it takes the approach that children develop understandings of number at a very early age and that it is the teacher's role to draw these understandings out and to develop them. There are contributions from a wide range of teachers and other mathematics educators who describe how they put these ideas into practice in their classrooms.

Atkinson, S. (ed.) (1992) *Mathematics with Reason: The emergent approach to primary maths.* Abingdon: Hodder and Stoughton.

Teaching and Learning Early Number

IAN THOMPSON

This has been described as a radical and influential book by the *Times Educational Supplement*. Although solidly based in research, it is very accessible and offers lots of practical ideas which teachers of young children can use to support young learners in the early stages of learning about number and counting. It includes chapters exploring learning and teaching number through play and assessing pupils' knowledge of number skills through interviews.

Thompson, I. (2008) *Teaching and Learning Early Number.* Maidenhead: Open University Press.

Self-audit

1   This question allows you to develop your use of number lines to explore ideas of rounding and estimation.

Each of these numbers is the answer to a question asking you to round a number. You should draw a number line to show the range of possible numbers you could have started with. For example, 2300 has been rounded to the nearest 100 so the smallest number I could have started with would be 2250 (we always round up from 5) and the largest number I could have started with could be 2349 (as I would round 2350 up to 2400):

2250 _____

2300_____ 2349

a)   570 has been rounded to the nearest 10.
b)   3000 has been rounded to the nearest 100.

c) 7.8 has been rounded to the nearest tenth.

d) 10.75 has been rounded to the nearest hundredth.

e) 0 has been rounded to the nearest whole number.

2 These questions explore your skills in expressing numbers as decimals, percentages and fractions. It is important that you feel comfortable moving between these three representations of numbers. Children who can move easily between fractions, decimals and percentages are better able to carry out complex calculations, and have a clearer sense of number.

a)

20%	5/8	0.25
9/10	2.8	2/3
5/9	75%	1/3
30%	½	0.7

Use the fractions, percentages and decimals to make questions with the following answers (e.g. 75% of 12 is less than 10 and 0.7 × 20 is between 10 and 25):

i.   < 10

ii. > 25

iii. between 10 and 25

iv. between 5 and 6

v.   < 1

vi. = 15

vii. = 0

viii. = 0.5

ix. = 20%

x.   = 4/5

b) Draw this number line:

Add the following numbers to the appropriate place on the number line:

5/8, 0.9, 1/3, 0.66, 75%, 65%, 8/9, 15%

The next question introduces proportionality. This is the final key idea within counting and understanding number.

3 Look at the following information about a group of students on a teaching training course:

There are 25 students on a teacher training course:

20 are female;
10 are from minority ethnic groups;
5 have a mathematics A-level;
8 are living with their parents;
4 are mature students.

I can write the following statements from this information:

- 1 out of 5 of the students has mathematics A-level.
- The ratio of students from minority ethnic groups is 2:3.
- 32% of students are living with their parents.

Write ten more statements using this information. Use fractions, decimals, ratios and proportions.

CHAPTER 5

NUMBER
Knowing and using number facts

Introduction

Mathematics is about much more than knowing facts. However, there are some facts that are useful as they support us in carrying out calculations quickly and in being able to check that our answers to problems are accurate.

You may have played 'Guess my number' with classes that you have taught. This is when you think of a number and the children in your class have to guess the number by asking questions. You can only answer 'Yes' or 'No' to their questions. The following exchanges probably ring true too:

Tony: OK, I've written my number down on this piece of paper. Tom, you start asking the questions.

Tom: Is it 57?

Tony: It might take quite a long time if you just guess numbers. Michelle, have you got a question?

Michelle: Is it even?

Tony: Well done, that's a great question. No it's not even. Megan, you next.

Megan: Is it odd?

Just as with the games where we ask people to guess famous people, the game above relies on good subject knowledge, here knowledge of number facts, for success. It also relies on good questioning. My class got much better at questioning, and very quickly. After each game we talked about what the best questions were – that is, which questions narrowed down the choices best. I asked the children to work in pairs to come up with good questions before we started the next game. As an extension we tried to use the minimum number of questions possible. We also had a 'number of the day' and during the day, in a spare moment, children wrote down any number facts they could about this number.

Starting point

The story above is an illustration of 'knowing number facts', and, of course, we need to know number facts before we can use them. One of the most useful ways we can use number facts is to 'derive' new facts. This is sometimes referred to as having good 'number sense'. When we look at a number we get a 'sense' of that number. So I might look at 36 and see a number that has a lot of factors, that is a **square number**, that is divisible by 12, and so on. If we see numbers in this way we are better able to work with the numbers, calculation becomes more straightforward, and estimation comes easily.

Most importantly this chapter emphasises how important it is to be able to use the facts that we can remember to work out new facts. For example, if I can remember that $2 \times 6 = 12$ I can work out that $4 \times 6 = 24$ and $8 \times 6 = 48$ by doubling and that $9 \times 6 = 54$ by adding another 6, and so on.

I want to emphasise that your pupils do not have to memorise a huge range of facts whilst they are being taught by you. Rather they have time to make sense of the number facts they have been previously introduced to and you can work with them to use the facts that they already know to derive new sets of facts.

TAKING IT FURTHER: **FROM THE RESEARCH**

The term 'number sense' was introduced by A. McIntosh, B. J. Reys and R. E. Reys in 1992 in their article 'A proposed framework for examining basic number sense'. They explored the link between informal methods and the formal calculation procedures. This issue is analysed in detail by Ian Thompson in the paper 'Narrowing the gap between mental computational strategies and standard written algorithms' presented to the International Convention on Mathematics Education in Denmark in 2008.

The idea of 'number sense' has been discussed widely and is an important area for further exploration if you wish to develop your understanding of how children draw on their own informal methods to come to an understanding of formal written methods.

There is currently a debate about how much children should commit to memory. Professor Jo Boaler has written a paper titled 'Fluency without fear'. This revolutionary paper debunks the myths that we have to able to have all our number facts at the tips of our fingers in order to succeed in mathematics. I imagine that many of you reading this book will not feel as though you can instantly recall all the facts you wish you could. In the paper Jo writes,

Some students are not as good at memorizing math facts as others. That is something to be celebrated, it is part of the wonderful diversity of life and people. Imagine how dull and uninspiring it would be if teachers gave tests of math facts and everyone answered them in the same way and at the same speed as though they were all robots. In a recent brain study scientists examined students' brains as they were taught to memorize math facts. They saw that some students memorized them much more easily than others. This will be no surprise to readers and many of us would probably assume that those who memorized better were higher achieving or 'more intelligent' students. But the researchers found that the students who memorized more easily were not higher achieving, they did not have what the researchers described as more 'math ability', nor did they have higher IQ scores.

The most important job for you is to develop 'numbers sense' in and with your learners. Developing this ease with numbers is what 'knowing and using number facts' is about. Sometimes our learners seem to treat numbers with suspicion – as if they can't be trusted. This happens if mathematics is presented to them as a series of tricks and rules to be learnt. If they can be presented with mathematics as inherently logical they may begin to trust numbers, to see that they always behave in the same way. This chapter gives a wide range of examples of how mathematics is logical – and how you can convince yourself and your learners that it is logical.

The next section shows the development of children's knowledge of number facts as learners move through primary school. It also shows you what you might expect the learners in your class to have experienced before they meet you. These are the number facts that you can build on, the facts you can draw on as you encourage your learners to deepen this knowledge. Of course, the easiest way to see what 'facts' children bring with them is to have conversations with your learners which allow them to demonstrate what they already know before you move on to teaching them 'new' facts.

Progression in knowing and using number facts

Foundations for knowing and using number facts

At the early stages you should work with young children to help them observe relationships and patterns in numbers they see in their everyday environment, like house numbers, the numbers in blocks of flats, numbers on classroom doors, numbers in nursery rhymes, and so on. In particular you could work with them on finding one more or less than a number, at this stage only working with numbers up to 20, so they will know that one more than 5 is 6, and one less than 9 is 8. In addition to this, through using number lines, they will begin to see how the process for finding one more or less remains the same whatever number you start with. This is the beginning of seeing mathematics as logical and consistent.

Beginning to understand knowing and using number facts

At this stage you will be introducing children to all pairs of numbers that total 10. You should also look at addition facts to at least 5 and be able to use this to work out the corresponding subtraction facts. Drawing on this pupils can begin to count on and back in 1s, 2s, 3s, 5s and 10s and through this notice the patterns in multiples of 2, 3, 5 and 10. Eventually they will be able to remember all the doubles of numbers to at least 10.

The next step is to learn how to derive and recall addition and subtraction facts up to 10, all pairs with totals up to 20 and pairs of multiples of 10 up to 100. So they will notice the patterns when you add

$$20 + 20 = 40 \text{ or } 50 + 50 = 100$$

and make the links with this pattern and the patterns of pairs up to 10 (2 + 2 = 4; 5 + 5 = 10). They will also begin to understand the difference between odd and even numbers.

At this stage pupils will be making the link between halving and doubling and remembering multiplication facts for 2, 3, 5 and 10. They will also be beginning to use this knowledge to estimate and check their answers are sensible.

Becoming confident in knowing and using number facts

Your next aim is for pupils to be able to derive and recall all addition and subtraction facts to 20, sums ('sum' means addition, although many teachers use it as a generic term for 'calculation'; try to avoid using 'sum' unless you mean addition – sums of multiples of 10 would be 30 + 30 = 60 and so on) and differences of multiples of 10 and number pairs that total 100 ('difference' is found by subtraction or adding on, so the difference between 50 and 60 is 10).

Once pupils have developed their ability to recall multiplication and division facts for 2, 3, 4, 5, 6, 10, 11 and 12 (you will see that this is different from simply being able to recite their times-tables) you can work with them so that they 'know their times-tables' up to 12. This means being able to derive multiplication and division facts of all the tables up to the 12 times-table, up to the 12th multiple. Pupils at this stage should also recognise the patterns which allow them to recognise multiples of 2, 5 or 10 up to 1000.

Drawing on their prior knowledge pupils will be able to derive sums and differences of pairs and multiples of 10, 100 or 1000. As previously they will see how these patterns build on patterns they have been introduced to earlier.

So if 3 + 3 = 6, then 30 + 30 = 60 and 300 + 300 = 600 and so on. Similarly, if 70 – 30 = 40 then 700 – 300 = 400. This is the way in which the consistency within mathematics begins to become clear.

Other facts that should be introduced at this stage include the doubles of two-digit numbers and using these to calculate doubles of multiples of 10 and 100 and derive the corresponding halves (so 52 is 26 + 26 which tells me 520 is 260 + 260 and that half of 520 is 260).

This will help pupils develop their knowledge of fractions to identify pairs of fractions that total 1 (e.g. 1/2 + 1/2 and 1/4 + 3/4).

All this prior experience will enable your pupils to derive sums, differences, doubles and halves of decimals. For example, if I know 38 + 25 = 63 then I know 3.8 + 2.5 = 6.3 , and I can work out that 6.3 – 2.5 = 3.8; or because I know 19 is half of 38, I also know 1.9 is half of 3.8.

By the end of their time in primary school learners will be able to recall their tables facts quickly and draw on this to multiply pairs of multiples of 10 and 100 (7 × 50 = 350 and 70 × 50 = 3500 and so on). They will be able to identify factors of two-digit whole numbers and use this knowledge to find **common multiples**. Factors of a number are the numbers that divide into that number. So the factors of 12 are 1, 2, 3, 4, 6 and 12. A common multiple is a multiple which is shared by two or more numbers. So a common multiple of 3 and 6 is 12 as 3 and 6 are both factors of 12. A common multiple is in the times-tables of both of the numbers.

Building on the understanding of decimals pupils will use their knowledge of multiplication facts to derive related number facts linked to decimals. (So, if I know that if 5 × 9 = 45 I can derive the following facts: 0.5 × 9 = 4.5, 4.5 ÷ 9 = 0.5.)

The pupils will also be able to derive square numbers (a square number is the result of multiplying a number by itself, so 9 is a square number because it is 3 × 3 and 25 is a square number because it is 5 × 5) and use this ability to derive squares of multiples of 10 (for example 80 × 8 = 640 and 80 × 80 = 6400). They will also be able to recognise prime numbers less than 100 and use this to find **prime factors** of two-digit numbers. A prime number is a number with only two factors, itself and 1. So 13 is a prime number because its only factors are 1 and 13. Another way of explaining this is that a prime number doesn't appear in any times-tables apart from its own. The first 10 prime numbers are 2, 3, 5, 7, 11, 13, 17, 19, 23; '1' is not a prime number as it only has one factor. A prime factor is a factor of a number which is also a prime number. For example, the factors of 18 are 1, 2, 3, 6, 9, 18. However, if you were asked to write 18 as a product of its prime factors you would write 2 × 3 × 3.

Extending learners' knowledge in knowing and using number facts

At this stage pupils should have a good grasp of all the number facts they will need to draw on during the rest of their mathematics education. A new idea you can introduce to extend your pupils would be the recognition of **square roots** of **perfect squares**. The square root of any number is the number which, if squared, would give you that number. So the square root of 16 is 4, and the square root of 100 is 10. A perfect square is the square of a whole number, so 36 is a perfect square as it is 6^2 or 6 squared.

The aim of this section is to support you in seeing how a child's knowledge of number facts gradually builds over seven or more years, and how it forms a coherent and consistent landscape in which numbers behave as we expect them to. We can use this consistency and our current knowledge to derive new knowledge.

Big ideas

I have called the two big ideas in this section 'Patterns' and 'Rules'. In the opening to the chapter I wrote about developing a 'number sense' in pupils. This sense of number develops with an understanding of the patterns that exist within the number system and the rules which our number system obeys. Noticing patterns allows us to derive new facts quickly from those which we know and applying rules appropriately allows us to use the facts accurately. This skill is vital when we begin to develop our algebraic thinking. The word 'algebra' is derived from the Arabic 'al-jebr' which means, literally, putting back together broken parts. Being able to notice patterns and seeing individual numbers in terms of their properties supports us when we need to create and solve equations.

There is a story of two famous mathematicians G.H. Hardy and Srinivasa Ramanujan who whenever they met used to pick numbers and see who could find the most interesting facts about them. On one occasion Hardy had travelled to meet Ramanujan in hospital in a taxi which had the number 1729. Hardy picks up the story:

> *I remember once going to see him when he was ill at Putney. I had ridden in taxi cab number 1729 and remarked that the number seemed to me rather a dull one and that I hoped it was not an unfavourable omen. 'No,' he replied, 'it is a very interesting number; it is the smallest number expressible as the sum of two cubes in two different ways.'*

We should not expect to know everything there is to know about every number, but being able to see numbers in many different ways allows us to manipulate them and to explore and understand pattern.

Patterns

The most important resources to support children in noticing pattern are number lines and 100 squares. At the early stages of learning we are encouraging children to notice what happens when we add or subtract 1 from a number. At this stage they will be using a number line to see that they move one digit to the right to add 1 and one to the left to subtract.

This image will support them as they explore more complex ideas but they have already learnt an essential image – we add and subtract by moving up and down a number line. This is the beginning of algebraic understanding. If I can see this pattern I will be able to solve the equation

$$x + 1 = 9$$

For learners in the primary school we would substitute a 'cloud' or a box for 'x' but the question remains the same. If I add '1' to a number and get the answer '9' what is that number? The portfolio task below asks you to notice the way that patterns on a 100 square can help learners carry out calculations. This discussion will be developed further in Chapter 7 which explores learning and teaching algebra in depth.

Portfolio task 5.1

Describe the following operations on a 100 square:

- adding 10
- subtracting 11
- adding 27.

Try to describe the 'move' you make – for example, to add 11, 'I move down one row and one column to the right.' Add these notes to your personal portfolio.

1	2	3	4	5	6	7	8	9	10
11	12	13	14	15	16	17	18	19	20
21	22	23	24	25	26	27	28	29	30
31	32	33	34	35	36	37	38	39	40
41	42	43	44	45	46	47	48	49	50
51	52	53	54	55	56	57	58	59	60
61	62	63	64	65	66	67	68	69	70
71	72	73	74	75	76	77	78	79	80
81	82	83	84	85	86	87	88	89	90
91	92	93	94	95	96	97	98	99	100

The patterns that we see are all linked to the idea of place value which was explored in the previous chapter, and a good understanding of place value is key in helping learners see the underlying reasons for the patterns that we notice. In the 100 square above all multiples of 10 end in a '0' and multiples of 5 end in '5' or '0'. Whenever you are introducing new ideas linked to number facts draw on these resources to give children images they can use to help them memorise the facts, but also for them to realise how the 'facts' link to the number system.

Other properties of numbers that we introduce to our pupils are the square numbers. These are also easily represented pictorially, as

The first square number is 1, the second is 4, and so on. We write

$$1^2 = 1$$

$$2^2 = 4$$

$$3^2 = 9$$

$$4^2 = 16$$

and so on.

There are also the triangle numbers. 1, 3, 6 and 10 are the first four triangle numbers.

You will see that we form the triangle numbers as follows:

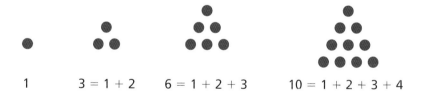

1   3 = 1 + 2   6 = 1 + 2 + 3   10 = 1 + 2 + 3 + 4

and so on.

The next portfolio task asks you to explore the relationship between square numbers and triangle numbers in more depth. In this way you get a better 'sense' of these properties.

Portfolio task 5.2

Explore the link between square numbers and triangle numbers. Let us call the square numbers S1, S2, S3, S4, and so on, so that

$$S1 = 1, S2 = 4, S3 = 9, S4 = 16 ...$$

and the triangle numbers T1, T2, T3, T4 so that

$$T1 = 1, T2 = 3, T3 = 6, T4 = 10 ...$$

Try to represent any square number as the sum of two triangle numbers.

Try to illustrate your answer with a picture.

Rules

The rules that are important to help children in applying their number facts appropriately are the commutative property of numbers, the distributive property of numbers and the associative property of numbers. These sound complicated but you will have been using them all your life, and as I have been saying throughout this chapter, they make absolute sense.

The commutative property

This means that for some operations it does not matter which order the numbers are used in the calculation. The numbers can 'commute' or change places. You may have already realised that addition and multiplication are commutative – if I am asked to add 15 and 12 I can either work out 15 + 12 or 12 + 15. Similarly, if I want to know 32 multiplied by 13 I can either work out 32 × 13 or 13 × 32. This property is useful as it means we can immediately halve the facts we need to learn! It is also helpful as we can encourage children to rearrange calculations so they can carry out mental calculations. We would use this property if we were to be asked to carry out the following calculation

15 + 7 + 14 + 3 + 5

as we could rearrange the numbers in the following way

15 + 5 + 7 + 3 + 14 = 20 + 10 + 14

to make it easier to add the numbers.

It is the commutative law that teachers are using when they suggest to pupils that they start counting on from the largest number first, when carrying out an addition by counting on a number line.

The commutative property does not hold for subtraction or division; the order of numbers cannot change. You will see that, for example,

15 − 8 is not the same as 8 − 15

and

28 ÷ 7 is not the same as 7 ÷ 28

The distributive property

The best way to illustrate the meaning of the distributive property is through an example. Often when we carry out mental calculations for multiplication we rely on this distributive property. For example, the figure below illustrates a calculation using an **array**.

Rather than calculate 13 × 8 I can calculate 8 × 10 and then add 3 × 8. Then I could write

13 × 8 = (10 × 8) + (3 × 8) = 80 + 24 = 104

Similarly, if I want to work out 28 × 7 I could write

28 × 7 = (30 × 7) − (2 × 7) = 210 − 14 = 196

Being able to draw on the distributive property is very helpful in order to develop your mental calculation skills. There are some examples below for you to try out in your portfolio. Always encourage the pupils you are working with to describe how they are carrying out their mental calculations. This will help all your learners come to terms with the distributive law.

Portfolio task 5.3

Use the distributive property to carry out the following calculations mentally.

Draw a sketch to illustrate the calculation:

18 × 8	34 × 7
29 × 14	48 × 6

Check with a calculator to convince yourself!

The associative property

As with the distributive property the best way to describe the associative property is through examples. Whenever we carry out a calculation we always begin with pairs of numbers. So if I ask a child to calculate the sum of 22, 14, 6, 3, 18 and 5 they have to decide which pair of numbers to begin with. For addition it does not matter which pairs of numbers we begin with. The same applies to multiplication. For example,

$$8 \times 5 \times 2 = (8 \times 5) \times 2 = 40 \times 2 = 80$$

or

$$8 \times 5 \times 2 = 8 \times (5 \times 2) = 8 \times 10 = 80$$

However, subtraction and division are not associative, for example,

$$18 - 7 - 3 = (18 - 7) - 3 = 11 - 3 = 8$$

but

$$18 - (7 - 3) = 18 - 4 = 14$$

so we have to carry out subtraction and division in the order the numbers are given.

These rules are very helpful in reorganising calculations to make them easier but can lead to some confusion as you will see later in the chapter. This is why it is always important for children to be checking that answers are sensible – then they will know if they have misapplied a rule.

The next section of this chapter explores common errors that you might notice children making or misconceptions that they may have developed. The aim of each teaching point is that you are able to use the error or misconception as a focus for teaching to move the pupils' learning forward.

Teaching points

Teaching point 1: Confusion in definitions of properties of numbers

You will probably have seen questions in test papers which ask children to sort numbers according to their properties either using a **Carroll diagram** or a **Venn diagram**. (Examples of Carroll diagrams and Venn diagrams are shown below.) For example, children were asked to sort 2, 7, 8, 9, 17, 20 using this Carroll diagram:

	Even	Not even
Prime		
Not prime		

The main confusion here involved 2 and 9. Children are introduced to odd and even numbers early in Key Stage 1 and so have a good sense of 'oddness' and 'evenness', but prime numbers are not introduced until much later. Because all prime numbers are odd, apart from 2, children often make the mistake that all odd numbers are prime, forgetting that 9 has three factors (1, 3 and 9) and so isn't prime. Similarly, many children don't see 2 as a prime number even though it has only two factors, 1 and 2.

Games like 'Guess my number' which opened the chapter are very useful for helping children become familiar with the wide range of properties of numbers. Another activity which is useful as a starter is to give children number cards – a different number for each child. Ask them to move around the room and ask them to form groups of three. The three in the group then have to find a property that is shared by all the numbers in their group. Another activity which can be repeated as often as you like is to draw a large Venn diagram on the board. One of the class comes up to the front and writes numbers in the appropriate part of the Venn diagram. As they are doing this the rest of the class have to guess what the properties are that are being used for the sort.

Sometimes these misunderstandings can be used directly by asking questions that the children may think are impossible:

Tell me an even number that is also a prime number.

Tell me a multiple of 3 that is even.

Tell me a multiple of 10 that is in the 3 times-table.

And so on.

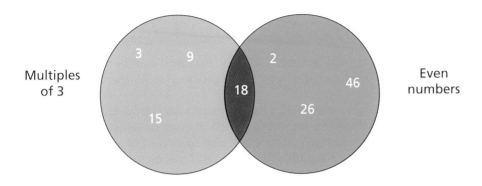

Teaching point 2: Errors in remembering multiplication facts

Most of us can remember that every multiple of 5 ends in a '0' or a '5' and that every multiple of 10 ends in a '0'. You will also probably remember that all the even numbers are multiples of 2. This sometimes leads to confusion for children who can overgeneralise. They notice that every even number is a multiple of 2 and so invent a new rule – 'every odd number is a multiple of 3', which sounds plausible, but unfortunately isn't true. This is a good example of a misconception.

It is very useful to try to discover the 'rules' that children are following so that you can ask them to find examples that show their 'rule' doesn't work. It is also helpful to introduce them to the patterns that do exist for other families of multiples. For example, let's look at multiples of 3:

3, 6, 9, 12, 15, 18, 21, 24, 27, 30

If I add up the digits of any number in the 3 times-table, and repeat this until I get a single digit, I always get 3, 6 or 9.

So 15 gives me 1 + 5 = 6, and 27 is 2 + 7 = 9.

I can tell you that 4341 is divisible by 3 (4 + 3 + 4 + 1 = 12 and 1 + 2 = 3).

Check it on a calculator if you don't believe me.

Asking children to explore the patterns in families of multiples is a good way of encouraging them to get a feel or a 'sense' of the properties of numbers.

Portfolio task 5.4

Explore patterns in the 4 and 9 times-tables. Are there rules that you can find so that you know if a large number is divisible by 4 or by 9?

For an example of how a Year 1 teacher explored number patterns using posters see Jill Russell's article 'Interactive pictures' in *Mathematics Teaching* 182.

She describes how she used sets of posters to support the children in 'telling stories' about the numbers, which in turn developed their understanding of number patterns. There are also examples of the posters in the article. One poster is called 'Animal fields' and has pictures of a wide range of animals in fields. Jill Russell asked her class to make up questions based on the poster. One child came up with the following story:

> *Seven rabbits were just finishing their breakfast when they spotted five sheep in the next field. Four of them ran away frightened so then there were only three of them left.*

It is a great idea to ask your learners to make up their own 'number stories' based on illustrations or photographs that you give them. This helps them become at ease with numbers, and also helps them when they come to interpret number problems that are set for them by other people.

Teaching point 3: Errors in estimation when deriving new facts

Sometimes the children I'm working with get very excited when they realise they can derive a huge number of new facts with the knowledge that they have. I had asked a Year 6 group to jot down as many new facts as they could given their knowledge that $8 \times 7 = 56$. This is the list that one group gave me:

$8 \times 7 = 56$	so	$80 \times 7 = 560$
and $80 \times 70 = 56\,000$	and	$800 \times 700 = 560\,000$
and $8 \times 0.7 = 0.56$	and	$0.8 \times 0.7 = 0.56$

I asked them if they were sure they were all right and they looked at me blankly – I think they had forgotten that they were looking for genuine new facts in their excitement and speed and had just been jotting down numbers that 'looked' right. I asked them to look at $80 \times 7 = 560$. They agreed this was correct because '80 is less than a 100 so the answer should be less than 700'. So then I asked them to apply the same logic to 80×70. 80 is still less than 100 so the answer should be less than 7000, as 100×70 is 7000. They spotted their error and checked the rest. You might like to do the same.

A useful strategy to get children to look carefully for accuracy is to give them lists like the one above with errors in them and ask them to find the errors and explain why the incorrect answers are wrong. If they can notice the sorts of errors that can be made they are less likely to make them themselves.

Teaching point 4: Children misapplying the commutative and associative laws

My son Sam once brought home the following calculation from school:

$$
\begin{array}{r}
584 \\
-376 \\
\hline
212 \\
\hline
\end{array}
$$

He said to me, 'I know it's wrong, the answer should be 208, but I've done it right.' Mentally he had counted on, he knew that 576 was 200 more than 376 so if he added another 8 he would get to 584, but frustratingly for him, using the method he thought he had been taught gave him the wrong answer. This is an example of why some children seem to see maths as fraught with confusion: you can do the right thing and still you get it wrong.

What had happened is that Sam had followed an instruction he may have been given by a previous teacher: 'you always take the smaller number from the larger number'. This works when you are trying to find differences between numbers, but not for column subtraction! Similarly, he may have been told '4 take away 6 doesn't go', so here he was trying to find a way to make it 'go' and so he subtracted the 4 from the 6 giving him the answer 2. We need to be very careful with the way we describe mathematical rules so that we don't unwittingly add to children's confusion.

He may also have remembered the commutative law and thought that it applied to subtraction as well as addition. If you remember the commutative law says that it doesn't matter which order you carry out a calculation. This is fine for addition and multiplication but not for subtraction or division. At least he had the knowledge to be able to carry out the calculation mentally and realise that something was going wrong.

Teaching point 5: Mental calculation errors in partitioning

The previous chapter introduced you to 'arrow cards' or 'place value cards'. You can use them to support learners in developing their mental methods by using partitioning. The activity below shows how place value 'arrow' cards can be used to support learners in using partitioning to develop their skills in mental calculation.

PARTITIONING NUMBERS

Use these place value cards.

| 300 | 200 | 70 |
| 50 | 9 | 6 |

1   How many different numbers can you find by combining these cards?
2   Find all the numbers using just two cards each time.
3   Find all the numbers using just three cards each time.

Here are some examples:

200 + 50 = 250   200 + 50 + 6 = 256

50 + 6 = 56

It is important that children working on this activity are given the cards to manipulate. The overlapping of the cards is a vital part of coming to an understanding of the concept of partitioning. So, for example, as the learner makes 256 by using the cards, they must be able to overlap the card so that they read 256 and not 200, then 50, then 6: this can lead to their developing misconceptions around place value and around partitioning.

Because children realise that partitioning offers them a powerful way of calculating mentally, they sometimes see it as a first port of call rather than one strategy to choose when appropriate. This can lead to the following misconception. A class I was working with had been looking at partitioning as a way of carrying out multiplication calculations mentally the previous week. This week, however, they were looking at division. I had asked them to use any strategies they wanted to calculate 280 divided by 14. Sohm had written this in her book:

$$280 \div 14 = 20 + 20 = 40$$

I asked her how she had done this. She said she had partitioned 280 into 200 and 80 and 14 into 10 and 4, and so 200 ÷ 10 was 20 and 80 ÷ 4 was 20 giving her the answer 40. The fact that both answers were 20 seemed to have convinced her even more that it must be right (there's something about round numbers in maths that feels right, isn't there?).

To encourage her to check, I asked her what 40 × 14 was; if her answer was correct this should have been 280. Very quickly she answered 560. I asked her how she had worked this out. Again, she had used partitioning, where she had calculated 40 × 10 and added 40 × 4 . This time she had partitioned correctly. She then realised that 280 ÷ 14 couldn't be 40, and should be 20 (because 20 × 14 = 280). The examples below unpick this in more detail:

280 ÷ 14

Partitioning 280 into 200 + 80 doesn't help as neither of these are easily divisible by 14; and as we saw above, splitting this calculation into

200 ÷ 10

and

80 ÷ 4

gives us a different calculation altogether. For this calculation it is easiest to notice that 28 is double 14 so 280 ÷ 14 = 20. This is an example of how 'memorising' our doubles can help us with mental calculations. However,

40 × 14 = (40 × 10) + (40 × 4) = 400 + 160 = 560

As I mentioned before the best way to work with the rules of number is always to question your learners about the strategies they are using whether they are correct or making errors. This way they will talk to you about the methods they are using, you can pick up the misconceptions and work with them. Very often children are giving you correct answers, they just aren't carrying out the calculation that you asked them to.

In practice

The following lesson plan was used to draw on pupils' current understandings of number bonds to 10 to begin to develop an understanding of place value in decimals.

I did this through asking them to find pairs and triples of numbers that total 10 or 100 including decimals. This allowed them to use the knowledge that 45 + 55 = 100 to deduce that 4.5 + 5.5 = 10.

Following the plan is an evaluation of the lesson which explores how successful the plan was in supporting the children to develop their knowledge, skills and understanding.

Objectives:	• Use knowledge of place value and addition and subtraction of two-digit numbers to derive sums and differences, doubles and halves of decimals • Explore properties of numbers and propose a general statement involving numbers • Identify examples for which the statement is true or false

Key vocabulary: Units boundary, tenths boundary, addition, plus, pattern

Context: This is the first lesson in a series of five. This lesson supports children in finding pairs and triples of numbers that total 10 or 100. Future lessons use this understanding to carry out calculations arising from word problems. This lesson should support the children in devising mental strategies so that they can effectively carry out the calculation

Resources: 0–9 digit cards, 6 × 4 grid

Starter activity: I will draw a 6 × 4 grid of pairs of numbers which add to 10 using whole numbers. I will ask the children to work in mixed ability pairs and give them one minute to find as many pairs as possible which add to 10. They will record this on mini-whiteboards. After a minute I will ask each pair to come up to the board and select a pair of numbers to check if they are right. I will repeat the activity using another grid I have prepared with numbers to one decimal place

I will introduce the term 'complement to 10'

Main activity	Teacher	Pupil activity
Group activity: Children operating above expected levels	The children will work in pairs. Each member of the pair creates a 'pairs' and 'triples' board so that it contains sets of numbers that add to 10. This should be decimals. They will then give them to a partner who will shade in the pairs	Pupils will list pairs and triples of numbers and decide how to make the board 'challenging'. The TA who is working with this group will ask the children to explain their thinking and to describe the patterns they notice when they are finding pairs and triples of numbers
Group activity: Children operating at expected levels	The children will work in pairs. Each member of the pair creates a 'pairs' board so that it contains 12 pairs of numbers that add to 10. This should include some that are decimals. They will then give them to a partner who will shade in the pairs on the number grid	Pupils will list pairs and triples of numbers and decide how to make the board 'challenging'. I will work with this group and will ask the children to explain their thinking and to describe the patterns they notice when they are finding pairs and triples of numbers
Group activity: Children operating below expected levels	This group will continue to use the program on the laptops. I will use the program which asks the children to find pairs of numbers that sum to 100	The children will record the pairs of numbers that they find sum to 100. They will organise this list so that they can report back on any patterns they have found

Plenary: The group who were summing to 100 will report back on the patterns that they have found. I will ask the other two groups if these patterns are reflected in the patterns that they have found. Hopefully they will notice, for example, 45 + 55=100 and 4.5 + 5.5=10. We will then revisit the activity from the starter. This time we will only use the decimal grid. As a child finds a pair they will describe to the group the mental process they are using

Rationale and evaluation

I realised very quickly that pairs to 10 in the introductory activity was not challenging any of the pupils so I quickly redrew the grid for pairs to 100. This was a little more challenging and I noticed that some of the children were making the mistake of just adding the '10s' digit. This was a useful teaching point. When we moved into the decimal numbers I was very pleased that Philippa noticed that 'the decimals are just the same as the normal numbers – if you just pretend the decimal point isn't there you can do them just the same'. I explained that we were dividing by 10, which is why the answer was 10 and not 100. I set her and Christine the challenge of finding three-digit numbers that sum to 1000. They went away on their own and very successfully completed this task. I was also very impressed by the way they explained their thinking to the rest of the class in the plenary.

I wonder if the activities were challenging enough – each group was very successful. It seemed that once they had found the pattern they managed to complete the task relatively straightforwardly. However, the pupils seemed to be engaged and motivated by the task. They were also very articulate in the plenary and were able to describe their thinking process well. For example, Hannah said:

If I've got 3.4 (three point four), that means I need another 0.6 (point six) to make 4 and then 6 to make 10. So that means 3.4 + 6.6 = 10. I can check this because 34 + 66 = 100.

At that point Philippa chipped in, 'and that means that 340 + 660 = 1000'.

Audit task

Devise a lesson plan which is appropriate for a group of learners you are working with. The focus should be an aspect of knowing and using number facts that is appropriate to the age group you are working with. Use the proforma that is available on the companion website. Make sure you think carefully about the context and evaluate the lesson. Try to use ICT to support the children's learning.

Add this lesson plan and evaluation to your subject knowledge portfolio.

Observing the teaching of knowing and using number facts

Watch the video 'Using a counting stick' on the companion website which shows a counting stick being used to support the learning of multiplication facts. A counting stick provides a powerful mental image which can support children in learning multiplication facts and in remembering them. They are easy to make by buying a 1 metre long piece of dowelling or a metre stick. Use coloured tape to define 10cm long sections on the stick.

While you watch the video try to learn the multiplication facts by putting yourself in the place of the learner. Reflect on the following questions in your portfolio.

- How does the counting stick support learners in memorising new facts by drawing on facts they already know?
- How might you use the counting stick to model other aspects of the number system? For example decimals between 0 and 1 or numbers between 0 and 1 million.

Assessing knowing and using number facts

The most effective way of assessing your learners' knowledge of number facts is on a day-to-day basis. Playing the 'Guess my number' game as in the example which opened the chapter is one way to get a sense of which pupils are at ease with properties of numbers.

Similarly, you can choose a 'number of the week'. This can be an individual, group or whole class activity. Simply select a different number each week and during the week the pupils have to list as many properties or facts as they can about the number.

'Loop cards' are a great way of assessing your pupils' current knowledge of number facts as well as supporting them in learning new number facts (through noticing patterns and hearing other children's responses). You can also see how they are using current facts to work out new ones by stopping the game and asking pupils how they arrived at an answer. Loop cards are a set of cards on which the answer to the question on one card leads to the next card; so for example one card might read, 'I am 15% of 200'; another card will have the answer '30' written on top of the card and a new question on the bottom of the card.

There are further examples of loop cards and a blank set on the website which accompanies this book.

Cross-curricular teaching of knowing and using number facts

The idea of these extended cross-curricular projects is to draw on the key ideas within the chapter to develop a cross-curricular project which you can explore with your learners over a series of lessons. This allows you and your class to develop your subject knowledge together.

Boxes for stock cubes

This investigation asks children to explore cuboids with constant volume. This involves them in looking at prime numbers, factors and multiples. It is most effective for children to work in small groups. Give each group enough multilink cubes to make a range of cuboids made from 36 cubes. You will need to encourage the children to keep a record of the cuboids they make – for example, $3 \times 4 \times 3$, and so on. They will probably notice that cuboids with the same dimensions look 'different' in different orientations.

Ask groups to explore the range of cuboids that can be made from different numbers of cubes; you could suggest they work systematically on this starting with one cube, then two cubes, then three, then four, and so on. They can then decide what 'sort' of numbers give the largest number of different cuboids. They will discover that numbers which have a large number of factors can be made into a large number of cuboids, and prime numbers can only make a single **cuboid**.

This leads them into exploring boxes of stock cubes. Bring a range of stock cube boxes into the class. Ask the groups to decide which cuboid they would use if they were packaging 36 stock cubes. They should create the packaging for this and prepare a 'bid' for the rest of the class to argue for their design. The whole class can judge the best designs as a concluding activity for the investigation.

Summary

The chapter opens with a discussion of 'number sense'. The development of this number sense is an underpinning theme for the chapter and I describe it as being 'at ease' with numbers, or trusting the internal logic of the number system. The progression section outlines which 'facts' are appropriate for each stage of learning, but the chapter also focuses on techniques you can use to support children in using the facts that they already know to learn new facts. Using patterns to remember and predict number facts is illustrated, and the rules which underpin the number system are carefully outlined. You will also have seen how this supports pupils in coming to an understanding of algebra. The teaching points illustrate how you can use children's misconceptions around number patterns and the rules of number to bring them to a better understanding of how the number system works. If they trust the number system they will also trust their memory!

Reflections on this chapter

I hope that this chapter has helped you see how you gradually build children's knowledge of number facts over seven years of primary education. Learners do not have to memorise a huge range of facts immediately – they have time to make sense of the number facts associated with their stage of learning and most importantly they come to see how they can use the facts that they already know to derive new sets of facts. You should now understand which facts you should help your pupils learn and which you should be working towards, and understand the difference between fluency, number sense and memorisation.

In terms of 'using number facts' this chapter has aimed to explain 'why' certain rules work – I hope you understand the commutative, associative and distributive properties of numbers, and how the misapplication of these rules can sometimes lead to errors. Finally, and most importantly, I hope you are beginning to see that the number system makes sense, and it is feeling less mysterious and more logical. In the foundation stage you teach your learners how to add 1 to a number below 10, so they understand that every time you add 1 to 8 you get 9. Armed with this knowledge you can carry out an infinite number of calculations – eventually you know that because $1 + 8 = 9$, then $100 + 800 = 900$, $0.1 + 0.8 = 0.9$ and $28.01 + 3.08 = 31.09$. What could be more logical than that?

Carry out this self-audit to examine how your learning has progressed as a result of working on this chapter. Include your results in your portfolio.

Going further

Fluency without fear

JO BOALER

'Fluency without fear' is available on the youcubed website at **www.youcubed. org/fluency-without-fear/**

Interactive pictures

JILL RUSSELL

This article shows the benefit of encouraging children to tell stories about numbers by talking about pictures.

Russell, J. (2003) 'Interactive pictures', *Mathematics Teaching* 182, March 2003.

Numbers: Facts, figures and fiction

RICHARD PHILLIPS

This is a useful book for giving you lots of facts about individual numbers. It isn't a research book, but you will find it useful as a resource book.

Phillips, R. (2004) *Numbers: Facts, figures and fiction*. London: Badsey Publications.

The Number Mysteries: A mathematical odyssey through everyday life

MARCUS DE SAUTOY

This is a book to engage and challenge you in learning more about number facts for yourself. It is a very accessible text and hopefully will fascinate you. You will be able to draw on much of what you learn from this book in your own classroom and it will certainly make you much more confident – and excited – about the properties of numbers.

De Sautoy, M. (2011) *The Number Mysteries: A mathematical odyssey through everyday life*. London: Fourth Estate.

Numbers: Their history and meaning

GRAHAM FLEGG

I once drew on this book to write a complete course for 11-year-olds. It is a 'history' of the development of numbers through their spoken and then written form. You will come to understand how calculation developed and realise that counting and number properties have developed differently across different cultures.

Flegg, G. (2003) *Numbers: Their history and meaning*. Harmondsworth: Penguin Books.

A proposed framework for examining basic number sense

ALISTAIR McINTOSH, BARBARA REYS and ROBERT REYS

This article introduces the term 'number sense'. The authors explore the link between informal methods and formal calculation procedures. Ian Thompson analyses the concept further in the paper 'Narrowing the gap between mental computational strategies and standard written algorithms' presented to the International Convention on Mathematics Education in Denmark in 2008.

McIntosh, A., Reys, B.J. and Reys, R.E. (1992) 'A proposed framework for examining basic number sense', *For the Learning of Mathematics*, 12(3), 2–8.

Self-audit

This activity asks you to use your knowledge of place value and multiplication facts to multiply 10 by 10 to derive related facts involving decimals.

I know that $8 \times 7 = 56$ so I can derive the facts $56 \div 7 = 8$ by rearranging the number sentence; $28 \div 7 = 4$ by halving 56; $2.8 \div 4 = 0.7$ by dividing by 10.

Start with 12×10 and write down ten other number facts you can work out from this starting point. Explain how you derived each new fact.

A report from Ofsted in England called 'Good practice in primary mathematics: Evidence from 20 successful schools' focused on calculation. The key findings in this report included the following recommendations:

- Children should focus on practical activities and developing mental methods in the early stages of their time in primary school.
- A good understanding of place value and the ability to recall multiplication tables and number bonds supports effective calculation. (This has been covered in the previous chapter.)
- Your learners' confidence and 'fluency' in calculating will be improved if you place a strong emphasis on problem solving and make the most of any cross-curricular links.
- A focus on misconceptions will make sure that these do not develop and impede next steps in learning.

This chapter follows these recommendations and it is worth spending a moment thinking about your own experience of learning how to calculate. Think about your own confidence in mental methods. How confident were you in carrying out the initial activity above? If you have good mental methods and can recall multiplication facts well then you are probably a fluent calculator. My guess is that if you are not yet confident in calculating you may not have learnt to calculate in a context which matched the bullet points above. So try not to replicate the way that you were taught with your pupils.

These schools did not teach 'chunking' as a method of division, nor did they teach the long division algorithm. The teachers in these schools had realised that neither of these approaches help children become efficient at calculations which involve long division. (You will read more about chunking and the long division algorithm later in this chapter.)

As you can see, there is much more to calculating than just knowing the written methods for adding, subtracting, multiplying and dividing – the message is clear: mental methods first, then a range of written methods to allow children to develop 'efficient, reliable and effective' methods when it is not possible to use mental methods. Chapter 13 looks at the use of calculators in detail and describes how you can introduce these to your learners so that they are supported in developing their mental methods and know when it is appropriate to use them. In this chapter you will read about the importance of developing a range of calculating methods so that your learners can make sensible choices over their methods when they are faced with a calculation to carry out.

TAKING IT FURTHER: **FROM THE RESEARCH**

In Chapter 4 you were briefly introduced to *Children and Number: Difficulties in Learning Mathematics* (1986, Blackwell) by Martin Hughes. It is worth revisiting this research at this point. There is an important section exploring calculation strategies and the way in which children invent their own forms of recording when carrying out calculations. Hughes suggests that, left to their own devices, children go through a series of stages in their responses.

An initial stage is the 'pictographic' response. At this stage children literally 'draw' the calculation. So if they are adding three multilink blocks to four multilink cubes they will draw the cubes in two groups and then count them up to add them together. Another stage is described by Martin Hughes as the 'iconic' stage. Here children represent the blocks by 'icons'. So for the calculation above a child might draw three sticks in a circle and four sticks in a circle and then add them. Again, there is a direct correspondence between the drawing and the physical act of counting. Both of these stages precede the use of formal symbols – here a child would write the symbol '3' and the symbol '4' to represent the calculation.

I have seen children using the number symbols as icons – for example, when working out

$3 + 4 =$

they will count each point of the 3 by tapping their pencil on the points and then tap each point of the 4 to carry out the calculation. They count the taps and reach 7. You may have seen children doing this – you may even remember doing it yourself!

Take the time to spend some time with early learners in your setting as they start to record their calculating process. Encourage them to use individual white boards to 'jot' down their 'working out'. It is likely that you will notice them developing in the way that Martin Hughes suggests.

Progression in calculation

Foundations for calculation

Counting is at the heart of calculating and initially you will be working with your learners on counting objects and using language such as 'more' and 'less' to introduce them to ideas of addition and subtraction. You should compare different groups of objects to find out how many more or less there are in each group and start to explore sharing by splitting groups of objects into equal parts.

Beginning calculation

The next step is to introduce your pupils to the idea of counting on. That is, if you are adding 5 and 3 you point to 5 on a number line and count on saying, 6, 7, 8. You can teach that addition can be carried out in any order and that you can carry out subtraction by finding the difference between two numbers through 'counting up'. This also shows them how addition and subtraction are inverse or opposite operations and the two operations should be taught together. You may introduce the number symbols to record practical activities but should ensure pupils are secure in their understanding before you do this.

You should develop grouping activities by combining groups of 2, 5 or 10 objects and by sharing into equal groups.

At this stage you can begin to introduce children to the four symbols, $+$, $-$, $\times$ and $\div$, as well as $=$. This will help children find unknown numbers in number sentences such as $20 - \uparrow = 12$, which is the early stages of algebra (see Chapter 7). Mentally they will be able to add and subtract:

- a two-digit number and ones
- a two-digit number and tens
- two two-digit numbers
- three one-digit numbers (adding only).

They will use concrete objects and pictorial representations to support them in this. Children should also understand that addition and subtraction are **inverse operations** and should represent multiplication as an array – for example,

4×3 is the same as

Becoming confident in calculation

At this stage you can support your pupils to add or subtract mentally one- and two-digit numbers and introduce them to practical and informal methods to multiply and divide two-digit numbers (these informal methods are described later in the chapter), teaching them that multiplication and division are inverse operations. Your pupils will also start to find unit fractions. Unit fractions have 1 as the numerator. So they will be able to find 1/2 of 5 metres or 1/6 of 18 litres, for example.

You can develop your pupils' use of written methods to record and explain multiplication and division of two-digit numbers by single-digit numbers and teach them to use written methods to add and subtract two- and three-digit whole numbers, including working in the context of money. You should expect your pupils to multiply and divide by 100 and 1000 and they will have developed their understanding of fractions to find fractions of quantities and shapes. You will explore the use of a calculator to help them carry out one- and two-step calculations involving all four operations, including understanding the meaning of negative numbers in the display.

The next stage is to develop calculation skills so they can use efficient written methods to add and subtract whole numbers and decimals up to two decimal places. You will have helped them extend their mental methods for whole number calculations including multiplying one-digit numbers by two-digit numbers; multiplying by 25; and subtracting near multiples of 1000. You will ask them to draw on their understanding of place value to multiply by 10, 100 or 1000 and be able to draw on a range of written methods to multiply and divide three-digit numbers by single-digit numbers. They will be able to find fractions and percentages by division including using a calculator.

By the end of primary school, children will be calculating mentally when appropriate and will be able to use a range of written methods for those calculations which cannot be carried out mentally. You will expect them to use a calculator to solve multi-step problems and find fractions and percentages of whole number quantities.

Extending learning in calculation

With these learners you can teach them to apply the commutative, associative and distributive laws that were described in Chapter 5, as well as using their understanding of inverses to calculate more efficiently. Look at these examples:

$$12 \times 13 = 156$$

$$13 \times 12 = 156$$

$$156 \div 12 = 13$$

$$156 \div 13 = 12$$

For example, multiplication and division are inverse operations; this means they are the opposites of each other. By knowing the answer to one of the above problems you can work out all the others.

The children will have developed their mental methods to include fractions and decimals and will be able to calculate percentage increases and decreases.

Big ideas

To introduce the big ideas in calculating try this activity:

Portfolio task 6.1

Work out 48 + 36 and record your solution using a pencil and paper method.

When I use this activity with teachers the most common response is

$$48$$
$$+36$$
$$\overline{84}$$

When I ask them 'how' they calculated the answer a common response is, 'I added 40 and 30 to give me 70 and then added on 14.' What is interesting here is that this calculation is not represented by the method they record. The written method records the question and the answer but does not 'represent' the method used. When I work with children they are more likely to use a number line to record the calculation. For example

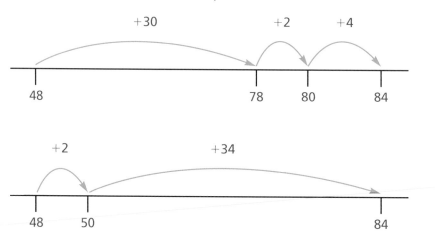

The big ideas in calculating are how children develop mental methods, which support them in understanding and developing formal written methods at an appropriate stage.

Children's development of mental methods

The reason that we encourage pupils to develop mental approaches to calculation is because it is much more efficient to work things out 'in our heads' if we can rather than immediately reverting to a pencil and paper or a calculator. If we are fluent in mental methods we carry this confidence over into other areas of mathematics. The reason to develop rapid recall of number facts is to help us become fluent in mental calculation – not so that we can pass our weekly times-tables tests. It is interesting that the poet Ted Hughes and the writer Jeanette Winterson both advocated the memorising of poems and other classic literature. Ted Hughes even put together poetry collections just for that purpose. They argue that having access to these memorised texts gives them easy access to a wealth of examples of great literature to support them in their writing. In the same way having access to a wealth of number facts, and key relationships between numbers means that we can quickly manipulate numbers in our heads. It is interesting that Ted Hughes describes how important it is to be able to draw on images in order to memorise text. This is just the same for number facts and mental calculations. The most appropriate strategy to support children in developing their mental methods is to use a wide range of images and models which children can draw on to enable them to 'see' calculations in their heads. Using number lines, number squares and empty number lines all support the development of mental methods.

Activities such as 'Guess my number' or 'loop cards', discussed in the previous chapter, give you plenty of opportunity to ask individuals how they are calculating mentally and also support your pupils in developing effective mental methods. You should join in these activities too and make your own thinking overt, sharing it with your learners. In this way you will make sure that you develop your own mental capacity too.

Pupils develop mental calculation skills as they progress through school. At each stage they should be using concrete materials and images and models of the number system to support them. The table below illustrates the progression in developing mental calculation skills and the mental images that you can use to support learners.

Mental calculation skill	Strategies and models
Adding and subtracting pairs of single-digit numbers Adding and subtracting single digits from 20	Use concrete objects – grouping together and removing from groups Use number lines and number tracks
Adding single-digits numbers to and from multiples of 10 Adding and subtracting single digits from two-digit numbers	Number lines 100 squares Empty number lines Partitioning
Adding and subtracting groups of numbers Adding and subtracting two-digit numbers from two-digit numbers	Reorder to make calculation simpler Number lines Empty number lines 100 squares Partition numbers
Adding and subtracting three-digit numbers and 1s and 10s and 100s Multiplying two-digit numbers by one-digit numbers	Empty number lines Use known facts to derive new facts Partition numbers
Multiplying three single-digit numbers Multiplying numbers by near multiples of 10 and 100	Empty number lines Use known facts to derive new facts Partition numbers
Using place value, known and derived facts to multiply and divide mentally	Empty number lines Use known facts to derive new facts Partition numbers

You will see that as the mental calculation becomes more complex we have to draw on an important skill. That is, we need to be able to use facts that we know to derive new facts. This is best described through an example.

By the later stages our pupils will have learnt that we can carry out mental multiplication by partitioning.

So

$$28 \times 7 = (20 \times 7) + (8 \times 7) = 140 + 56 = 196$$

So I know that

$$28 \times 7 = 196$$

Using this fact I can list the following facts

$$2.8 \times 7 = 19.6$$

$$0.28 \times 7 = 1.96$$

$$280 \times 7 = 1960$$

and so on.

Try this for yourself.

Portfolio task 6.2

Use mental methods to carry out the following calculations

$$36 \times 9$$

$$52 \times 6$$

$$84 \times 3$$

Derive at least five new facts from each calculation.

Children's development of written methods

There has been a long-held belief that young children cannot carry out calculation activities until they reach what Piaget called the 'concrete operational thinking' stage at around age seven. Martin Hughes, who carried out the research explored earlier in the chapter, challenged this view suggesting that very young children can begin to explore the underlying processes of calculating. He developed a 'box task' – in this task he worked with children aged between three and five. With some children he asked them to count a number of bricks into a box which he would then close – he would either add additional bricks to the box, or remove bricks, and ask the children how many were in the box now. The young children could understand and succeed on the task so long as the numbers were very small.

When working with one child he counted five bricks into the box, then removed three and asked the child how many were left. The young boy told him 'two'. Martin Hughes then records the following conversation (see page 27 in his 1986 book *Children and Number*):

MH: I want to take three bricks out of the box now.

Richard: You can't can you?

MH: Why not?

Richard: You just have to put one in, don't you?

MH: Put one in?

Richard: Yeah, and then you can take three out.

This suggests that Richard was capable of carrying out two successive mental calculations before he was five. Asking children to represent activities such as this early in their experience in school will help them see written methods as supportive of mental calculations rather than simply a record of the question and the answer.

They should be given the opportunity to develop pictographic recording of their calculations when the activities are predominantly practical; they will move onto iconic representations during the early years, but it is unlikely that formal written methods will be helpful until Year 3.

The next section of the chapter draws heavily on a series of articles written by Ian Thompson for the Association of Teachers of Mathematics (ATM). These appear in *Mathematics Teaching*, issues 202, 204, 206 and 208, and explore in detail an approach to calculation which has been drawn on by many effective schools. These are available from the ATM, and can be found online at **www.atm.org.uk/**. These articles and many others are also available at Ian's own website: **www.ianthompson.pi.dsl.pipex.com**

If you are working in a school or on placement at a school it is likely that there will be a school calculation policy. Read this section alongside your school's calculation policy. This will describe in detail the way in which your school teaches calculation. Whilst the series of steps will be very similar to that set out below, there may be more detail or slightly different expectations. There is a sample calculation policy on the companion website.

Addition

An initial approach to written calculation is the empty number line which I introduced you to at the beginning of the 'Big ideas' section. The empty number line is a useful 'record' of a mental strategy as you can use it to support any addition or subtraction calculation. We could view the conceptual structures for addition in the following way:

1   Combining two or more quantities

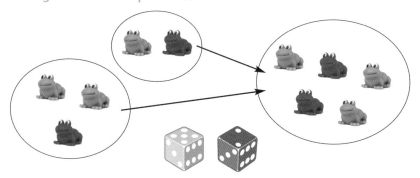

2   Augmentation of one quantity

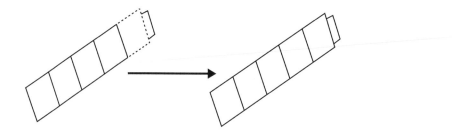

3   Comparative addition

3	2
5	

4   Using a number line

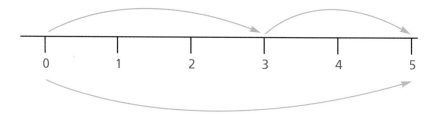

The next idea to introduce is the use of 'partitioning' for calculating with larger numbers. So for example

$$39 + 52 = 39 + 50 + 2 = 89 + 2 = 91$$

or

$$39 + 52 = 30 + 50 + 9 + 2 = 80 + 11 = 91$$

Can you see that only the first example of partitioning builds on the use of an empty number line? If you draw a number line you can sketch the calculation on that line. The second example changes the order of the numbers so that an empty number line would not model the calculation as you need to conserve the order of the calculation to sketch it in a number line.

In order to move towards formal written methods it is important to offer children practice in the second form of partitioning. This can then be represented in a more formal way as

$$
\begin{array}{rcl}
39 & = & 30 + 9 \\
+52 & & 50 + 2 \\
\hline
& & 80 + 11 = 91
\end{array}
$$

This leads children into the 'expanded column method' – this method would record the calculation above as either

$$
\begin{array}{r}
39 \quad \text{(adding 10s first, that is } 30 + 50) \\
+52 \\
\hline
80 \\
11 \\
\hline
91 \\
\hline
\end{array}
$$

or

$$
\begin{array}{r}
39 \quad \text{(adding 1s first, that is } 9 + 2) \\
+52 \\
\hline
11 \\
80 \\
\hline
91 \\
\hline
\end{array}
$$

It is helpful to work your examples both ways so that your pupils can see there is no difference to adding 10s first or 1s first. The final strategy to be taught to children is the column method involving 'carrying' with the 'carry digits' recorded below the line. In order to make sure that children make the links back to place value it is suggested that they are encouraged to say 'carry 10' or 'carry 100' rather than 'carry 1' as may have become a habit.

Chapter 6 Number: Calculation (addition, subtraction, multiplication and division)

Subtraction

We can view subtraction in two ways: subtraction as take away or as difference. Sometimes children will model a subtraction calculation such as 15 – 6 by placing 15 objects in a box and taking out 6 and then counting how many remain. This will give them 9. They may represent this by a jotting like this:

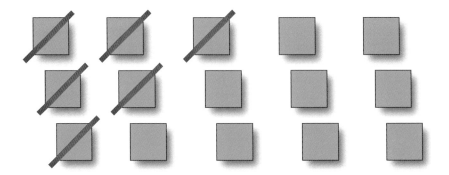

Subtraction as difference can be calculated using a number line. Here the pupil will start at 15 and count back 6 ending up on 9.

A way of thinking about the conceptual structures for subtraction is as follows

1   Partitioning

2 Reduction

3 Comparative difference

4 Additive difference/complementary addition

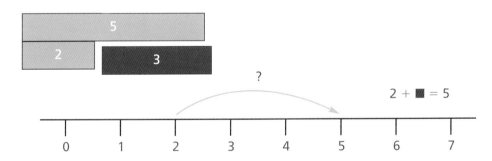

The stages for developing written methods to support subtraction also employ a progression through the empty line to partitioning before moving on to column methods. The first stage in the strategy involves counting back on an empty number line. So, for example, to calculate 74 – 27 we may write

or combine steps by initially subtracting 7 and then 20. It is important that children see the calculation can be carried out in any order.

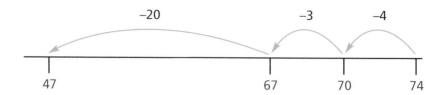

An alternative is to begin with the 27, and ask the children how many they would have to count up to get to 74. This can be recorded on an empty number line as follows:

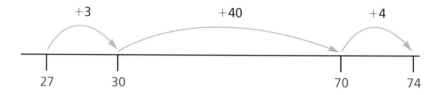

Ian Thompson suggests that if children can use the empty number line in this way there is no benefit in using partitioning to support subtraction. In fact, children are effectively partitioning if they are using the empty number line efficiently.

The final stage in moving towards a formal algorithm is the expanded layout. An example of this is 653 − 289:

$$600 + 50 + 3 \qquad 500 + 140 + 13$$
$$-200 + 80 + 9 \qquad -200 + \ 80 + \ 9$$
$$\qquad\qquad\qquad\qquad 300 + \ 60 + \ 4$$

In moving from one calculation to the other I have partitioned

$$600 = 500 + 100$$
$$50 = \ 40 + \ 10$$
$$3 = \ 3$$

So 653 can be written as 500 + 140 + 13.

TAKING IT FURTHER: **FROM THE CLASSROOM**

In his article 'The same difference' in *Mathematics Teaching* 202, published by the ATM in May 2007, Ian Sugarman describes a mental strategy for subtraction developed by children he was working with which does not appear in the National Strategy. He argues that this method is more appropriate for carrying out subtraction calculations than the decomposition method described by the Strategy. He worked with Year 4, 5 and 6 children and the activity he used with them involved transforming numbers that would be difficult to work with using the column method to a pair of numbers that could be subtracted mentally. So, for example, rather than trying to calculate 563 − 278 the pupils transformed this to 565 − 280 and then 585 − 300 by initially adding 2 to each number and then another 20. The children described this as the 'same difference' method.

They realised that if you add the same number to each number in the calculation, the 'difference' remains the same, and so the answer to the calculation is unaltered. This can be extended to four-digit numbers, for example,

2038 − 1757	= 281
2040 − 1759	= 281 (adding 2)
2000 − 1719	= 281 (subtracting 40)
2081 − 1800	= 281 (adding 81)

Multiplication

Ian Thompson suggests it is important to let children develop their own informal methods to record multiplication as with addition and subtraction. The first formal stage therefore would be the grid method. This approach is supported by the Ofsted review mentioned earlier in the chapter. The schools which were visited, all of whom were successful in supporting their pupils in becoming effective at 'calculating', used the 'grid' method to introduce the pupils to the ideas of 'long multiplication'. It is worth spending some time becoming secure with this method yourself so that you are able to introduce it confidently to your learners. It will also help you see why the more traditional long multiplication method 'works'.

You record the grid method as follows.

We would write 38×7 as

×	7
30	210
8	56
	266

The next step would be recording this as

$$
\begin{array}{r}
38 \\
\times\ 7 \\
\hline
210 \\
56 \\
\hline
266
\end{array}
$$

because it develops naturally from mental methods and the grid method shown above. The grid method can be extended to multiply a two-digit number by a two-digit number. For example,

$\times$	20	9	Total
30	600	180	780
7	140	42	182
			962

It is important to remember that by the end of primary school the most complex calculation that pupils would be expected to carry out is a two-digit by three-digit one. There are three ways to carry out this calculation.

Firstly, consider 286×29

$\times$	20	9	
200	4000	1800	5800
80	1600	720	2320
6	120	54	174
			8294

or writing the same calculation in column

286 × 29		
	200×20	4000
	80×20	1600
	6×20	120
	200×9	1800
	80×9	720
	6×9	54
		8294

or finally

$$
\begin{array}{r}
286 \\
\times\ 29 \\
\hline
\end{array}
$$

5720 (286 × 20)
2574 (286 × 9)

8294

Division

When I talk to people about why they do not feel confident about teaching mathematics they often describe 'long division' as a hated memory. This is not something that many pupils should be exploring before Year 6. It is interesting that not a single school that Ofsted identified as being effective in teaching calculation expected their pupils to use the long division algorithm, which you probably remember.

$$
\begin{array}{r}
27 \\
\hline
3\ )\ 8^21
\end{array}
$$

It is important to allow children to explore mental methods and also their under-standing of division as the inverse of multiplication. For example you can use a number line to show a range of strategies for division (see the examples below).

Empty number line strategies for division:

a) Using repeated subtraction

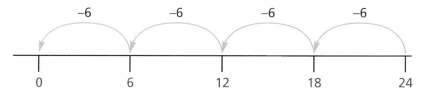

So 24 ÷ 6 = 4 because 24 − 6 − 6 − 6 − 6 = 0

b) By 'chunking'

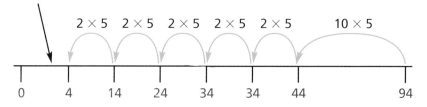

c) Using multiplication (as repeated addition) as the inverse of division

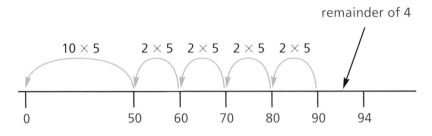

$94 \div 5 = 18$ r4 because $(18 \times 5) + 4 = 94$

It is also important not to rush into any formal recording of division. I still hear children in schools, or my students, describing this process in the following way: '81 divided by 3. So 8 divided by 3 goes 2 carry 2; 3's into 21 goes 7. So the answer is 27.'

The problem with this form of calculation is that the actual place value of the numbers is forgotten: 80 becomes 8 and 20 becomes 2. This can lead to children not noticing if answers are incorrect as they do not return to think if 27 is a sensible answer to 81 divided by 3. Estimating first can help this process.

I would expect the answer to be less than 390 because 90 divided by 3 is 30. I would also expect it to be more than 275 as 75 divided by 3 is 25. The answer should therefore be between 25 and 30, so 27 seems about right!

Initially pupils can use partitioning to carry out division calculations.

For example if they are calculating $75 \div 3$, the dividend of 75 is split into 60, the highest multiple of 3 that is also a multiple 10 and less than 75, to give $60 + 15$. Each number is then divided by 3.

So

$$75 \div 3 = (60 + 15) \div 3$$
$$= (60 \div 3) + (15 \div 3)$$
$$= 20 + 5$$
$$= 25$$

This short division method can be recorded as

$$\begin{array}{r} 20 + 5 \\ \hline 3\,\overline{)\,60 + 15} \end{array}$$

which can be shortened to 25

$$3\,\overline{)\,6\,{}^{1}5}$$

Here the 'carrying' digit 1 represents the 'ten' in the 15.

As pupils become more confident they can move onto the 'chunking' method for division.

For example to calculate find 226 ÷ 6, we start by multiplying 6 by 10, 20, 30, ... to find that 6 × 30 = 180 and 6 × 40 = 240.

This means that the answer to 196 ÷ 6 is somewhere between 30 and 40.

So we can start the division by first subtracting 180 from 226 leaving 46.

We know that 7 × 6 = 42.

So we have

   6 × 30 = 180

   6 × 7 = 42

Adding gives us 222 (so there will be a remainder of 4).

This can be written as

```
    _____
6 | 226

    −180   (6 × 30 = 180)
    ____
     46
    ____
     42    (6 × 7 = 42)
    ____
      4
    ____
```

Answer: 37 remainder 4.

Using manipulatives and practical resources to support calculation

All teachers are happy to use practical materials to aid calculation at the earliest stages. We would think it was silly to take away practical materials from a learner who was just beginning to combine sets to understand addition or taking objects out of a set to begin to understand subtraction. Unfortunately we often reduce their use as children move through school even though they can act as incredibly useful models to help us understand calculation strategies and in particular written calculation strategies. I would hope that every classroom would have Diene's blocks freely available.

These are invaluable in modelling addition and subtraction as you can physically exchange 10 'ones' for a ten rod. Similarly it is clear that 10 ten rods make 100 and then 10 one hundred 'flats' make 1000.

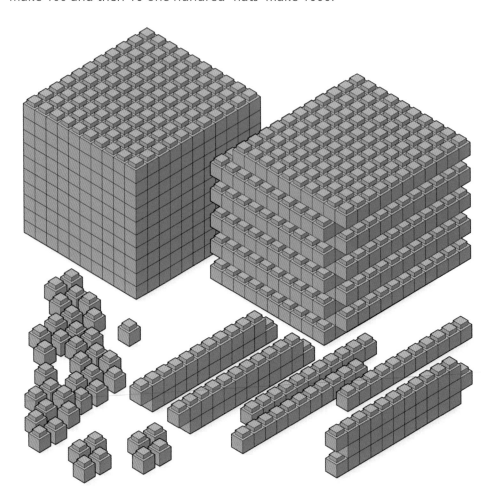

Similarly, cuisenaire rods can be used to model a wide range of calculations.

For example:

$$5 + 8 = 13$$
$$13 - 8 = 5$$

$$8 \times 3 = 24$$
$$4 \times 6 = 24$$
$$6 \times 4 = 24$$

$3 \times 2 = 6$ $2 \times 3 = 6$

Cuisenaire rods can also represent fractions easily.

Finally, place value counters – which are now to be found in many schools – also offer a physical way for children to represent calculations, with written and mental methods.

Teaching points

Teaching point 1: Misapplying algorithms

I often tell teachers that children very rarely make mistakes – they can come up with an answer that doesn't seem quite right but when you ask them what they have done, they have answered a question correctly – it just isn't the question you have asked them. For example, Sam, aged nine, had been asked to calculate

$$
\begin{array}{r}
85 \\
-48 \\
\hline
\\
\hline
\end{array}
$$

and gave the answer 43. He was irate when his teacher suggested this was 'wrong'. It isn't,' he said, 'I took away 8 from 5 by "finding the difference" so I put 3 down and 80 take away 40 is 40 so that gives me 43'. Whenever you are asking children to calculate using a formal algorithm it is useful to have them 'talk it through', sometimes at the front so that the rest of the group can see the approach and sometimes in a one-to-one situation with you. This way you will begin to understand whether your learners understand the mathematics behind the algorithms or whether they are simply following, or misapplying, a rule. This is where having secure mental methods is helpful as this can help the pupils see when they have misapplied an algorithm as they will have a good sense of what the answer should be. In this case Sam could work out that the answer should be 37. (He counted on, 48 + 30 is 78, 78 + 2 is 80, and another 5 is 85. So the answer is 30 + 5 + 2 = 37.)

Teaching point 2: Not checking calculations

We all remember putting our hands up to tell a teacher we had finished our calculations, or completed a test paper, only to be told by the teacher to check our answers carefully. Be honest with yourself – did you always check carefully? It is important to try to get children into the habit of checking as a first step. So when Helen came up to the board and wrote

$$3 \times 142 = 126$$

I said, 'I don't know what the answer is but I know that it isn't 126.' She looked at me and then said, 'Oh no – it should be more than 300, shouldn't it?' She was then able to find her mistake and carry out the calculation. Sometimes when pupils are following algorithms they lose track of the numbers they are working with and so forget to estimate and use this estimate as a check. By encouraging pupils to estimate as a first step you will help them get into this habit.

In the activity below the pupils are being encouraged to look for errors by drawing on their knowledge of odd and even numbers. It is important that the pupils are not asked to carry out the calculation.

1   Will the results of these calculations be odd or even?

    a) $4861 + 3758$ b) $7052 - 507$ c) 34×57

    d) $711 - 296$ e) 72×28 f) $461 + 836$

2   Which of these are incorrect? Use rules for odd and even numbers to check.

    a) $30 \times 91 = 2730$ b) $9072 - 978 = 8272$

    c) $826 + 7095 = 7922$ d) $68 \times 47 = 3196$

3   Which of these are incorrect? Use rules for odd and even numbers to check.

    a) $76 + 128 = 204$ b) $241 - 129 = 111$

    c) $97 - 38 = 58$ d) $50 + 503 = 553$

4   Will the results of these calculations be odd or even?

    a) $419 + 282$ b) $174 - 86$

    c) $347 + 63$ d) $70 - 47$

Teaching point 3: Not understanding written symbolism

The research by Martin Hughes described in some detail earlier in the chapter (page 114) suggests that often children's errors in calculations are not because they do not understand the mathematical concepts, rather they get confused with how the written symbolism relates to the calculations they are carrying out. It is a problem of 'translation' rather than a problem of mathematics.

The best way to support pupils in making this translation is to work with the pupils as they say number sentences and to write calculations down for them. In this way they will begin to see the + sign as simply shorthand for saying 'add'.

Another activity to help children begin to understand the use of the multiplication sign 'x' is to introduce them to arrays. An array is simply an 'orderly arrangement of objects'. Arrays can help us understand multiplication by lining up objects in rows and columns. So, for example, 4 × 3 can be shown as

When I look at a box of eggs I can see both 6 and 3 × 2.

Similarly, for a box of a dozen eggs I see 12 and 2 × 6.

If I buy a book of stamps arranged in the way they are in the image below I see both 24 and 3 × 8.

This sense of multiplication as an array helps me both with multiplication and with rapid recall of number facts. It is worth drawing on the many examples of arrays that your pupils see around them every day. The milk bottles in the crate; desks if you organise them in rows on occasions; lining up in pairs. Making physical arrays is a great activity. Get a group of 12 of your class, or 24, and see how many different arrays they can form. Ask the pupils to make sketches of these arrays.

Teaching point 4: Carrying out the wrong operation when solving number problems

I recently picked up a greeting card from my local farm shop. It is headed 'Rural Maths' and contains the following text:

> 'Jack,' said the teacher, 'you have 30 sheep in your field, two escape through a hole in the wall, how many are left?'
>
> 'None,' Jack replied instantly.
>
> 'No Jack, it's 28!' the teacher replied sounding cross, 'I thought you knew your maths!'
>
> 'Yes Miss, I know my maths alright, it's you that doesn't know sheep.'

This is a great example of a child solving a mathematics problem in their 'actual' real world than the pseudo reality of a maths problem. Children who are successful solvers of word problems realise that these are very rarely 'real' problems but are mathematics problems set in a context. The first skill for your learners to develop is to decode such problems so that they apply the correct operations to solve the problem and then check the answer. Many teachers use the acronym RUCSAC to help their learners solve such problems. This acronym stands for:

R – Read the question carefully
U – Understand the question – what do you have to find out?
C – Choose the correct operations to solve the problem
S – Solve the problem
A – Find the answer
C – Check your answer – is it sensible?

It is helpful to just focus on a series of questions without solving them to teach your pupils to select the operation which will solve the problem. Spend some time simply underlining key pieces of information in questions in order to help pupils see through all the extraneous information that is contained in word problems. Focusing on selecting the correct operation without having to carry out the calculation allows your pupils to see the importance of this step.

Another useful classroom activity is to provide your pupils with a sketch or an image from which they can devise their own word problems. For example an image of a pot containing six pencils with two pens lying by the side of the pot will allow learners in the early years to devise several different word problems. The answers might be 6 + 2 = 8 or 8 – 2 = 6 or even 2 + 2 = 4 (there are two pencils outside my pot, I take another two out how many are outside the pot now?). If you visit **www.oxfam.org.uk/education** you will find many images illustrating global issues which can be used for your learners to devise number problems with the added bonus of developing their global awareness.

Portfolio task 6.3

1   The grid method: Calculate the following using the grid method. Before you carry out the calculation estimate the answer. Which two numbers do you think the answer should be between?

$$358 \times 34$$

×	30	4	
300			
50			
8			

Then use the expanded method shown on page 128.

In practice

The following lesson plan and evaluation describe a lesson taught to a group of pupils who had been introduced to pencil and paper procedures. The particular focus was developing skills in multiplying and dividing using mental methods to support their use of pencil and paper methods for more complex procedures.

Objectives:	• Develop and use written methods to record, support and explain multiplication of two-digit numbers by one-digit numbers	
Key vocabulary: Digit, multiply, product, estimate	**Context:** This is the second lesson exploring the grid method for multiplication. The group worked on differentiated examples using the grid method in the last lesson. The children who needed extra support found the concept of the grid difficult although they were able to carry out the individual calculations	
Resources: Two sets of 0–9 digit cards	**Starter activity:** Working in pairs use any operation with a two-digit number and a one-digit number to make 100	
Main activity:	**Teacher:** Model 'grid multiplication' to introduce multiplying through partitioning. Use the examples 13 × 6; 18 × 4; 24 × 7 and 32 × 5. Partition using the 10s. So 24 × 7 = 20 × 7 + 4 × 7 and so on	**Pupil activity:** Before carrying out the calculation ask pairs to estimate to the nearest 10 using individual whiteboards
Group activity: Children operating above expected levels	This group can work with four digits and carry out TU × TU as well as HTU × U	Pupils should estimate before carrying out the calculation. They should try to explain why a particular arrangement of digits gives the largest answer, drawing on their understanding of place value
Group activity: Children operating at expected levels	The group should pick any three cards from the two sets of 0–9 digit cards and write down all the multiplication calculations that can be formed from these numbers. Working in pairs within the group they should carry out these calculations and see which gives the largest product	Pupils should estimate before carrying out the calculation. They should try to explain why a particular arrangement of digits gives the largest answer, drawing on their understanding of place value
Group activity: Children operating below expected levels	This group should be supported by the teacher. The group should just work on two-digit multiplied by one-digit numbers. The teacher should model each calculation on a whiteboard	Estimate which calculation will give the smallest answer and which will give the largest. Pupils should 'tell' the teacher how to proceed throughout the calculation

Plenary: Each group feeds back one of their calculations – the core group and the extension group explain why the particular arrangement of digits gives the largest answer

Rationale and evaluation

My aim was that, by presenting this as an investigation into which arrangement of digits would give the largest product, I would encourage the pupils to estimate first. This worked very well – it also encouraged them into checking as they went through the grid multiplication. The extension and the core groups didn't share out the different multiplications as I suggested – rather they took it in turns to calculate whilst the others in the group watched to see what the answer would be. This was actually a useful way of organising the activity as those who weren't carrying out the calculation were checking as they went along.

I worked alongside the support group so that I could model the process for them carefully. This group still isn't making the connection between the grid method and the numbers they are working with. So for example Parmjit carried out the calculation

23×4

×	4	
2		
3		

and Jay wanted to put a '2' instead of '20' and was quite happy with the answer 20 as a result: $(4 \times 2) + (4 \times 3) = 20$. This was despite the group agreeing that the answer should be bigger than 80. As a result I have suggested that they use the 'grid multiplication' program in the next lesson so that they can have an image of how partitioning works to support the grid method. I am also going to focus on multiplication of multiples of 10 by single-digit numbers with this group before coming back to the grid multiplication with them.

Troy seems to be understanding how the grid method can help, though – in the plenary he showed everyone how you can write it 'without the grid'. He wrote:

$$\begin{array}{r} 27 \\ \times\ 4 \\ \hline \end{array}$$

80   (saying 'that's 4 times 20')
28   ('and that's 4 times 7')
_____
108 ('so that's 108 altogether which is about right cause it's a
     bit more than 100 and 4 times 25 would be 100')

Observing the teaching of calculation

On the companion website find the clip called 'How many peas fill the classroom?' This is a fascinating activity in which the teacher works with her class to try to calculate how many peas it would take to fill the classroom. As well as developing and practising children's calculation skills it also develops the idea of very large numbers in a real context. Children often find it very difficult to visualise very large numbers. The task also requires the pupils to break down a complex problem into small steps.

Although this clip is from a Year 7 group I have carried out very similar activities with learners in primary schools. Focus particularly on the segment from 4 minutes onwards which shows the teacher taking feedback from the groups. What might you do differently as a result of observing this section of the lesson? One concern might be that the large numbers they were working with did not carry very much meaning to the children as they didn't break the task down into chunks which they could visualise. Perhaps dividing the classroom up into more manageable 'chunks' to start with would have allowed the learners to make more sense of the answers they were coming up with.

Imagine you are feeding back to the teacher. What are three things that you feel were strengths in the lesson, and what is one key thing that you would suggest the teacher does differently?

How would you adapt this activity for the group that you are currently working with?

Assessing calculation

The 2011 Ofsted report mentioned earlier in this chapter described 'problem solving' as being at the heart of learning arithmetic. This supports the argument presented to you in Chapter 3 and suggests that the ability to solve problems should also be central to assessing your pupils' calculating skills. This can be carried out in a wide range of contexts. It is helpful if these contexts are genuine 'real-life' contexts rather than the pseudo reality I referred to earlier in the chapter. Examples that you can use could include:

- Calculating the best value purchase. Bring in a range of cereals, or drinks in different sized containers. The pupils have to calculate which size offers the best value.
- Calculating the costs to redecorate the classroom. Include the costs of paint for the walls and carpet for the floor.
- Calculating costs of fruit for younger pupils. Make sure you let the pupils devise their own ways of recording their calculations at this stage. It is likely that these learners will begin with repeated addition and will sketch the fruit they want to buy and 'attach' a price to it.

Ask very young learners to work out how many raisins there are in a packet. Observe how they group the raisins. Some may choose to count in 2s or 3s or even 5s.

Cross-curricular teaching of calculation

The idea of the extended project is to draw on the key ideas within the chapter to develop a cross-curricular project which you can explore with your learners over a series of lessons. This allows you and your class to develop your subject knowledge together. The examples given above in the assessment section all offer cross-curricular routes into calculating. I have found that developing the assessment activity around redecorating the classroom is a very fruitful cross-curricular activity which involves all learners in developing their calculation skills.

You need to begin this investigation in an open space.

Ask 24 pupils to come to the centre of the space. The rest of the pupils stand in pairs. They take it in turns to tell the 24 pupils how to arrange themselves in an array, for example 2×12 or 3×8.

Keep going until you have exhausted all the possibilities. Repeat for a range of other numbers – some that give a large number of possibilities and some that only offer one.

Return to the classroom and ask the pupils to explore how many different 'arrays' you can make for each number from 1 to 36.

At this stage you can ask pupils to identify other arrays that they notice around them, for example carpet tiles on a floor, or panes in a window.

This allows you to begin to think through different ways of organising the classroom. How many ways could the desks be arranged – what is appropriate in the space, and which arrangements work for which parts of the curriculum? Depending on the time you have you can develop scale models either 2D or 3D.

Summary

The key focus for this chapter is the link between the mental methods we employ as a first choice and how these can be formalised into written algorithms when the calculations become too complex for us to hold in our head. You have read how the four operations link together and how you can use your knowledge of one of the operations to support calculations using another operation. Our aim for children leaving school is that they have a good understanding of the four operations and that they can carry out calculations mentally, when possible, and can employ a range of written methods, making sensible choices depending on the calculation they are carrying out.

I have emphasised the importance of children approaching calculation practically and through activity – this allows you to support them in developing the vocabulary of calculation. They should also be encouraged to develop their own informal records for calculations. The key to understanding the more formal algorithms is to build carefully on previous understanding so that your pupils understand the reasons that the algorithms 'work' and don't just apply them unthinkingly. Most of the misconceptions come from losing sight of the value of the numbers in the calculation so that children don't notice they have an answer that doesn't make sense.

Work your way carefully though the progression of written methods – the grid method may be an idea that you are not used to. If the written methods make sense to you, you will be able to share this with your learners.

Reflections on this chapter

My guess would be that many of you have found this chapter the most challenging in the book – not because the ideas are more complex but because the methods of calculation may well be different from those that you were taught. My hope is that you can see that the rationale for teaching these methods of calculation is that pupils will be able see why the methods are effective and will begin to move away from simply trying to remember how you carry out a calculation to understanding why a 'rule' works. If you understand how the calculation is carried out you can make effective decisions about which method to use, and are also more likely to notice when you have made a mistake.

I also hope that you have become able to notice the choices that you are making when you carry out calculations, whether mentally or on paper. In a sense you have 'relearnt' the algorithms for the four operations, noticing, maybe for the first time, why you carry out calculations in a particular way. This process of revisiting your own learning should support you in explaining methods of calculation – both mental and written – to your learners.

Going further

Issues in Teaching Numeracy

IAN THOMPSON

This title contains a very useful section on calculation which outlines progression in written and mental calculation in much greater detail than there was space for in this chapter. There is also a very helpful chapter on using the empty number line which you will find invaluable in supporting your learners in developing mental methods.

Thompson, I. (2010) *Issues in Teaching Numeracy in Primary Schools*. Buckingham: Open University Press.

Teaching and Learning Early Number

IAN THOMPSON

This is the forerunner of the text above. It is important for all teachers not just those who teach learners in the early years as Thompson outlines in detail the ways in which early learners begin the process of learning to calculate. These two books will expand the research base on which you can draw to develop your practice as well as offering lots of practical approaches to learning and teaching calculation skills.

Thompson, I. (2008) *Teaching and Learning Early Number*. Buckingham: Open University Press.

Good Practice in Primary Mathematics: Evidence from 20 successful schools

OFSTED

This report offers useful small-scale case studies on how to teach calculation. There are several vignettes from classrooms which are enlightening, as well as evidence from children. This is particularly helpful in seeing how learners can develop their own written methods for calculating.

Ofsted (2011) *Good Practice in Primary Mathematics: Evidence from 20 successful schools*. Manchester: Ofsted.

Self-audit

Carry out this audit to explore how your learning has progressed as a result of working on the ideas in this chapter. Include the results in your portfolio.

1   Make a copy of this table.

Just know it	Need to think a bit	Need to work it out on paper

Using the digits 1, 3, 5, 7, 8, 9 make up a range of addition and subtraction calculations. Make sure you have some calculations that you would place in each column. Write the calculations in the appropriate column together with a rationale for your choice.

2   Set yourself the following tasks:
   - a column addition involving decimals
   - an addition involving decimals you would calculate mentally
   - a column subtraction involving decimals
   - a subtraction involving decimals you would do mentally
   - a short multiplication involving decimals you could do mentally
   - a multiplication involving decimals you would do using pencil and paper
   - a short division involving decimals you could do mentally
   - a division involving decimals you would do using pencil and paper.

Complete the calculations and write a commentary outlining your thought processes and the points at which you think pupils may make a mistake.

3 Spot the mistake: These three long multiplication calculations have got mistakes in them. Write down the mistake that the pupil has made, then complete the long multiplication correctly.

$$
\begin{array}{r}
135 \\
\times\ 62 \\
\hline
270 \\
710 \\
\hline
980 \\
\hline
\end{array}
\qquad
\begin{array}{r}
270 \\
\times\ 30 \\
\hline
710 \\
\hline
\end{array}
\qquad
\begin{array}{r}
452 \\
\times\ 18 \\
\hline
324016 \\
452 \\
\hline
324468 \\
\hline
\end{array}
$$

CHAPTER 7
ALGEBRA

Introduction

I remember sitting with a young woman called Natalie who was in Year 9. I knew that she was not normally in the group I was working with. She told me that she had been sent to this group as 'the teachers said I was being disruptive'. She also said, 'I can't do this work – they are doing algebra – I'm in the bottom set usually so we just do easy stuff like adding and taking away.' The problem she was working on was

If you cook a chicken for 20 minutes a pound and then an extra 20 minutes, how long would it take to cook an 'n' pound chicken?

'This is stupid', Natalie told me, *'there is no such thing as an "n" pound chicken.'*

I asked how long it would take to cook a 3 pound chicken. Natalie said,

'Well, that's easy – it would be 1 hour 20 minutes because 3 lots of 20 minutes make an hour and another 20 minutes make 1 hour 20 minutes.'

'So, how about a 5 pound chicken?' I asked.

This took a bit longer. Natalie wrote down,

$$20 + 20 + 20 + 20 + 20$$

Then drew a circle around the first three twenties.

> *'That makes 1 hour 40 minutes,'* she said, *'then another 20 minutes is 1 hour 60 minutes, that's the same as 2 hours.'*

> *'So how do you work it out?'* I asked.

> *'You count up the 20 minutes – one for every pound and then add another 20 minutes on at the end'.*

I looked delighted.

> *'You see you can do it',* I said.

Natalie looked at me askance.

> *'Maybe – but there's still no such thing as an "n" pound chicken!'*
> she said.

I am always reminded of this story when people talk to me about their image of algebra. In the United States the ability to pass tests in algebra is one of the gatekeepers for moving on in mathematics. In fact they have invented a topic called 'pre-algebra'. I am avoiding this term. There is no such thing as pre-algebra in the same way as there is no such thing as 'pre-counting'. The moment we start to operate algebraically we are 'doing algebra'. Let's try to demystify the term.

For some this is the moment when mathematics became hard. It is seen as impenetrable. Others wear it as a badge of pride. 'Well – I was really good at algebra' they will tell me. All of these responses come from a misunderstanding of what algebra actually is. Many people see algebra as simply substituting letters for numbers – and being good at algebra is being able to decode strange sentences such as

$$3x - 7 = 29$$

Algebra is so much more than this. In fact we are all doing algebra from the moment that we start to notice patterns in numbers and in things like bead strings. My grandson is 'doing algebra' when he lines up his cars on the back of the settee and starts to move them around and classify them according to his own criteria.

This chapter will show you what algebra really is. It will describe how you can introduce algebraic ideas from the moment that pupils start school and how you can draw on pupils' intuitive algebraic understandings. It will show you the power that algebra has in generalising patterns that you notice and how it can help you come to a better understanding of the number system. Let us start with an activity.

Starting point

Look at this 100 square.

1	2	3	4	5	6	7	8	9	10
11	12	13	14	15	16	17	18	19	20
21	22	23	24	25	26	27	28	29	30
31	32	33	34	35	36	37	38	39	40
41	42	43	44	45	46	47	48	49	50
51	52	53	54	55	56	57	58	59	60
61	62	63	64	65	66	67	68	69	70
71	72	73	74	75	76	77	78	79	80
81	82	83	84	85	86	87	88	89	90
91	92	93	94	95	96	97	98	99	100

Take any 2 × 2 grid in the square. For example:

12	13
22	23

What do you notice about the numbers in this square?

You probably quickly realised that numbers increase by 1 as you move 1 column across the 100 square and increase by 10 as you move down the rows. Because of this the number across the diagonal from the number in the top left-hand square is 11 more.

Before you read on think if you can calculate the total of the numbers in the 2 × 2 square if you are given the number in the left-hand column. Work on this in your notebook.

Now let me use the information from the paragraph above to 'generalise', that is to write down the numbers that appear in any 2 × 2 chunk of the 100 square:

n	$n+1$
$n + 10$	$n + 11$

This simply says that if the number in the top left-hand square is 'n' (any number) we can find the number to its right by adding 1, the number below it by adding 10 and the number across the diagonal by adding 11.

I can find the total of all 4 numbers by adding them:

$$n + n + 1 + n + 10 + n + 11$$

We know that it doesn't matter what order we add in so we can rearrange this as

$$n + n + n + n + 1 + 10 + 11$$

which is the same as

$$4n + 22$$

So I can find the total of any 2 × 2 chunk in a 100 square by multiplying the number in the top left square by 4 and adding 22. Try it. Try it for several 2 × 2 chunks. See – it always works. We have just used 'algebra' to generalise a result.

Algebra can be described as the ability to understand patterns and relationships. In the example above we used algebra to describe the patterns in a 100 square and to generalise about the relationships between the numbers in the 100 square. It is also the ability to use symbols to represent and analyse these patterns and relationships. The moment we moved to generalisation we used the symbol 'n' to represent 'any number'.

TAKING IT FURTHER: **FROM THE CLASSROOM**

In 2009 a team of researchers including Anne Watson shared the research they had carried out exploring how children learn mathematics. A section of this research discussed the learning and teaching of algebra. They described the nature of school-level algebra. This consists of:

- generalising laws about patterns and number
- modelling mathematical situations
- transforming and solving equations
- manipulating symbolic statements about relationships
- learning how to describe change and relationships using algebraic symbols.

They also suggested that learners have natural propensities that can support them in learning algebra. These include:

- interpreting symbols and diagrams in terms of their previous experience of similar symbols and forms
- looking for patterns all around them – very young learners have a natural propensity to classify and sort
- the development of personal mental calculation strategies that they can generalise across similar situations
- the ability to connect, relate to and compare different representations of the same situation.

You may find it useful to reflect on the times that you have noticed the pupils that you have worked with showing the natural propensities that Anne Watson describes in the research above. Although 'algebra' as a topic does not appear until the Year 6 Programme of Study in the UK there are elements of algebra through both the English Curriculum and the Cambridge Curriculum Framework.

Progression in algebra

Foundations for algebra

Young learners will describe and make repeating patterns. They will be able to tell you what shape or colour should come next in a pattern. Learners will use everyday language to talk about a wide range of measures. They will use properties of objects to solve problems and make comparisons. This is the beginning of algebraic thinking.

Beginning algebra

Pupils begin to identify and represent numbers using objects and pictorial representations. They read and write mathematical statements involving $=$ signs and can solve missing number problems such as $7 = \_ - 9$. They come to understand that addition can be carried out in any order but not subtraction and can use the inverse relationship between addition and subtraction to solve missing number problems. They will be beginning to explore number patterns and be able to describe them.

Becoming confident in algebra

As pupils become more confident with the number system they can identify, represent and estimate numbers using different representations. They use number facts and their knowledge of place value to solve missing number problems. They begin to solve scaling problems and can use ratio and proportion in simple contexts. They can also work on correspondence problems – for example, 'If I have three hats and four coats how many different outfits can I put together?' As they extend their understanding pupils will be able to solve more complex scaling and correspondence problems such as the number of choices on a menu. They will also begin to generalise mathematical situations such as the example used in the starting point to this chapter. They will begin to express area and perimeter as a formula (perimeter $= 2(a+b)$ where a and b are the lengths of the sides). At this stage pupils will be able to describe and continue number patterns identifying the relationship between each number.

Extending learning in algebra

The progression described above will support learners in meeting the requirements of the curriculum in Year 6 which are that they can use simple formulae and that they can generate and describe numbers sequences. They will also be able to solve and create missing number problems of increasing complexity and find pairs of numbers that can satisfy an equation with two unknowns, for example:

$$\bigcirc + 8 = 10 + \triangle$$

They will also be able to describe the relationship between these two unknowns. In the above example the circle is always 2 bigger than the triangle

Big idea

One book that has been a great influence on my own learning and teaching of algebra is *Developing Thinking in Algebra* by John Mason, Alan Graham and Sue Johnson-Wilder. The writing team suggest that:

> *Expressing generality is entirely natural, pleasurable and part of human sense making. Every learner who starts school has already displayed the power to generalise and abstract from particular cases and this is the root of algebra.*

But what does this mean, I hear you say.

Maybe three stories about my own children beginning to express generality will help. Our youngest son is Sam – he is now 28 and well into his PhD in politics but age three he was just starting to make sense of the world. We were having breakfast one morning and as he ate his cereal he looked at a photograph sitting on top of the piano. This was a photo of my wife, Helen, as a teenager with her pet beagle, who was called Sam. He glanced down at his cereal, looked back up at the photograph and with that look young children have which suggests great wisdom asked, 'How old was I when I was a dog?' In the world of a three-year-old it would make much more sense if everything called Sam was the same thing rather than having lots of different things called Sam. There is a kind of sense to that – and there is also the idea of generality. At a similar time our daughter Holly was out for a walk with us and caught sight of a cat. 'Oh look', she said, 'a Henry.' At that time we had a dog called Henry – I am sure that Holly had seen a small furry animal with four legs and a tail and assumed that all these creatures were called 'Henry'. This is generalisation.

And finally, two weeks ago I was playing with an old model railway with my grandson Felix, age two and a half. We started to get the model trains out of their boxes. The first was a 'diesel locomotive' and I read the label on the box to Felix. This was followed by two 'steam locomotives'. Felix lined them up on the train track – 'Look Grandad,' he said, 'all locomotives.' This is what John Mason is describing above.

So – the big idea in algebra is...

Generalisation

Professor Jo Boaler from Stanford University has put together a MOOC (massive open online course) called 'How To Learn Math' and several of the videos (available on YouTube) explore the learning and teaching of algebra with a focus on generalisation. Jo argues that the current teaching of algebra is an equity issue as the proportion of learners who fail examinations due to their lack of confidence in algebra come disproportionately from low income families. She argues that the current teaching of algebra focuses on procedural algebra (finding a single unknown number) rather than structural algebra where we use symbols to express generality. You will notice that I chose to start this chapter with a piece of structural algebra. You may also notice that curriculum documents tend to focus on procedural algebra such as finding a missing number, which is unfortunate. Try this portfolio task as a way of seeing what I mean by structural algebra. It is a task you may recognise from GCSE and is commonly used in the later stages of secondary school. I would argue that these sort of tasks can be worked on with learners in primary school – in fact I have used this task and other very similar ones with Year 3/Stage 3 learners.

Portfolio task 7.1

Look at this series of shapes:

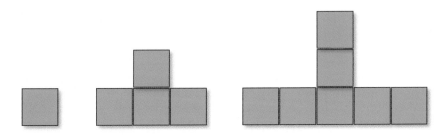

- How do you see the shape growing?
- How many squares would be in the 100th shape?
- How many squares would be in shape 'N'?

If you don't know where to start on this get yourself some cubes and begin to build the shapes. What would be the next shape in the sequence? Write down everything that you notice about the shapes in your notebook. Imagine that you are trying to give someone else instructions on how to create the sequence.

If you worked on this in secondary school you were probably asked to complete a table such as this one rather than exploring for yourself.

Shape number	Squares
1	1
2	4
3	7
4	10

You then will have noticed that the number of squares was increasing by 3 each time. This is called a linear relationship. You will also have realised that this didn't really help you find how many squares were in shape 100 or in the nth shape as all you could do was add 3 on to the previous shape. This comes from jumping straight to procedural algebra.

Rather than this, think about the first question: 'How do you see the shape growing?' When I work with primary learners on activities such as this they do not feel bound by having to jump straight to an equation and so they will say things like,

> In the third shape there are 3 legs that are 2 squares long and a square in the middle. In the 4th shape there are 4 legs that are 3 squares long and a square in the middle.

Here they are expressing generality. For any shape the length of the leg is one less than the shape number. So for the 100th shape the 'legs' would be squares 99 long. And then there is the square in the middle. So I can find out how many squares by calculating

$$99 + 99 + 99 + 1 \text{ or } (3 \times 99) + 1 = 298$$

If I want to describe the nth shape each leg would be n-1 squares long and then there is the square in the middle so I can write

$$3(n-1) + 1$$

And this formula works. Try it for the numbers in the table. So this is how we can begin with structural algebra and focus on generalisation rather than only allowing pupils to see algebra as a procedure in which we have to find missing numbers or in which letters stand for numbers that we have to find.

TAKING IT FURTHER: **FROM THE CLASSROOM**

In a paper called 'Algebra in the Early Years: Yes' published in 2003 in the US journal *Young Children*, Jennifer Taylor Cox describes a wide range of activities that she engages in with very young learners to support them in developing early algebraic thinking in the first stages of schooling. She describes what algebra in the early years looks like, showing how young children can describe position patterns using vocabulary such as 'up, down; up, down' or 'top, side, front, top, side, front'.

You will recognise this use of language from the young learners that you work with or maybe from your own young children or nephews and nieces that you play with. Teachers can build on this intuitive use of language by looking at other attributes such as shape or colour.

She also shows that young children are able to build 'growing patterns' using cubes following patterns that teachers set up or by making their own growing patterns.

She also uses pan balance scales to introduce the idea of equality. If things balance then they are 'equal'. The children also realise that sometimes things need to be added to one side of the balance to make it equal.

Finally, she shows that using pictures such as images of cats can support us in asking questions such as – if we have four cats how many ears are there? How many paws? This is another early algebraic activity.

I have used this article on many occasions with early years practitioners and they are always convinced that they can begin to introduce algebraic thinking into the activities they provide. In fact, the most common response is – we have been doing algebra for years and we didn't realise it.

The following teaching points suggest ways that you can introduce algebra to pupils in your classrooms and develop all pupils' capacity for algebraic thinking.

Teaching points

Teaching point 1: Describing and creating patterns

Young learners will sort and classify objects intuitively. As John Mason pointed out earlier in the chapter many children come to school with this as a behaviour that they have developed at home. It is helpful to join in young children's play and try to continue their patterns.

It is also helpful to join in the play and create your own bead strings, talking about the pattern as you go along. 'I'm putting two blue, then two red, then two green and then another blue – what should I put next?'

Encourage learners to talk about the patterns that they make and to work with each other to copy and re-create patterns. You can develop this using shapes that repeat, or colours, or even a mixture of shapes and colours.

It is important to show the children that the pattern repeats so you have to see the repeat rather than just show them the first part of the pattern.

As pupils move through school they can move on from this to look at the sort of growing patterns that you saw earlier in the chapter. For example they could describe how this pattern grows.

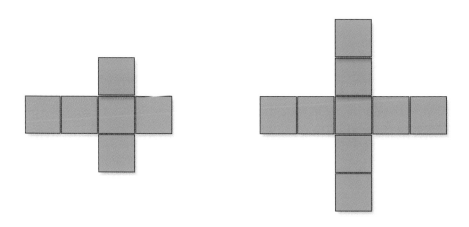

Teaching point 2: Developing an understanding of the 'equals' sign and equations as 'balanced'

As I suggested earlier, balance scales are a great way to begin this process. Children can use a range of objects to balance against each other. They could see how many cubes will balance a toy bus and begin to record this using pictorial representation. Here they might actually draw the scales with images of the bus and the cubes on each balance pan. Some will use iconic represent-ation – so they may draw lines for the cubes on one scale and a box for the bus on the other scale.

Some pupils may even write B = 4C!

This type of activity supports learners when they meet the missing number problem such as

$$8 - \boxed{} = 2$$

as they have an understanding of the importance of 'equality'. Activities which allow children to see that symbols can 'stand for' a range of different numbers are also important.

$$\bigcirc + 8 = 10n + \triangle$$

Teaching point 3: Modelling quantitative relationship

I have a young grandson called Felix. He is just approaching his third birthday. He currently spends most of his time playing with toy cars and trucks. He classifies then in many different ways and will explain the criteria by which he is sorting them in great detail. We have started to 'model quantitative relationships' by exploring how many wheels there are on different numbers of cars. His mum has four dogs. This gives us lots of opportunity for counting ears, eyes and paws. This is the beginning of seeing the relationships between quantities.

Try this portfolio activity to see how this type of activity can be developed.

Portfolio task 7.2

A farmer has only goats and chickens. She has 28 animals and there are 72 legs altogether.

How many chickens and goats are there?

You may find it helpful to model the animals.

I have used play dough and modelling sticks to make the animals so that pupils can exchange one goat for two chickens until they reach the required number of animals.

Teaching point 4: Describing change

Quantitative changes are an everyday part of children's lives. They realise that their shoe size changes as they get older. They may well have a measure on the wall at home which shows how their height changes over a period of time. You can draw on these experiences at school. You can also set up activities involving change such as growing sunflowers and measuring the rate at which the height changes. Similarly science experiments such as exploring how much further a toy car will travel if you increase the slope of a ramp introduce pupils to the notion of describing and recording change. The following portfolio task requires several friends. This is one of the few activities I have carried out in a pub! I had used the activity with a friend in her classroom during the day and she was so excited that she made me repeat it in the pub that evening, and the whole pub joined in.

Portfolio task 7.3

What do you think the ratio of the circumference of your head to your height is?

Make an estimate and then collect the information from lots of your friends.

You could construct a scatter diagram to work out the relationship.

Do you think the ratio would be the same for the children that you teach?

What about the children in the nursery?

In practice

The following lesson plan and evaluation describe a lesson taught to a group of pupils. They were in Year 3, or Stage 3 in international schools. They had not been prepared for the activity but carried it out just before their Christmas party, so it became part of their party planning.

Objectives:	• Develop and use written methods to record, support and explain multiplication of two-digit numbers by one-digit numbers • Some pupils will begin to generalise the solution

Key vocabulary: Number patterns

Context: The pupils are planning a Christmas party and wanted to have crackers to pull as a part of the celebration. They had asked how many crackers I thought they should buy. This activity was to help them come to a decision

Resources: Rolled up paper to model crackers, mini whiteboards to draft ideas on. Large pieces of paper to represent the problem

Starter activity: Pose the question 'how many crackers should we buy' back to the pupils. Ask pupils to come up with estimates in pairs. Keep the opening section of the lesson brief so different groups can approach the problem in different ways

Add the constraint that every pupil should pull a cracker with every other child

Group activity:

Teacher activity: Arrange pupils in their 'collaboration groups', that is, all attainment groups. This will allow a wider range of ideas to be drawn on to solve the problem

Pupil activity: Pupils use rolled up paper as crackers. Give groups 10mins to think about how they might go about it

If groups are finding it difficult to get started suggest they try the simple cases first and model it physically. So how many crackers for one person, for two people and so on

Encourage groups to use large sheets of paper to draw the solution either using dots for people or by marking off points around a circle

Plenary: Bring the groups back together and ask each group to use their large sheets of paper to show what they have found out. Focus on the process and the learning that has been taking place rather than emphasising a solution. At the end of the lesson point out that this is a piece of GCSE coursework. So they have been working at the same level as Year 11 or Stage 11 pupils.

Rationale and evaluation

It was great to be able to use a question that had come from the group themselves to introduce this investigation. As we had begun to discuss the question in a previous lesson the 'talk partners' at the opening of the lesson proved an effective way of generating lots of different answers. Some pairs started off by thinking it would just be one cracker each so gave the answer 28 (the number of pupils in the class). Amina quickly countered this: she said it would be loads more than that because you will use up your cracker straight away on the first person and there would still be 26 people left to for you to pull a cracker with. This seemed a good point to set the groups off on the investigation.

We worked in our 'collaboration groups' and spent some time discussing the different roles people would take. The groups all chose someone to 'lead' the group. It was their job to make sure that everyone was listened to. The groups all chose someone else to keep notes of the discussions. I had been concerned that some of the groups might not get started but Rupna's group immediately used the paper to make pretend crackers and then stood in a circle to count how many crackers they would need. Most of the other groups followed this lead as they saw what they were doing.

Simon's group operated slightly differently and wrote their names down on a piece of paper and drew lines to connect each name to every other name. They quickly came to an answer for their small group (of five) but were struggling to think about generalising this.

At this point I drew the whole class back together and asked Rupna and Simon to share their approach to the problem. This led to some really useful discussion about how best to work on an answer for the whole class. No one had thought about starting with the simplest case and working up from that. I suppose this isn't a surprise as it's not necessarily something that the pupils are used to. So I modelled this with the whole class. We agreed that if there was 1 person there would be no crackers, and for 2 people it would be 1 cracker (at this stage Amina immediately shouted out – 'it's just one less!'). Then we looked at 3 people and this gave us 3 crackers. Amina realised she wasn't correct. Some of the groups had already worked out the answer for 4 and some for 5 so I asked all the groups to go back and explore the answers for groups of 6 and 7 people. I didn't specify that they should put the results in a table. Some groups used a table to collate the results whilst some used a circle to illustrate the answers with the total underneath. For example this is the diagram for 6 people.

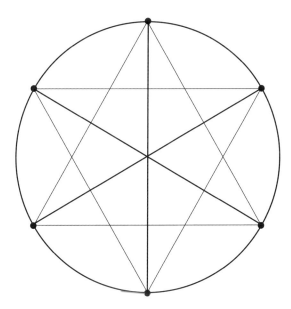

I pointed out that this way of illustrating the problem is called the 'mystic rose'. It also quickly shows that the answer for 6 people is $6 \times 5 = 30$.

We all came back together again and shared our learning. I wanted the focus to be on learning rather than simply the answer, although Amina was very quick to point out her 'mystic rose' and how it had given them the answer very quickly.

Finally, we decided it would be too expensive to buy 276 crackers so we would make do with 1 cracker each!

Portfolio task 7.4

Devise a lesson plan that is appropriate for a group of learners that you are working with.

The focus should be an aspect of algebra.

You could choose from some of the ideas in the 'Teaching points' section of this chapter or find another appropriate activity.

Think carefully about the pupils' previous experience to make sure that the activity is accessible and challenging.

Once you have taught the lesson evaluate it carefully and add this evaluation to your portfolio too.

Observing algebra

On the companion website you will find a video which shows a visiting teacher 'Mr Numbervator' exploring a very similar activity. He calls it the handshake problem. As he is a visiting teacher there is an interview with the class teacher and with a visiting advisor who help Mr Numbervator evaluate his practice.

As you observe this lesson think back to the lesson plan above.

- How would you plan and teach a lesson exploring this algebraic pattern?
- At what stage would you introduce the learners you are working with to the language of algebra?

The room was organised in a different way.

- How would you group the pupils in your class for this activity?
- How would you make sure that they all take an active role?

You could use your response to this video to support you in planning a lesson for the portfolio task above.

Assessing algebra

The focus on assessing algebra should be practical tasks which move from specialising to generalising. These will take a different form depending on the age of the learners that you are working with, however make sure that the tasks are sufficiently open so that you can observe and question the pupils to elicit their current level of understanding and move them forward in their thinking.

So for the youngest learners focus on making repeating patterns with coloured beads and with shapes.

You can use the sand and pastry cutters or different styles of potato prints. You could even make very simple repeating patterns with the numbers of cherries on cakes.

You can also see which criteria learners are using to classify objects. Developing language such as bigger and smaller, shorter and taller is important for the development of algebraic ideas. You could also use the pan balance as discussed earlier in the chapter.

As learners develop their understanding focus on the structural aspects of algebra rather than the functional aspects in your assessment of algebraic thinking. So whilst the missing number problems can help you see how well learners can remember number facts at this stage they do not really help you support algebraic thinking.

Instead, develop the types of activity discussed earlier by forming patterns of cubes or squares. Use the activities introduced earlier in the chapter which allow you to move from specialisation to generalisation. This is the big idea we discussed earlier and this is the skill that your assessment should focus on.

Cross-curricular teaching of algebra

The idea of the extended project is to draw on the key ideas within the chapter to develop cross-curricular activities which you can explore with your learners over a series of lessons. This allows you and your class to develop your subject knowledge together.

The lesson plan above shows you one possible activity built around a celebration.

Another activity which you could develop could be constructed around a play or other entertainment at the festive party. For example you could devise a play that includes angels (with two wings); sheep (with four legs); and spiders (with eight legs), and plan correspondence problems using these facts.

If it is winter celebration you can construct many different patterns using a snowflake as an inspiration. This allows the pupils to predict how the pattern would grow and to explore generalisation within the growing pattern.

Summary

The key focus for this chapter has been the all-pervasive nature of algebra within mathematics. You have been shown how algebraic thinking can be developed from the moment that a learner enters school and that young children have a natural aptitude towards classifying and then making generalisations based on their observations of the world around them. This natural aptitude can be drawn on in school to develop their algebraic thinking further. The progression section illustrated how these ideas are developed as learners move through school.

The big idea is specialising and then generalising, noticing what is particular about a pattern and then being able to generalise this so that we can continue to build the pattern. There were examples used from a paper which illustrated how early years teachers can use algebra in a very practical way and these were developed into the series of teaching points. These teaching points all offered starting points for your own algebraic activity in your classroom.

Reflections on this chapter

My hope is that this chapter has demystified algebra for you. If you are one of those people who loves algebra and remembers feeling a great sense of achievement as you solved complex equations I hope that you can see how you can begin to share this excitement with young learners. They do not have to wait until secondary school to engage with algebraic ideas and to experience the delight of being able to explain how a pattern is growing and explain the generalisation that they are seeing.

Or you may be one of those people who has always been scared of algebra; who remember it as a puzzle that you could never solve or a strange language that you did not have access to. I hope that this chapter has shown you how you can explore algebraic ideas with your leaners and so become algebraic thinkers together. Try the activities for yourself, complete the portfolio tasks and then enjoy working with the learners in your class.

Going further

Developing Thinking in Algebra

JOHN MASON, ALAN GRAHAM and SUE JOHNSON-WILDER

This is one of a series of three books written by the team at the Centre for Mathematics Education at the Open University in the UK. The series was written for teachers both to support them in teaching and to help them develop their own mathematical thinking. The books integrate mathematics and pedagogy in the way I have attempted to do in this book. If you only buy one book on algebra make it this one!

Mason, J., Graham, A. and Johnson-Wilder, S. (2005) *Developing Thinking in Algebra*. London: Paul Chapman Publishing.

'What's × got to do with it?'

ANNE WATSON

This article appears on the Nrich website. In the article Anne aims to outline the aspects of algebra that should be introduced to young children if they are going to adopt an algebraic approach to their mathematics. Anne explores the 'threads' of algebraic thinking from primary into secondary education. There are also links to a much wider research project into children's mathematical thinking published by the Nuffield Foundation.

Watson, A. 'What's × got to do with it?', available online at **http://nrich.maths.org**

Self-audit

Look back to the first portfolio task. If you remember you were asked to explore 2 × 2 chunks of the grid like:

12	13
22	23

1	2	3	4	5	6	7	8	9	10
11	12	13	14	15	16	17	18	19	20
21	22	23	24	25	26	27	28	29	30
31	32	33	34	35	36	37	38	39	40
41	42	43	44	45	46	47	48	49	50
51	52	53	54	55	56	57	58	59	60
61	62	63	64	65	66	67	68	69	70
71	72	73	74	75	76	77	78	79	80
81	82	83	84	85	86	87	88	89	90
91	92	93	94	95	96	97	98	99	100

Explore shapes like this within the grid. Can you find a generalisation to give you the total if you know the number in the middle square?

What about a cross with 4 squares in each leg, or 5?

What about shapes like this?

CHAPTER 8

GEOMETRY
Properties of shapes;
position and direction

Introduction

I remember working in a mixed age class in a small school in North Yorkshire. There were children aged from 7 to 11 in the class and the teacher was working on an activity I had suggested which involved visualising whether or not a range of nets of cubes would 'fold up' to make a cube. The children had created the **nets** by drawing all the different arrangements of six squares they could think of. Once they had decided which they thought would fold up into cubes they cut them out to check their conjectures.

At the end of the session the teacher said to me, 'What was interesting to me was that some of the less able children did best on that activity.' I often question the unthinking use of the word 'ability'. If someone has been successful in a mathematical activity linked to shape surely they are 'able' even if their achievements in other areas of mathematics are not at similar levels. Some of you will be more comfortable with this area of mathematics, and for some of you it will present a challenge. I hope that this simply illustrates the breadth of the mathematics curriculum and how there will be areas of mathematics in which we feel comfortable and areas in which we struggle. The important point is that we are able to make connections between all areas of mathematics so that we become confident mathematics teachers and learners.

Starting point

Close your eyes. That may seem a strange request to someone reading a book so let me expand. First, find a friend, then ask them to read the next section whilst you have your eyes closed. If we are going to think about how you teach and learn 'geometry' we need to begin with a visualisation.

Create a large red rectangle that you can see clearly in your mind's eye.

Stand it on its end so that you can see it standing on its shortest side.

Then slowly rotate it so that it is laying on one of the longest sides.

Now rotate it again so that it is balancing on a corner.

Move the rectangle round and round in your mind's eye and make a decision about which way round you want finally to picture the rectangle and stop it in that orientation.

Now imagine a small, blue **right-angled triangle** that will fit inside the rectangle.

Picture it inside the rectangle and slide it so that the right angle fits exactly into one corner of the rectangle.

Imagine another small, blue right-angled triangle, which can be a different size from the first one you thought of.

Slide it into one of the other corners of the rectangle. Notice the red shape that is left inside the rectangle.

Open your eyes and sketch what you see.

Talk to your friend about the shape you have sketched. How many different properties can you describe? What do you notice about its properties? Are there **parallel lines** (like railway lines) or **perpendicular lines** (lines at 90° to each other)? What can you say about the angles: are they **acute** (less than 90°), **obtuse** (between 90° and 180°) or **reflex** (more than 180°) angles? Do you know what the shape is called?

This simple activity embraces two of the key skills you need to teach children to help them understand shape. They need to be able to visualise the shapes that we are working with and they need to be able to describe them so that someone else can 'see' the same shape. We do this by having a clear understanding of the properties of different shapes.

These are both skills that we can teach – although visualisation is not always a skill that we will have been taught. As I suggested in the opening of the chapter the interesting thing is that sometimes those learners who have not excelled when working with numbers will be able to visualise and manipulate shapes very quickly. These learners are good at maths too!

Portfolio task 8.1

Look at the polygons below:

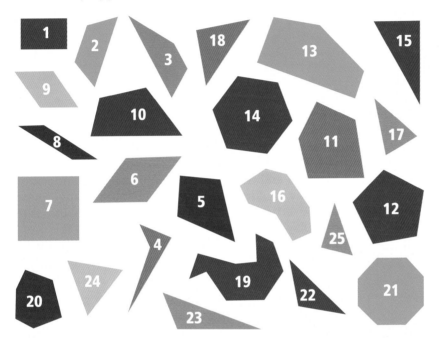

Classify them in any way you like, into as many groups as you like. When you have completed this task explain your classification to a friend. Then classify them in a different way.

Finally, name as many of the polygons as you can.

(This activity is taken from many of the free online resources provided by the National Council of Teachers of Mathematics in the USA.

This activity can be found at http://illuminations.nctm.org/LessonDetail.aspx?ID=L277.)

See page 193 for the solution.

You will have noticed that you are having to draw on language that you may not have used for a while. There are the names of the shapes (all provided in the answers at the end of this chapter) and perhaps, more importantly, ways to describe their properties. We have already used parallel and **perpendicular**. Other vocabulary you may have drawn on for the activity above is **congruent shapes** (two shapes which will fit perfectly on top of each other) and **similar shapes** (these are shapes whose sides and angles are all in the same ratio).

For example the two right-angled triangles below are similar as one has each side three times bigger than the other one. This also means that the corresponding angles in each triangle are the same size.

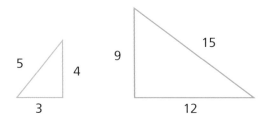

Taking care to develop children's vocabulary of shape is vital, so make sure there are plenty of displays utilising the vocabulary and also that there is plenty of opportunity to talk about the shapes we are working with.

In the 1950s Pierre van Hiele and Dina van Hiele-Geldof, two Dutch mathematics teachers and husband and wife, identified five levels of understanding that help us appreciate how children come to understand shape. These are described in Pierre's 1999 article 'Developing geometric thinking through activities that begin with play' in *Teaching Children Mathematics*. It is useful for us to explore these levels in some detail before exploring how progression is described by the strategy:

Level 0:   *Visualisation – at this stage learners can name and recognise shapes by their appearance. They cannot yet describe properties or use properties to sort shapes.*

Level 1:   *Analysis – at this stage children identify properties related to shapes and use these to classify them.*

Level 2:   *Informal deduction – at this stage learners can use the properties that belong to classes of shapes to problem-solve. So they will be able to talk about **regular** and **irregular shapes**, and about triangles in general, or specific types of triangle. This is the furthest we would expect most learners to progress within primary school.*

Level 3:   *Deduction – at this stage learners use their understandings about shape to construct geometrical proofs. That means that they can use their understanding and knowledge about the properties of shapes to convince others that new understandings are true.*

Level 4:   *Rigour – at this final stage students would be constructing rigorous proofs about the geometrical properties of shapes. These proofs will follow mathematical conventions rather than the more informal proofs at level 3.*

This research suggests that the visualisation and analysis stages of learning are key to understanding shape. This has become the focus of most of the teaching throughout the early and primary years of education. The teaching points later in the chapter emphasise the importance of the development of the vocabulary to allow children to be able to talk about what they are noticing at the visualisation stage. You will notice that many children will move between the visualisation level and analysis level as their vocabulary develops to describe particular concepts within understanding shape. As with many 'schemas' for learning, this can be seen as dynamic rather than a stepladder. That is, children do not rigidly move through the four stages – rather, they will move backwards and forwards through the stages depending on the particular idea they are exploring.

TAKING IT FURTHER: **FROM THE RESEARCH**

Penny Coltman, Dinara Petyaeva and Julia Anghileri have explored how best adults can support young children using 'building blocks' to carry out problem-solving activities which help them come to an understanding of three-dimensional (3D) shape. In an article 'Scaffolding learning through meaningful tasks and adult interaction', published in the *Early Years Journal*, in 2002, they suggest that young children between three and six, although operating at the first of the van Hiele levels, are limited by their experience and language and that through careful adult intervention children can learn effectively.

The children were given 'poleidoblocks', a set of wooden 3D shapes, and toy animals and cardboard models to produce 'playful' contexts which made sense to the young children. Children were allowed to become familiar with the blocks through free play and constructed their own stories using the blocks and the other resources. However, after this free play the researchers then used practical activities to support the children's learning.

For example, children were introduced to cylinders and cuboids. The children were told a story about cylinder birds loving to roll – the children could use this idea to see the difference between cylinders and cuboids and to begin to sort them according to this property of 'rolling'.

This research emphasises the importance of exploring properties of shapes by manipulating the shapes themselves. Shapes are dynamic, they move in space: 2D shapes move so that we can see them in any orientation, 3D shapes can roll and slide and build and balance. By working practically with shape, children are much more able to 'see' their properties.

The next section outlines the development of children's understanding about shape as they move between foundation stage and the end of their time in primary education. You should keep in mind the advice from the research above that as much of this as possible should be explored actively and dynamically.

Progression in geometry

Foundations for geometry

The initial focus should be to provide children with common objects and shapes so that they can make and re-create patterns, build models and talk about what they are doing to begin to develop the language of shape, size and position. You can then start asking children to visualise common 2D and 3D shapes and use them to make patterns and models.

Children should be introduced to ideas of whole, half and quarter turns as an introduction to angle. They can be introduced to the difference between things that turn about a point (like a pair of scissors)

or about a line (like a door). You can help them develop their use of language to describe position, using vocabulary like in front of, behind, next to, on top of, and underneath.

Later you can teach children to recognise shapes in different orientations and use their properties to classify them. This was the activity you carried out as Portfolio task 8.1. This will help them notice **reflective symmetry** in patterns and draw lines of symmetry on 2D shapes. Teach them to give instructions using the language of position and understand the difference between clockwise and anti-clockwise. By this stage children will understand that a quarter turn is equivalent to a right angle.

Becoming confident in geometry

At this stage children will be able to match 2D and 3D shapes to drawings of them. They will also be able to use **mirror lines** to draw **reflections** and use compass directions to describe movement about a grid. Pupils will be able to draw and classify **polygons** and describe their properties. The children will visualise nets of D solids. A net is the 2D shape that you can 'fold up' to make the 3D shape. They will know that angles are measured in degrees, that a whole turn is 360°, and they will be able to compare and order angles less than 180°.

Pupils at this stage will read and plot coordinates in the first **quadrant** (see below), and recognise parallel and perpendicular lines. They will use their understanding of symmetry to complete patterns and draw positions of shapes after reflections and **rotations**. They will also be able to estimate, draw and measure angles and calculate angles on a straight line using their understanding that angles on a straight line add up to 180°.

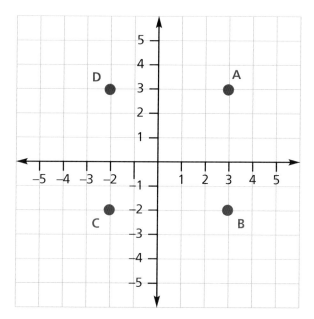

Here **A** is in the first quadrant, **B** in the second quadrant, **C** in the third quadrant and **D** in the fourth quadrant.

Extending learning in geometry

Pupils at this stage will recognise **vertically opposite angles,** use this to find 'missing angles' and will be operating in all four quadrants with coordinates.

This diagram shows vertically opposite angles, made where two lines cross. The angles have the same value.

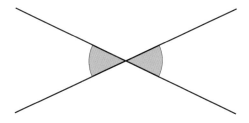

The children will be able to transform images using ICT and to construct a triangle given two sides and the angle between them.

Big ideas

Properties of shapes

A young man in a lesson I was observing about algebra once said to his teacher, 'That's what maths is all about, isn't it Sir? It's about saying complicated things very simply.' Being able to classify and order sets of objects fits this perfectly. And we classify and order shapes using their properties. A property of a shape is something that doesn't change. It might be 2D (having length and width but not depth) or 3D (having length, width and depth); shapes can be closed (all sides join together) or open (there is a gap between two corners); they may have sides which are all straight or some curved sides; shapes can be **convex** (all the interior angles are less than 180°) or **concave** (at least one interior angle is greater than 180°); or they may be regular (all sides the same length and all interior angles the same size) or irregular (having sides and angles which are different lengths and sizes).

Closed shapes with straight sides are called polygons and these are listed below.

Number of sides	Names	Regular	Irregular
3	Triangle		
4	Quadrilateral		
5	Pentagon		
6	Hexagon		
7	Heptagon		
8	Octagon		
9	Nonagon		
10	Decagon		
11	Hendecagon		
12	Dodecagon		

It is important to use both regular and irregular versions of the polygons with children, otherwise they only link the name to the regular version of the shape.

Look at the shapes you sorted earlier in the chapter. For your portfolio sort them into groups using the vocabulary you have been introduced to above – so you may sort into concave and convex, regular and irregular, and so on – and draw them.

Within the set of polygons there are further classifications. So, for example, triangles can be:

Equilateral   All angles are 60° and all the sides are the same length.

Right angled   One angle is 90°.

Isosceles   One pair of sides are the same length.

Scalene   All sides are different lengths.

A triangle can be right angled and isosceles or right angled and scalene.

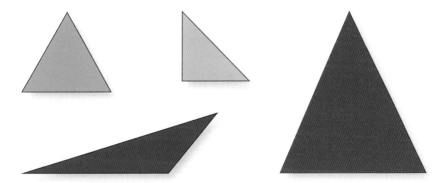

Similarly, several quadrilaterals have special names:

Square   A quadrilateral with four equal sides and four right angles.

Rhombus   A quadrilateral with four equal sides; the angles do not all have to be 90° (so a square is a specific version of a rhombus).

Rectangle   Any quadrilateral with four right angles. An **oblong** is a rectangle that isn't a square.

Parallelogram   A quadrilateral with opposite sides parallel.

Trapezium   A quadrilateral with only one pair of parallel sides.

Kite   A quadrilateral with adjacent sides (i.e. sides that are joined at a point) of equal length.

Portfolio task 8.3

Try this activity – the folding helps you understand ideas of symmetry and the surprises when you unfold the shape support you in 'noticing' the properties of the shapes. Children find it motivating too as it develops their skills of visualisation as they have to try to 'picture' the shape that will emerge when they unfold the paper.

Take a piece of A4 paper and make one fold anywhere – you do not have to fold it in half. Make a cut so that you form two shapes out of the piece of paper. Sketch the two shapes that you have made and name them. Can you find ways to fold and cut the paper so that you make a square, a rhombus, a rectangle, a parallelogram, a trapezium and a kite?

3D shapes can also be classified in several ways. **Prisms** and **pyramids** are some-times confused. I remember a 14-year-old pupil of mine describing the difference as 'a prism is where you find naughty people and a pyramid is where you find dead people'. The difference is to do with the cross-section. You can slice a prism at any point, parallel to the face at the end, and you will always get the same cross-section, whereas if you slice a pyramid you will different sizes of the same shape.

Regular triangular pyramid   Regular square pyramid   **Regular hexagonal pyramid**

Two prisms you might recognise are a **cube** and a cuboid. The most common 3D shapes are shown below.

One way of classifying 3D shapes is by the numbers of **faces**, **edges** and vertices (singular **vertex**). The faces of a shape are the flat regions. The edges are where two faces meet and a vertex is a point at which two or more edges meet.

Face

Cube

Edge

Cuboid

Triangular prism

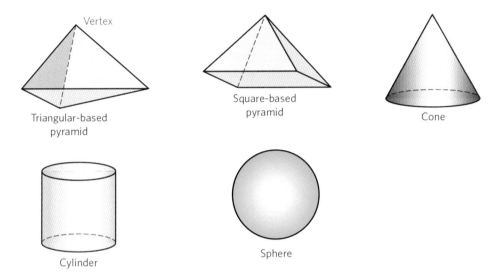

Vertex

Triangular-based
pyramid

Square-based
pyramid

Cone

Cylinder

Sphere

Position

When we want to define, or locate, a point mathematically we use coordinates on a pair of axes (you pronounce this 'axees' – not like the implement you chop wood with). These **axes** cross each other at what is known as the **origin**, which has coordinates (0,0). The four areas created by the axes are known as the four quadrants. The best way to explain these terms is by a diagram. In the diagram below the x-axis is the horizontal axis and the y-axis is the vertical axis:

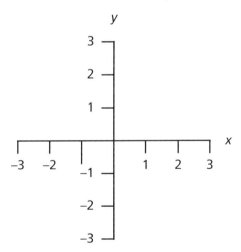

The two axes are labelled x and y. We write coordinates as a pair of numbers in brackets separated by a comma, for example (2,3) or (21,4). The first number always refers to the x-coordinate and the second number refers to the y-coordinate.

Primary pupils are also introduced to defining direction by compass points.

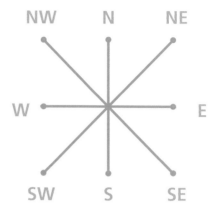

There are four points of the compass: north, south, east and west. The direction halfway between north and west is described as north-west. Similarly, the direction halfway between south and east is described as south-east, the direction halfway between south and west is south-west, and the direction halfway between north and east is north-east.

Once we have placed a shape on a grid we can change its shape through a **transformation**: this is the process of moving a shape on a grid. The three transformations are translation, reflection and rotation.

A translation leaves the shape's dimensions and its orientation unchanged. In other words, it is the same as sliding the same shape across the grid. Here is an example from a Year 6 girl:

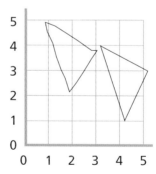

This shape has moved −2 in the x direction (ie. backwards along the x-axis) and +1 in the y direction (i.e. upwards along the y axis) and so you would write

$$\begin{pmatrix} -2 \\ 1 \end{pmatrix}$$

A negative sign in front of the number would represent a move backwards along the x-axis or down the y-axis.

A reflection moves the shape using a mirror line, as below:

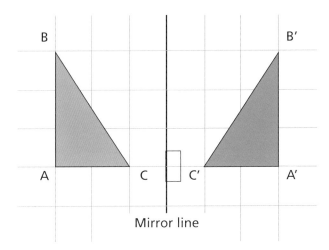

Mirror line

When reflecting in a mirror line you need to take care to check that all points are the same distance from the mirror line. So, in the example above, points A and B are three squares from the mirror line and C is one square away.

You must always measure at right angles to the mirror line.

Finally, we can rotate shapes.

When we rotate shapes we have to define the point we are rotating about, called the **centre of rotation**, and say the angle we are rotating through.

So, for example, if we rotate this triangle about the origin the dimensions of the triangle will stay exactly the same. It is as if we have fixed a 'stick' to the corner 'A' and moved it through x degrees:

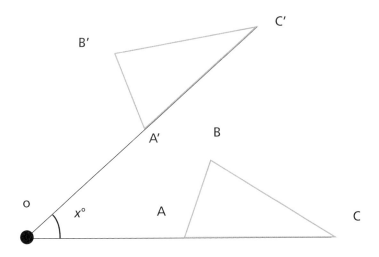

Symmetry

The use of the mirror line gives us a link into the idea of symmetry. The form of symmetry here is called reflective symmetry. The best way to explore line symmetry is through folding shapes. If you can fold the shape in half so that the pieces fit exactly on top of each other you have found a **line of symmetry**. For example,

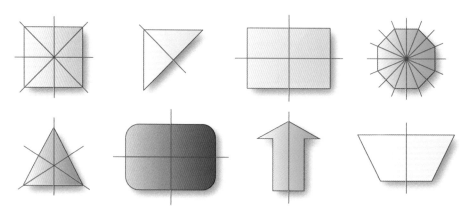

A shape can also be described as having **rotational symmetry**. This means that you can rotate the shape and it will look the same before you have rotated the shape through 360 degrees.

The **order of rotational symmetry** is the number of times the shape is repeated before it makes a complete turn and the **degree of rotational symmetry** is the amount of turn you must make for a repeat to take place.

Portfolio task 8.4

Draw the **regular polygons** given in the table on page 172. Find all the lines of symmetry for each shape. What do you notice about the result? Why do you think this is the case?

Teaching points

Teaching point 1: Issues with language – describing properties; positional language

Find a couple of friends – or phone a couple of people up. Ask them to find a scrap piece of paper and draw a triangle. My prediction would be that they draw an equilateral triangle.

I have tried this out with very large groups of students, teachers and children and this is always the case. Of course, there is a huge range of triangles to choose from (isosceles, scalene, right angled) but it appears as though the default option is equilateral. Indeed, many young children find it difficultto see a shape like this as a triangle as it looks very different from the triangles that they have previously seen.

This looks very 'different' from the shape they were first introduced to as 'triangle'. This takes us back to the discussion about generalisation at the beginning of Chapter 8. When introducing shapes to children it is very important that they see the whole range of shapes. So rather than offering one example of a triangle, offer a whole range and ask children what all the shapes have in common. In this way they will see that what makes a triangle is a triangle having three straight sides all joined together.

Similarly, when introducing vocabulary which may have a range of meanings such as 'face' or 'edge', take time to find out the children's meanings before imposing a new definition on them. A simple activity to help with this is to ask children to draw or write a definition for a set of key words. These might be face, edge, vertex, corner, line, straight. You can then use the children's definitions to help explain the mathematical definition.

Teaching point 2: Orientation of 2D shapes

I once carried out some work for an examination board looking at GCSE scripts. One of the criteria which was used to help decide borderline cases was whether or not the pupils could use Pythagoras' theorem effectively. It was clear from looking at the scripts that if a triangle such as this

appeared in the question most pupils realised that they should try to use what they knew about right-angled triangles. However, when faced with a triangle such as this

pupils seemed not to recognise the shape as a right-angled triangle. This is a similar issue to the one mentioned in Teaching point 1. Children get used to seeing a single representation of a shape and cannot transfer their learning when faced with an unfamiliar version.

An activity such as 'Shapes in a bag' can help with this.

Get yourself a cloth bag and a set of large shapes. Gradually and slowly reveal a shape. When the children can only see a small portion of the shape ask what different shapes it could be, slowly reveal a little bit more and ask again.

As you reveal the shape it will become clear what the shape is, but the children's focus is on noticing the properties of shapes rather than simply remembering names.

Teaching point 3: 2D representations of 3D objects

Try to sketch a sphere. Did you draw

rather than something like this?

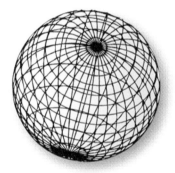

Children find it very difficult to sketch 3D shapes. It is difficult after all – in trying to draw a 3D object using only two dimensions we will often draw represen-tations such as a square for a cube. This can lead to difficulties when working with more complex shapes, and the ability to sketch 3D objects supports us in visualising.

The activity below introduces isometric paper as a way of sketching 3D cuboids. It also raises the importance of orientation.

We need to look at 3D shapes such as this in different ways if we are to be able to reproduce them exactly. I often find that the children who can quickly grasp sketching on isometric paper may not have as quick a grasp of other areas of mathematics.

This is an important skill, so it is good for these children's views of themselves as mathematicians to see themselves as the experts in this particular area. A helpful extension of this activity is to draw the plan view and the two side elevations of each shape. These are the two dimensional views that you get if you look directly down onto the shape and directly at the front and the side.

BUILDING SHAPES OUT OF CUBES

You will need:

THERE MAY BE SOME HIDDEN CUBES

- interlocking cubes
- dotty paper

1 Build each of these shapes using the numbers of cubes shown.

a) 8 cubes

b) 10 cubes

c) 9 cubes

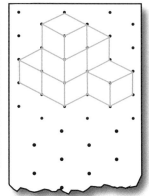

2 Can you find more than one way to build each shape?

3 a) Make this shape.
    b) Add a cube to make a new shape.
    c) Draw your new shape on dotty paper.
    d) How many different shapes
       can you make using the extra cube?

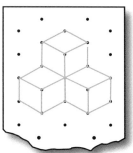

4 a) Make this shape.
    b) Add a cube to make a new shape.
    c) Draw your new shape on dotty
       paper.
    d) How many different shapes can you
       make using the extra cube?

Teaching point 4: Errors in not seeing angle as dynamic

One of the early activities I work on with children is asking them to order angles intuitively in terms of their size. This follows discussion of angle as a measure of turn using strips of card pinned at one end.

Alfie was looking confused the last time I worked with his group on this.

He looked at this angle

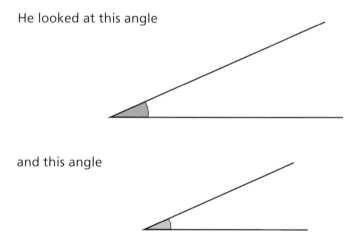

and this angle

and said, 'The first angle is much bigger but it's the same size.' He was confused as he was noticing the length of the lines and equating that with the 'size' of the angle as well as realising that angle is a measure of turn. I was able to convince him that they were actually the same angle by extending the 'lines' on the second angle so that it appeared identical to the first angle.

Teaching point 5: Estimating and measuring angles

There are two common mistakes when using a protractor to measure angles. The first error is using the wrong scale to measure the angle. The two scales are often referred to as the 'inner scale' and the 'outer scale'. Asking children to estimate angles before measuring them will help them decide which scale they need to use.

So if we were measuring an angle of 63° using this protractor we would know that we should be looking for 'about' 60° rather than using the wrong scale giving an answer of 123°.

The second error to look out for is when children place the bottom of the protractor on the vertex rather than the point where the '0–180' line and the 90 line cross.

The first angle that most children are introduced to is a right angle or 90°. Using this fact we can help children estimate many other angles. They will be able to see that two right angles – which make a straight line – are 180°. Similarly, half a right angle must be 45°. Also, if they divide a right angle into three they will get an angle of 30°. It is helpful to ask children to sketch as many different angles as they can given angles of 30°, 45° and 90°. They can then classify these angles as acute and obtuse. If they get used to having a sense of angle this will help them when they are using protractors to measure angles to 1° of accuracy.

Teaching point 6: The language of coordinates

I have heard many teachers remind children to 'go along the corridor and then up the stairs' as a way of reminding them to write down the x-coordinate first and then the y-coordinate. Many children remain unconvinced that it really matters in which order you write the coordinates and so seem to forget. I once observed a teacher convince children that order matters, and that the positive and negative signs are important when working in four quadrants. He drew a set of axes on the board and marked a point A in the first quadrant. He then asked the group, 'What shall I call the point A?' One of the group immediately shouted out 'Alisha'. Rather than show any irritation the teacher asked another pupil to come up to the front, drew another set of axes and asked them to draw 'Alisha'. The pupil said, 'But it could go anywhere.' The teacher then asked for other ways to describe the point. Pupils responded with answers such as, 'It's 2 along and 3 up,' or 'Its x-coordinate is 2 and its y-coordinate is 3.' This allowed him to draw up all the possible ways of 'naming' the point, illustrating the importance of coordinates as giving information.

Teaching point 7: Confusions with mirror lines

There are a number of errors you may notice pupils making when using mirror lines to explore symmetry. Earlier in the chapter I suggested asking children for their own definitions of key terms as a way of finding out what their current understandings are. I recently asked a group of Year 3 pupils what 'mirror line' meant to them. Ben suggested that 'it is something that splits a shape in half'. This was accepted by the group. So I asked them to draw me the lines of symmetry on this rectangle.

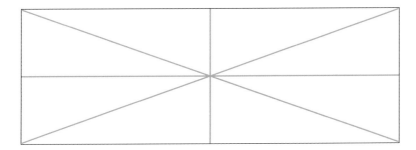

Again, they were all happy that this showed a rectangle had four lines of symmetry. It was only when I asked them to try to fold the rectangle along the diagonals so that the halves 'matched up' that they agreed these were not lines of symmetry. (Try it if you don't believe me!)

Similarly, if a shape is to be reflected in a mirror line and the original shape is placed some distance away from the line, children often place the reflection flush to the line. Simply remind them that the 'reflected' shape should be the same distance from the mirror line as the original shape.

Whilst I usually suggest using practical materials in this case I would advise against actually using a mirror to explore line symmetry. Mirrors are often very difficult for children to use effectively – I would avoid using mirrors at this stage and reinforce the importance of reflections being equidistant from the mirror line. Pupils benefit from plenty of practice in drawing shapes and their 'mirrors'.

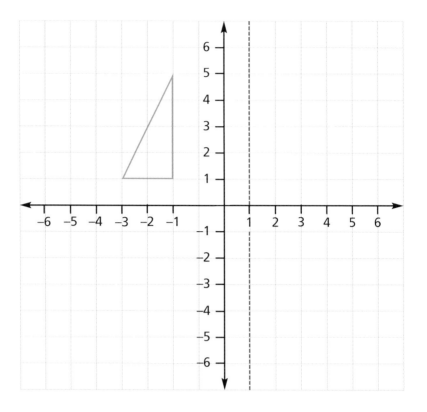

As well as providing pupils with a starting shape and a mirror line in which to reflect it it is helpful to give pupils an initial shape and a reflected shape and remove the mirror line. The task is to find the mirror line. This helps reinforce the notion of equal distance.

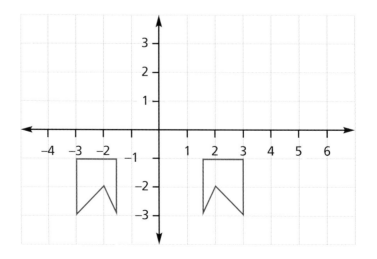

Teaching point 8: Rotations about vertices and centres of shapes

As with all areas of geometry it is important to focus on the dynamic. If I want to explore 'rotation' with a group of learners they need to rotate a shape about either the centre of the shape or one of its vertices, and then sketch the result.

In that way they will be able to describe what is happening for themselves rather than simply trying to remember 'rules' they have been told.

A useful strategy is to ask the pupils to work in pairs or groups so they can check each other's answers.

They very quickly see if they are getting the same results, and, with encouragement, support each other in identifying their errors.

In practice

The following lesson plan and evaluation describe a lesson taught to a group of pupils who have some understanding of the language of shape. I wanted them to develop their language in order to be able to identify and describe the properties of shapes in greater detail.

I also wanted them to become increasingly sophisticated in their use of technical vocabulary. The particular focus for this lesson was developing skills in visualising and naming 2D shapes and describing their properties.

The open questions I could ask meant that I was able to see what their current understandings were and so I could model more sophisticated vocabulary in my 'interpretation' of their answers.

Objectives:	• To visualise and name common 2D shapes and describe their properties
Key vocabulary:	**Context:**
2D shapes/ properties: Circle, triangle, square, parallel, perpendicular	This is my first lesson with this group of pupils exploring their understanding of shape. My aim was to discover the pupils' prior knowledge to support me in developing their understanding of properties of 2D shapes
Resources:	**Starter activity:**
Collection of shapes – regular and irregular Mini-whiteboards	Pupils sat in pairs with their talk partners to play the 'shape in the bag' game. I gradually revealed a shape and the pairs had to discuss what the shape might be. Each pair had to justify their guess by describing a property of the shape they were guessing. On each occasion we explored all the shapes that it might be as well as the shapes that were not possible. For example, 'that can't be a square because it has got curved lines'

Main activity:	Teacher:	Pupil activity:
	I asked the whole group to sit in a circle with all the shapes in the middle of the circle. I asked one of the group to sort the shapes in any way that they liked. The others in the group had to guess what the criterion for sorting was. If they guessed correctly they took over and had to sort the shapes according to a different criterion. This allowed me to point out the different properties of shapes and model the geometrical language that I wanted to encourage the pupils to use	Sitting in a circle observing the sorting and deciding on possible criteria Hearing and using a range of geometrical language
Small group activity:	I used all attainment groups to ensure that those pupils with less prior experience could hear a wide range of vocabulary being used to describe the properties of shapes	
	The groups continued to play the game that I had introduced until each member of the small group had taken a turn to sort the shapes. The next activity involved one of the group describing one of the shapes so that the others in the group could sketch it on their mini-whiteboards	
	As I moved around the groups I made a note of the range of vocabulary being used. I shared this with the class at the end of the lesson and used it to construct a vocabulary display	

Plenary: I drew a square and an irregular quadrilateral with one right angle on the whiteboard at the front of the class. In pairs the pupils had to discuss the ways in which the shapes were similar and the ways in which they were different. I took feedback from the class and each pair had to sketch two shapes and talk about the ways in which they were the same and different. I then shared my list of vocabulary with the pupils. They had to name one shape which had each property and a shape which did not have this property

Rationale and evaluation

My aim was to discover the pupils' current knowledge and I was pleased that I left the lesson with a clear understanding of the range of prior experience. Some of the pupils are secure in their knowledge of triangles, squares and rectangles – Bartek even knew the difference between isosceles and equilateral triangles. However, Malc thought that the scalene couldn't be a triangle because it was 'all wonky'. I will introduce a group to the different sorts of triangles next time through a classification exercise.

Most of the group found the irregular shapes difficult to work with – they are obviously more used to working with regular shapes. I will start every day this week with an example of an irregular shape and a regular shape so that they get used to seeing irregular shapes.

I was particularly pleased with the way that the all attainment groups operated.

The pupils listened carefully to each other and I could see that some of the children who had a more developed vocabulary were using it – almost to show off – but I was pleased that the other pupils were exposed to a wide range of vocabulary. I made a rule that if anyone didn't understand a word they had to ask – and that the person who had used the word had to explain what it meant by drawing an example.

My teaching assistant and I made sure that we asked pupils what they meant when they introduced some new vocabulary.

The pupils were very impressed with the long list of vocabulary I shared with them at the end. You could see a sense of pride in their knowledge of the vocabulary of shape.

Observing geometry

On the companion website there is a video which shows a teacher working with her class of seven- and eight-year-olds in describing and constructing three-dimensional shapes from two-dimensional drawings.

I would like you to focus on the section from 4 minutes 30 seconds into the video. This is the point at which the children are hiding 3D shapes behind a board and describing them to a friend who then has to guess which shape is hidden.

Listen to the extract and jot down all the technical language that the pupils are using to describe the shapes.

If you were planning this activity which shapes would you use in order to maximise the vocabulary that could be developed? What do you see as the teacher's role in this sort of activity?

A useful way of adapting this activity is to ask the children what the shape could be after each question so that they begin to notice the sorts of properties that shapes have in common.

So, for example, if a shape has eight vertices it may be a cube, or another kind of cuboid. The children have to ask another question to be certain which shape it is.

Assessing geometry

The activity above is a very useful assessment activity as you can observe the use of the vocabulary of shape as well as getting a sense of children's understandings of the properties of shapes through the questions that they ask.

Another very useful assessment task is to ask your pupils to classify shapes in a number of ways. Use a wide range of concrete shapes which the children can sort physically. These are available from many suppliers of mathematical resources. Using sorting 'grids' is a useful technique as this requires the pupils to look at properties very carefully. You could use properties of symmetry – for example

	No rotational symmetry	Has rotational symmetry
No lines of symmetry		
One line of symmetry		
Two lines of symmetry		
More than two lines of symmetry		

or ideas of regularity

	Regular	Irregular
Triangle		
Quadrilateral		
Pentagon		
Hexagon		

This allows you to focus on the wide range of varieties of polygons that exist and use specialist language where appropriate. So a regular triangle is an equi-lateral, a regular quadrilateral is a square and so on. This same activity can be adapted for three-dimensional shapes.

Cross-curricular teaching of geometry

The idea of this section is to draw on the key ideas within the chapter to develop a cross-curricular project which you can explore with your learners over a series of lessons. This allows you and your class to develop your subject knowledge together.

The ideas of design and packaging are ideal for developing into a cross-curricular project for your class. This sort of activity is useful for an end of term celebration. Perhaps the school is holding a summer fair and needs to award prizes or 'wrap' surprises for some of the games. The pupils need to work out how they can design the nets which will 'fold up' to make the packages which will hold the prizes as securely as possible. They will also need to visualise the 3D shape which will result from the 2D net so that they can decorate the net before making it up into the package.

Other possibilities are designing patchwork quilt. Many patchwork quilts are made up of a central pattern of squares with triangular surrounds. If the class were to make four pieces of patchwork each they would need to work out how big a quilt they could make, and how many squares and triangles would be required to make the quilt.

A final possibility, which also asks the pupils to use the idea of tessellations, is to calculate how much it would cost to make and hang bunting around the classroom. Tessellation is the process of covering a two-dimensional space with repeating two-dimensional shapes.

Most individual pieces of bunting are isosceles triangles so the pupils will need to work out the most efficient way to cut these out of pieces of material. There is also much scope for measurement to differing degrees of accuracy in this activity.

Summary

This chapter has shown you how the ideas of visualisation, categorisation and position underpin geometry. To be able to understand geometrical ideas you need to be able to see and manipulate shapes in your 'mind's eye'. This is a skill that can be developed – you may need to develop it in yourself before you can work with your pupils. Or, it may be that by helping your pupils to become better at visualising you become more skilled yourself. The chapter opened with an example of a visualisation activity you can try with your pupils – it is well worth building your own bank of these activities and using them regularly.

There has been a focus on the properties of shapes – a knowledge of the range of possible properties is important in order to be able to classify shapes. So another area to concentrate on with your pupils is developing their vocabulary of shape. Use posters and displays to make sure the vocabulary is clearly displayed so it becomes a part of the language of the classroom. It is important that you model the language of shape as often as possible – in the same way that you will often use number facts when taking a register, you can use the language of shape whenever you notice new shapes, whatever the subject.

Finally, the language of position has been emphasised. You have seen how important the four quadrants are in placing a point in space and how shapes can be transformed into new shapes by reflection and rotation.

Reflections on this chapter

I wonder if you see the learning of geometry in a slightly different way than you see learning and teaching aspects of number? Sometimes my students don't regard the topic as 'important'. But it is – not only in terms of being successful in assessments which all include shape, but also as a way of viewing and describing the world. You may well have discovered a new skill – that of visualisation. I find it very difficult to visualise things, maybe as a result of not learning it at school, and this inhibits me when I am trying to solve practical problems around the home, such as deciding how I might pack the car boot, or arrange a room in the best way.

Learning about geometry also seems to motivate children – they enjoy talking about the shapes, they enjoy making new shapes, they enjoy describing what they are seeing. I hope that you feel able to draw on all the practical aspects of shape in your work with your pupils. Don't forget that geometry is a dynamic and practical area of mathematics, and we can't learn about it without being dynamic and practical.

I also hope that you feel the language of shape has been demystified. It isn't complicated, but there is a lot of vocabulary to learn and remember. However, this is just a matter of regular use. Talk about shape with your pupils on a daily basis. Have a shape of the week and add a property a day. Play the 'shape in a bag' game whenever you have to fill five minutes at the end of a lesson and soon you will all have really well-developed vocabulary of shape.

Going further

Shape and space at Key Stage 2

JENNI BACK, CHRIS BROOKSBANK and GEOFF FAUX

This short article is available online at **www.secondarymathsite.co.uk/Primary/ Organisations/ATM/ATM5/MT201%20Back,%20Brooksbank%20&%20Faux.pdf** or from the Association of Teachers of Mathematics. It is in *Mathematics Teaching* 201, March 2007. It consists of three experienced mathematics teachers discussing how they approached a particular task involving pattern making and the different resources they brought to the task. They all use the same task with their pupils and describe the learning which took place.

Back, J., Brooksbank, C. and Faux, G. (2007) 'Shape and space at Key Stage 2', *Mathematics Teaching* 201, 27–31.

Mindstorms

SEYMOUR PAPERT

This seminal text brings together Papert's vision for the ways in which computers and ICT can transform the ways that children learn and how the programming language of Logo, which is predominantly used to explore shape and space, can be utilised to support children in developing independent thinking skills. Whilst this is a research text there are lots of immediately applicable ideas.

Papert, S. (1993) *Mindstorms: Children, computers and powerful ideas*. London: Basic Books.

Answers (to question on page 167)

Possible properties to sort the shapes by:
- Opposite sides parallel
- Opposite sides congruent
- At least one obtuse angle
- At least one right angle
- All sides congruent
- All angles congruent
- Two consecutive sides congruent

Solution to the 'name the polygons' task
- Parallelogram
- Quadrilateral
- Regular polygon
- Opposite angles congruent
- Pentagon
- Hexagon

- Octagon
- Rhombus
- Isosceles
- Trapezoid
- Concave polygon
- Convex polygon

Self-audit

Carry out this audit to explore how your learning has progressed as a result of working on the ideas in this chapter. Include the results in your portfolio.

1   Draw four sets of axes in all four quadrants with the coordinates labelled up from −5 to +5 (see page 171).

    For each question you should draw the initial shape on the set of axes in one colour and the second shape in another colour. Then write down instructions which explain how to move from the first shape to the second shape. You should use at least two sets of instructions each time and include reflections, rotations and translations if you can.

    a) Initial shape, right-angled triangle (−1,1), (−1,5), (−5,−1); dotted shape (1,−1), (5,−1), (1,−5).

    b) Initial shape, rectangle (−2,3), (−2,5), (−5,5), (−5,3); dotted shape (0,−2), (0,−5), (−2,−5), (−2,−2)

    c) Initial shape and 'L' shape (2,1), (5,1), (5,4), (4,4), (4,2), (2,2); dotted shape, rotate through 90° about (2,1) then translate 6 in the direction −X.

    Now draw your own starting and finishing shape together with instructions of how to get from one shape to the other.

2   Draw four shapes. They should include at least one triangle, one quadrilateral and one pentagon. Underneath the shape write the instructions to help a friend draw the shapes. You will need to include the length of the sides and the approximate angle at each vertex.

    Underneath the shapes write down a list of each shape's properties and the shape's name.

CHAPTER 9
MEASUREMENT

Introduction

All of the activities that I have introduced you to in this book are activities I have used in my own teaching. I find that I learn most about how to teach mathematics from teaching mathematics. And that there is always more to learn! For example I was working with a group of six- and seven-year-olds in a city school in Leeds using balance scales and exploring the relative **mass** of beans and pulses when I noticed one of the teaching assistants using her hand to measure out pulses. I talked to her later and she explained that when she was cooking she used her hand, cupped to a greater or lesser amount, as a measure which would compare to a teaspoon, or a tablespoon, or any measure in between. I realised that this was a 'unit' of measurement that I hadn't seen used before but which many of the children I worked with would be used to. It reminded me of the importance of learning from the cultural diversity within the classrooms that I work in.

As with activities involving shape and space, activities involving measuring allow us to notice pupils excelling, who have not always succeeded immediately when working with number. I often start to see those learners who have a well-developed sense of spatial awareness coming to the fore, and those who have experience outside the classroom of constructing, or cooking, are able to bring this prior experience to bear. Those children who sometimes struggle to remember their multiplication facts can easily estimate how long a shelf needs to be to fit into a space, or can quickly stack building blocks into a box – another reminder that we should not use the term 'ability' in an unthinking way.

Reflecting on the story with which I opened this chapter, it is worthwhile pausing for a moment to think about the measures we have a good sense of. I could probably estimate a pint and half a pint fairly accurately, but I still forget whether I need to order half a litre or a litre when I am drinking abroad, so I default to 'large' or 'small'. In my spare time I run, so I have an understanding of distances like 10km. It is 8 miles from my house to work, a cricket pitch is 22 yards long, and so on. The starting point to this chapter reflects on which units of measurement we have a good understanding of and those which we cannot 'picture'.

Starting point

Portfolio task 9.1

Write a list of the units of measurement you have a sense of as I did above. Try to complete the list below – what do you think weighs about 1kg, has a capacity of about a litre or measures about 1cm?

1mm	1g	1ml
1cm	1kg	10ml
1m	100kg	500ml
1km		1 litre
10km		100 litres

Which measurements did you find easy and which did you find hard?

Talk to your friends about it and think about how your prior experiences have informed your knowledge of measurements.

Measuring is not just about units of measurement; other key skills are reading scales and measuring instruments, including clocks, and understanding concepts such as area and perimeter. We will explore all of these areas in detail throughout the chapter. First, let us see how children's understanding of measuring is developed during their time in primary school.

TAKING IT FURTHER: **FROM THE RESEARCH**

In their book *Children Doing Mathematics* published in 1996, Terezinha Nunes and Peter Bryant show how children can be very successful in mathematical activities outside the classroom as they bring their intuitive understandings to bear on everyday problems. However, when they are faced with the same problems in school they often struggle as they try to apply 'school learning' to the problem rather than following their own strategies. Chapter 4 in the above book describes how children's prior experience impacts on their learning of measurement, and offers suggestions for the ways that teachers can draw on children's own understandings in the classroom. This book explores children's prior understandings of measurement in the way that Martin Hughes, whose book you have been introduced to in Chapters 5 and 6, examines young children's capacity to develop calculation skills outside of the formal classroom.

The most important message from the book is that children's understandings of mathematics are not generative. That is that children cannot generate knowledge they have not learnt through engagement in teaching activities. This challenges a traditional Piagetian viewpoint. However they also produce evidence that shows that children bring with them well-developed understandings of aspects of mathematics and that teachers should draw on these to support children in their learning. They also suggest that children will respond to mathematical problem solving in a different way if the problem occurs outside the classroom, often employing a wide range of reasoning skills, rather than in the mathematics classroom where they may try to use rules that have previously been imposed by a teacher. This reminds us that when teaching measurement we should spend time finding out how and when our learners measure outside the classroom and use this learning as our starting point. We should also draw on as many real-life, practical contexts as possible when teaching the skills of measurement.

Progression in measuring

Foundations for measuring

Initially children will begin to understand the language of measurement and comparison using vocabulary such as 'greater', 'smaller', 'heavier', 'lighter' to compare quantities. They will compare relative lengths, mass and capacity. To introduce children to ideas of time you should also use vocabulary such as 'before' and 'after'. You could also introduce money through a role-play area such as a shop. So, at this stage children should be engaging in a wide variety of practical activities which allow you to develop this vocabulary with them.

Beginning to understand measuring

At first children should carry out activities which involve measuring and weighing in order to compare objects. They will use suitable **uniform non-standard units** and then **standard units** for this comparison. (In non-standard units, uniform means that we use something that has a uniform measurement, so we can measure length using multilink cubes, or use a fixed number of wooden blocks to compare weights. Standard units are those in common usage, such as metres, litres, and kilograms and all the related units.) Once children have an understanding of using non-standard units to compare they can start to use a range of measuring instruments such as metre sticks and measuring jugs. Pupils will continue to estimate, compare and measure, but now relying on standard units. They will be able to choose suitable measuring instruments to help them. At this stage you should introduce them to scales and teach them how to read the numbered divisions on a scale, such as a weighing scale or measuring jug. They will also be using a ruler, which is another scale, to draw and measure lines to the nearest centimetre.

To build children's sense of time you can introduce them to vocabulary related to time such as days of the week and months. They can also begin to tell the time to the hour and to the half hour. You will develop their sense of time using seconds, minutes and hours. They will then be able to tell the time to the nearest quarter of an hour and be able to identify time intervals even across an hour. So, for example, they will know that it is 15 minutes between five to six and ten past six. Once they have a good grasp of telling the time to 15 minutes you can work on telling the time to the nearest 5 minutes. They should use both analogue and digital clocks.

When working with money pupils will recognise and use the symbols for the currency of their country and be able to find different combinations of small denominations that equal the same amount. They will also be able to carry out simple addition and calculation problems involving total amounts of money or giving change.

Becoming confident in measuring

At this stage pupils will come to understand the relationships between the standard units – kilometres and metres, kilograms and grams, and so on. They will be able to record their measurements using appropriate units. They will develop their skills reading scales, becoming able to read them to the nearest division and half division, including reading scales that are only partially numbered. As a next step they will learn the abbreviations for standard units and will understand the meanings of 'kilo', 'centi' and 'milli'. The basic units are metre, litre and gram – these are the basic units as they do not have a prefix. The prefixes tell you what multiple of the unit you require. So 'kilo' tells you that you need 1000 of the unit; 'centi' tells you this is 1/100 of the basic unit and 'milli', 1/1000. This leads on to decimal notation, so your learners will understand that 1.5 metres is the same as 1m 50cm. They will be reading scales and recording readings to the nearest tenth of a unit.

Pupils will be reading the time on 24-hour digital clocks and to the nearest minute on an analogue clock, as well as measuring time intervals so they can work out beginning and end times for given time intervals. For example they will know that if a TV programme lasts 30 minutes and starts at 9.40 it will end at 10.10. Once they have an understanding of this pupils will move on to be able to read timetables and time using the 24-hour clock and use a calendar to work out time intervals.

You will also introduce measurements linked to rectangles, including measuring the perimeter and finding the area of **rectilinear shapes** by counting squares in a grid. The perimeter of a shape is the distance all the way around its outside edge – this is measured in mm, cm or km. The area of a shape is the amount of space it takes up – this is measured in square mm, square cm or square km, written mm², cm² or km². A rectilinear shape is one that can be split up into a series of rectangles.

Developing these ideas pupils will be able to convert larger to smaller units using one place of decimals. For example, they will be able to change 7.3kg to 7300g. They will be able to interpret readings that lie between two divisions on a scale and draw and measure lines to the nearest millimetre.

They will also be calculating the perimeter of regular and irregular polygons and using the formula for the area of a rectangle to calculate area. A polygon is any shape with straight edges – a regular polygon must have all sides the same length and all the angles between the sides the same, otherwise the polygon is irregular. The formula to find the area of a rectangle is length multiplied by width.

Extending understanding of measuring

At this stage pupils will be operating up to two places of decimals – for example, changing 4.82m to 482cm. They will be able to read a wide variety of scales and will understand that the measurements made on scales are only approximate to a given degree of accuracy. They will be able to calculate perimeters and areas of rectilinear shapes and estimate areas of irregular shapes by counting squares.

Developing these skills pupils will operate up to three decimal places knowing that 2541ml is the same as 2.541 litres. They will apply their knowledge of measuring to solve a range of problems, and will also be able to calculate using imperial units (such as pints and ounces) still in everyday use, having an understanding of their approximate metric values.

Pupils will also be able to calculate the area of a right-angled triangle given the length of two perpendicular sides and be able to calculate the volume and **surface area** of a cube and cuboid. A right-angled triangle is a triangle in which two of the sides join at a right angle. The two perpendicular sides are the two sides that join at right angles – perpendicular means 'join at right angles'. The surface area of a 3D shape is the total area of all the faces of the shape. A cube is a 3D shape. All its faces are squares. A cuboid is a 3D shape with all its faces rectangles.

This section illustrates how, from the building blocks of the foundation stage where children are developing the language of comparison, they progress to the stage where they are accurately estimating, measuring and comparing up to two decimal places; reading any scale accurately; telling the time; and calculating area and perimeter of rectilinear shapes. The next section outlines the big ideas and key skills which underpin measuring.

Big ideas

Conservation and comparison

We measure in order to compare objects. We need to see if something is the right length to fit in a particular space, or if it will hold objects of a certain length. One of the earliest principles children come to understand is that the measurements of a particular object stay the same wherever we place it. Young children may describe something as longer than something else if they are not aligned.

In this case they may say that the shorter pencil is 'bigger' or 'longer' than the other. Young children need to use non-standard units such as pencils, wooden rods and cubes to come to an understanding that measurement is conserved, or stays the same, before they move on to using standard units. These difficulties with ideas of conservation are discussed in more detail later.

Units of measure

Units of measurement have been agreed by mathematicians and scientists in order to make measurement consistent throughout the world. In the UK imperial and metric units are used, but metric units, first introduced in eighteenth-century France, are the system taught in most schools. Metric units are in common usage as they are based on powers of 10 and so are easier to work with. The imperial units which are in the current English National Curriculum and the Cambridge International Programmes of Study are:

Length 12 inches in 1 foot; 3 feet in 1 yard; 1760 yards in 1 mile.

Area 144 square inches in 1 square foot; 9 square feet in 1 square yard; 640 acres in 1 square mile (an acre is about 4840 square yards).

Volume 1728 cubic inches in 1 cubic foot; 27 cubic feet in 1 cubic yard.

Capacity 5 fluid ounces in 1 gill; 4 gills in 1 pint; 8 pints in 1 gallon.

Mass 16 ounces in 1 pound, 14 pounds in 1 stone; 8 stones in 1 hundredweight (cwt); 20cwt in 1 ton.

Looking at this list you can probably see why the decision was made to focus on metric units! Metric units are sometimes referred to as SI units (Système

Internationale d'Unités). The table below shows the SI units together with the conversions to imperial units.

Attribute	SI unit	Abbreviation	Imperial units	Abbreviation	Conversion
Length	Metre	m	Inches, feet, yards, miles	in, ft, yd	1in = 2.54cm 1ft = 0.3m
Mass	Kilogram	kg	Ounces, pounds, stones	oz, lb, st	1oz = 28.35g 1lb = 0.45kg
Time	Second	s			
Area	Square metre	m²	Square inches, acres	sq in	
Volume	Cubic metre	m³	Cubic inches, cubic feet	cu in, cu ft	
Capacity	Litre	l	Pints, gallons	pt, gal	1pt = 0.56l

As you read in the opening section to the chapter, metric units are easy to use as the prefixes (kilo, milli, centi) tell you the conversion between the units.

Scales

All measurement is against a scale based on the unit we are using for comparison. Measurement is against a continuous scale, that is, we are always measuring approximately. If we say a line is 3.2cm long, what we are actually saying is that it is 3.2cm long to the nearest tenth of a centimetre. It may be 3.21cm or 3.19cm but we have decided that saying 3.2cm is accurate enough. Reading scales is one of the key skills to teach children – it is also useful to teach them how to create their own scales to measure. This helps them see the importance of standardisation and also the approximate nature of measurement.

Teaching points

Teaching point 1: Conservation of mass and capacity

In the 'Big ideas' section earlier in the chapter I suggested that young children do not always remember that you need to place the ends of two objects together to compare length. Similarly, if you move an object so that it is in a different orientation, the children may need some convincing that the length of the pencil has remained the same (or been 'conserved').

Before we explore children's understanding of conservation of mass it is worth defining mass. In everyday usage, mass is more commonly referred to as weight, although the precise scientific definition is the strength of the gravitational pull on the object, that is, how heavy it is. The distinction between mass and weight is important for extremely precise measurements which may be affected by slight differences in the strength of the Earth's gravitational field at different places, and for places far from the surface of the Earth, such as in space or on other planets. This means that you can convert exactly between weight and mass on the Earth's surface. This confusion between mass and weight is heightened by the fact that in much of the metric world, weight is not dealt with, and mass is used in its place almost exclusively. The main difference is that if you were to leave the Earth and go to the Moon, your weight would change but your mass would remain constant.

Conservation of mass is an even more difficult concept for young children. An activity I use which begins to get children thinking about this is to put four or five boxes of different shapes and sizes on a table and ask the group to place them in order of mass. I will have deliberately placed the heaviest object in the smallest box. Once we have ordered the boxes I will get the group to compare the masses of the boxes by lifting them up. They are often amazed that the smallest box is the heaviest as they have the misconception that the mass of an object is directly linked to its volume.

Another activity which deals directly with this misconception is to take a large spherical piece of play dough and place it in a balance so that it exactly balances with a counterweight. Then move the play dough from the scale and roll it flat. Ask the group if they think it will be lighter, heavier or the same. Children will often think that it will now be lighter, as it is 'thinner'. They will be surprised that this is not the case.

Another example of this is to place three or more containers in front of the children. The containers should range from very wide-based containers to long thin ones. Pour the same amount of liquid into each container. The liquid will not come very high up the wide-based container and the same volume may fill the container with the smaller base.

 Lots of practical experience of weighing a wide range of objects, and measuring capacity, are the most effective way to deal with this misconception.

Teaching point 2: Conservation of area

I was working with a small group of children finding the areas of rectangles by counting squares. After we had agreed that the area of this shape was 18cm²

I asked the group to make new shapes by cutting across diagonals of the squares. We created three new shapes, all including triangles:

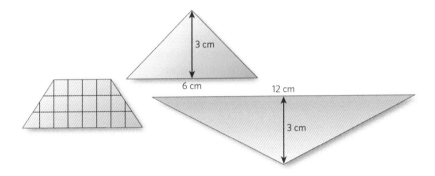

I then asked the group what they thought the areas of these shapes would be. None of them believed that the area would still be 18cm². In fact Helen had to count each one three times to convince herself. She said, 'That can't be right. Look, this one is much more spread out and so it should have a bigger area.' In Helen's view the fact that one of the shapes was longer suggested that it should have a greater area.

   A good way to develop children's understanding of conservation of area is to use tangrams

A tangram

or other tessellating activities

A tessellation
of triangles

A tessellation
of squares

A tessellation
of hexagons

to create a wide range of shapes with the same area. A tangram is a Chinese puzzle consisting of a square which is cut up into seven pieces. These pieces can be used to make many different shapes. As these are all made from the same pieces they will all have the same area.

In the activity below children are asked to rearrange 4cm squares to make different shapes. Although the shapes look very different, they all have the same area as they are all made up from the same 4cm squares. The link is made to perimeter as a way of supporting children in coming to an understanding that shapes with the same area can have different perimeters. This also consolidates the children's understanding of perimeter.

AREA AND PERIMETER

If two centimetre squares are put together, there is only one way to link them:

The perimeter is (2 × 2cm) + (2 × 1cm) = 6cm

If you put four squares together, you can make these shapes:

A

B

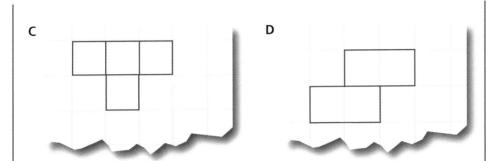

C   D

1   Find the perimeter of each of these shapes.
2   There is one more four-square shape you can make. Make this shape and record its perimeter.
3   Which four-square shape has the shortest perimeter?
4   Use six squares. How many different perimeters can you find?
5   Repeat with eight squares, then try ten and twelve squares. Find all the possible perimeters for each number of squares.
6   Look for rules or patterns to predict which shape gives the longest perimeter and which shape gives the shortest.

Portfolio task 9.2

A similar activity for more experienced learners can be set as the following open-ended investigation.

Explorers in a gold field are each given 100m of rope and 4 stakes.

Each explorer uses the 4 stakes and the rope to section off the piece of land they will dig in order to find gold.

What are the dimensions of the shape they should make to enclose the largest area they can?

Teaching point 3: Using appropriate units

The activity that opened the chapter was designed to start you thinking about appropriate units. It can be very confusing that length can be measured in millimetres, centimetres, metres and kilometres. Then when we measure area we can use the equivalent measures, although we tend mainly to use square centimetres and square metres. The best way to support children getting used to appropriate units is to use contexts which they are familiar with and ask for appropriate units rather than asking them to carry out the measuring activity. In this way they can focus on the units, rather than the act of measuring.

Teaching point 4: Relationships between dimensions and length, area and volume

Your pupils may simply try to remember a process when you ask them to solve problems to do with perimeter, area and volume rather than think through what the problem is asking them to do. I can think of occasions when learners have asked me if perimeter is 'that one where you add everything together' or simply multiplying any numbers that they can see on a diagram when asked to find an area as they remember that you 'multiply to find area'.

Try this activity with the class you are teaching as a way of supporting them in coming to a deeper understanding of the relationship between perimeter, area and volume. In this way the language of area, perimeter and volume will make more sense to them as well as the relationships between these three ways of describing measures.

Portfolio task 9.3

Decide which of these statements are true and which are false:

- If you double the dimensions of a rectangle you double its perimeter.
- If you double the dimensions of a rectangle you double its area.
- If you double the lengths of the sides of a rectangle, but leave the width the same, you double the area.
- If you double the dimensions of a cuboid you double its volume.

For the false statements write down an equivalent statement which is true. Try to describe why this is true.

Teaching point 5: Misreading scales

Children can make a range of errors reading scales. First, you will have noticed children not always measuring accurately because they don't line up their ruler correctly. They may start from the edge of the ruler rather than the zero point (this is not always at the end of a ruler), or sometimes you may notice children starting at the 1cm point and so will add 1cm to the true measurement.

An activity which can help children correct this for themselves is to have a series of lines down one side of a page and a series of measurements down the other side. Children have to measure the lines and match them to the appropriate measurement. Avoid using the answer which an error of measuring starting at the 1cm mark would give the pupil. Any child who is habitually making this error will then have to self-correct in order to 'match' the correct answer.

Children also sometimes forget to make sure that a measuring cylinder is placed on a flat surface when they are reading the scale. They move the cylinder to their eyes rather than their eyes to the cylinder. You need to check that children are placing their eyes level with the liquid so that they read the scale accurately. You can illustrate this to the children by tipping a cylinder and showing them how 'inaccurate' the reading can be.

Teaching point 6: Misreading clocks

The best way to support children in learning to tell the time is to have both analogue and digital clocks in the classroom, and to refer to them as often as possible. Some children rarely see analogue clocks – they will have a digital reading on their mobile phone, or on a TV at home, so you may need to model using an analogue clock frequently.

TAKING IT FURTHER: **FROM THE CLASSROOM**

In *Mathematics Teaching* 209, Rona Catterall describes the way she introduced 'telling time' to her class of six/seven-year-olds. This is a detailed article about the methods Rona used after she became frustrated with her children struggling with the skills of telling the time and is available on the companion website.

One example she uses is how you can use a child's understanding of their age to help with telling the time. She reminds us that a child sees their age to be of great importance. So she asks one of her class how old they are. 'I'm six,' they reply. The teacher asks if they can say they are seven? 'No,' says the pupil, 'I'm not seven until my next birthday.' 'It's just the same with this clock,' says the teacher, with the time set at half past six. 'We can't say its seven o'clock until the hand has gone all the way round.'

I introduced a class of mine to an analogue clock a few years ago and they laughed almost as if I had brought in an ancient timepiece. I set the clock at half past twelve (12:30) as this was lunchtime and asked the group what time was shown by the clock. The range of answers included:

6 past 12

6 to 12

12 and a half

All of these were sensible ways of interpreting a new scale. When we are introduced to a new scale out of context we decode it the best we can. I decided the best thing I could do was to discover all the possible errors with the children and so I set them the task below.

Portfolio task 9.4

This clock is showing 3:45.

Write down all the ways you could say this time.

These are some of the answers that my class gave – explain the errors the children are making:

- 45 minutes to 4
- 9 minutes to 4
- 9 minutes past 3
- 18 minutes past 9

One of the changes I have noticed over the last few years is that the number of different ways of describing the time has reduced. As people become more used to reading digital clocks and move away from analogue clocks the descriptions of time are always accurate to the nearest minute. So if I ask a pupil in my class what the time is they will tell me, 'It's eleven forty-seven' rather than 'just after quarter to twelve'. This is an interesting illustration of how technology imposes itself on our day-to-day mathematical practices.

In practice

The following lesson plan and evaluation describe a lesson taught to a group of pupils who had been working on measuring using uniform standard units.

As they have developed an understanding of the relationship between centimetres and metres the particular focus was developing their understanding of the relationship between grams and kilograms.

This will help them to make connections between the units of measurement of length and of mass. I particularly wanted to focus on the fact that there are 100cm in a metre but 1000g in a kilogram.

This will allow me to introduce the meanings of the prefixes 'kilo' and 'centi'. I am making sure that the children work practically so that they come to have an understanding of 'how much' 1kg, 500g and 10g is.

Objectives:	• Know the relationship between grams and kilograms • Choose and use appropriate units to estimate, measure and record measurements	

Key vocabulary:	Context:	
Gram, kilogram, weight, heaviest, lightest	This is the fourth lesson of the week and so far we have used hand spans to measure lengths and widths and then measured hand spans to the nearest cm to calculate lengths. We have estimated lengths to the nearest centimetre and then moved on to using metre sticks. This should support the children in making connections between kilograms and grams in this lesson	

Resources:	Starter activity:	
Mini-whiteboards and pens; 1kg, 500g, 100g, 50g and 10g weights; pan balances; collection of items to weigh; large sheets of paper	I'll ask the children to sit in their 'talk partner' pairs. The pairs have two minutes to write down as many different units of measurement as they can think of. After two minutes I will go round the pairs getting one unit from each pair to record on the board until we have collected everyone's answers. I'll draw a table on the board – length, capacity, mass and time. Individuals then pick a unit and tell me which column to put it in. I'll then ask pairs to think of things that they use the units to measure	

Main activity:	Teacher:	Pupil activity:
Whole group activity	I will ask the children to move to their numeracy tables which I have set out with the balances and a range of everyday items to weigh. Groups should estimate which item on their table is the heaviest and bring it to the scales at the front to weigh. I will ask the class if they think it will weigh more or less than 1kg. I will also ask if they think it is heavier/lighter than the previous item and model how to write down the weight	Pupils pick up the objects to estimate the weight in terms of heaviness/lightness They will draw on their previous knowledge as more items are weighed They will observe the way I am using the different weights to balance and then the method I am using to record the weights
Group activity: Children operating at above expected levels	I will ask members of the group to estimate the weight of the objects before they weigh them, encouraging them to draw on their previous measurements to come up with sensible estimates	This group will weigh all their objects and record the weights. They will then arrange them in order of weight and complete a table allowing them to record the measurements systematically

Group activity: Children operating at expected levels	This group will work with the 1kg, 500g and 100g weights only	I will focus my attention on this group and encourage them to estimate the answers first before measuring. If necessary I will fetch extra weights and move on to measuring more accurately.
	They will weigh the objects and complete the following chart:	
	Objects less than 100g	
	Objects between 100 and 500g	
	Objects between 500g and 1kg	
	Objects heavier than 1kg	
Group Activity: Children operating below expected levels	This group will work with the 1kg, 500g and 10g weights. I will give them three large sheets of paper labelled 1kg, 500g, 10g. Pairs of children from the group will find objects that weigh approximately 1kg, 500g and 10g and place them on the appropriate piece of paper	Pupils will draw on prior experience to estimate the mass of the objects. When they use all the objects I have given them I will ask them to find other objects which weigh approximately 1kg, 500g or 10g. The teaching assistant will accompany them on a walk to find objects in the environment and create a display table

Plenary: I will rearrange the groups so that each small group has representatives from the groups engaged in different activities. Pupils will discuss the activities that they have been engaged in, focusing on things that surprised them. Which things were heavier than they expected? Which were lighter? When I take feedback from these groups I will make sure that pupils use the units of kg and g to describe how heavy the 'surprising' objects were. We will discuss why they think that some 'small' objects can be 'heavy'

Rationale and evaluation

The talk pairs generated a lot of discussion. Talk pairs are always a good way to get responses and I could see pairs noticing each other's units and 'copying' and building on each other's ideas, which I encouraged. I made the point that it is very useful to use each other's ideas to develop our own thinking and I tried to discourage pairs from hiding their boards to keep their answers 'secret'. The classification activity was also useful – I moved this on so that we looked at the units within each classification and talked about what we might measure with each unit. This did mean that I spent much longer on the starter than I meant to, but I decided that, as understanding the relationships between units was a key idea, it was a good decision.

As I had extended the starter I decided to move straight into the group activities, otherwise I felt the children would not have sufficient time using the scales, which was important. I was able to move quickly between the tables to set up the activities and quickly realised that there was sufficient expertise within my higher attaining groups to carry out the activity. This suggests that the activity wasn't challenging enough for them, although they were well motivated and engaged with the activity. I extended this activity by asking the group to record the measurements in two ways – 1kg, 300g or 1300g. This did challenge them, although Megan also suggested 1.300 as a measure which impressed me. I asked them to focus on using kg and g as I think the idea of 1.300 being equivalent to 1.3 at this stage could lead to misunderstandings.

The groups who were estimating gradually became more effective in their estimation. Initially it appeared as though they were making 'random' guesses, but with support from me and the teaching assistant they were able to draw on their prior experience and by the end of the session had a sense of more and less than 1kg, as well as being able to compare weights.

Because of this I changed my planned plenary and used the introductory activity I had planned as a plenary. Each group used a different set of objects and this helped me both consolidate the learning of the children and assess their development during the lesson.

Portfolio task 9.4

Devise a lesson plan which is appropriate for a group of learners you are working with.

The focus should be an aspect of 'measuring' that is appropriate to the age group you are working with.

Make sure you think carefully about the context and evaluate the lesson.

Add this lesson plan and evaluation to your subject knowledge portfolio.

Observing teaching measurement

On the companion website you will find a video which shows a teacher introducing an activity which involves her pupils in measuring 500 millilitres of fluid. She sets an imaginary context for this by dressing up as a 'witch' who requires the potion. Watch the clip from the beginning and think through other contexts you could use to motivate the pupils. Could you enter into the role more convincingly? In this role play the teacher does not play a role; she is really just the teacher dressing up.

Observe the different ways in which the children record their five measures which will total 500 millilitres. How could you encourage them to think of as many different ways as possible?

How might you adapt this lesson for use with the pupils you are currently teaching?

Assessing understanding of measurement

The most effective way of assessing your pupils' measurement skills is to observe them engaging in activities which involve measuring. For early learners this will involve you asking questions about how many small containers your pupils might think will pour into larger ones, or how many hand spans will measure a table, or strides there will be across a classroom. For older learners this can take the form of using containers with a given capacity and estimating the capacity of larger containers using this knowledge. As learners become more skilled at measuring using scales you can ask them to create a measuring jug, including calibrating a scale on the jug. You might perhaps ask them to create a 1 litre measuring jug with 50 millilitre divisions given a 100 millilitre measure.

You can assess pupils' early understanding of time by asking them to order events during a typical day and assign a time to them to the nearest hour. This can become increasingly sophisticated in terms of the accuracy of the time. If you draw on the pupil's own experience this is even better. Later you can use timetables to ask pupils to plan appropriate journeys given set criteria.

Cross-curricular teaching of measurement

As I suggested above, a useful way both to develop and reinforce the skills of measurement through a cross-curricular project is by asking children to make containers of appropriate sizes. The two ideas below should motivate both your younger learners and those in Key Stage 2.

Younger learners

Bring three teddy bears into the class. One should be very small, one 'medium' sized and one larger. If you want, you could link this to the 'Three bears' story. Each group needs to make different objects for the three animals. For example, you might ask one group to make a chair, one a plate and bowl, and even an appropriate shelter. This will involve them in comparing measurements and using the language of comparison.

Older learners

Bring in a range of cereal boxes. The pupils should find ways of measuring the capacity of the box and their task is to design a box which is a different shape but which will hold the same amount. Ask them to design the net for the box, including logos, as this means they have to think through how the net fits together to form the final box. An alternative to this is to ask the groups to design and create carrier bags for particular objects.

Summary

The emphasis within this chapter is on the practical nature of measuring and the importance of drawing on learners' intuitive understandings and knowledge of measurement in order to develop their skills. The progression section illustrates the importance of developing a language of 'measurement' in young children and engaging them actively in carrying out measurement as the only way to learn about 'measurement'. The key ideas which the chapter then builds on are ideas of conservation and comparison – everyday skills we will use all the time but may not have put a name to before. The teaching points emphasise the fact that we can and need to teach these skills to our learners – they aren't simply common sense. Other big ideas such as the units we use to measure and compare objects, and the scales we use to support measurement, are also described.

Reflections on this chapter

The important thing to take away from this chapter is the small number of skills we are trying to teach our pupils in order to help them become effective in measurement. The basic foci are 'units' and 'scales'. Pupils need to have a sense of what a measurement means – if your pupils leave primary school with an understanding of what a litre looks like, how far 500m is, what 50g feels like, and so on, they will be able to estimate measures effectively. And if you have taught them how to read and create a range of scales, they will be able to transfer this skill into many other areas of mathematics.

If you did not attempt the 'Portfolio task' activities in teaching points 4 and 5, complete them at this point. This will allow you to assess your understanding of the relationship between area and perimeter.

Going further

Progression in Measuring

MARGARET BROWN AND HER COLLEAGUES

This report on a research project explores the extent to which learners' progression in learning measurement can be described. As you might expect there are idiosyncratic patterns to individuals' progression in their learning. However the team is able to outline a general framework to describe progression in this area. It is interesting to compare this to any progression described in other curriculum documents.

Brown, M., Blondel, E., Simon, S. and Black, P. (1995) 'Progression in measuring', *Research Papers in Education* 10(2), 143–170.

Primary teachers' perceptions of their knowledge and understanding of measurement

MICHELLE O'KEEFE AND JANETTE BOBIS

This paper was presented to the Mathematics Education Research Group of Australia. This study focused on primary teachers' perceptions of their knowledge and understandings of length, area and volume. It also explored their understanding of how children's growth of measurement concepts and processes develops. Data gained from in-depth interviews revealed that teachers' knowledge was often implicit and that they struggled to articulate their knowledge of measurement concepts and children's trajectories of learning.

O'Keefe, M. and Bobis, J. (2008) 'Primary teachers' perceptions of their knowledge and understanding of measurement', available at **www.merga.net.au/documents/RP462008.pdf** (accessed 18 July 2012).

Self-audit

These activities focus on estimation of distance, mass and capacity. Through working on the ideas you should develop your understanding of these concepts and be better able to support those you teach.

1   Complete this table. The first column is a measurement; in the second column write down an object that is approximately that length and in the final column rewrite the measurement in either cm or m, whichever is most appropriate.

Length		
1mm		
10mm		
100mm		
1000mm		
10 000m		
100 000m		

2   Repeat this activity for weight, using g or kg.

Weight		
1g		
10g		
100g		
1000g		
10 000g		
100 000g		

3   And capacity, using ml or l.

Capacity		
1ml		
10ml		
100ml		
1000ml		
10 000ml		
100 000ml		

CHAPTER 10

STATISTICS AND HANDLING DATA

Introduction

Several years ago I carried out some work in a Year 5 class in Leicester. The class I was working with included children from a wide variety of backgrounds. I was interested in the group posing their own problems and using their own mathematical skills to come up with solutions. One group suggested carrying out a survey into attitudes towards racism.

They designed a questionnaire, decided who they would use this questionnaire with and then analysed the responses and reported back to the class. They reported back using **bar charts**, **line graphs** and pie charts, with each group describing why they had chosen particular representations to illustrate their data. Some of their results are given below:

How would you feel if someone made fun of your skin colour?

I would hit them	16%
I would be sad	34%
I would be angry	38%
I would think they were ignorant	12%

What would you do if no one would let you play because you looked different to them?

I would ask them why	42%
I would let a teacher know	58%

Two people wrote, 'I would be sad and play with someone else', and another wrote, 'I would wish I could change my skin colour'.

If you were on a bus and you had a spare place next to you how would you feel if there were lots of people standing and no one would sit next to you?

I would think they didn't like me because I am different	64%
I would ignore it and be happy because I wasn't squashed	36%

This approach to handling data made direct links to the children's lived experience; it also allowed the teacher to bring mathematics directly into the personal, social and health education (PSHE) curriculum which focused on these issues for the next three weeks. It opened the teacher's eyes to issues they hadn't been aware of – the day-to-day prejudice impacted on their learners when they travel on public transport, and the damage to self-esteem suffered when children are made to feel that 'they want to change their skin colour'.

I would suggest that the children came to understand the mathematics of data handling more deeply from this project than they would have done from surveying shoe sizes. It was a question that they were committed to, and they had to decide how to 'tell the story' accurately with the data so that people could understand the issue.

Starting point

Let us start wth an activity. Work on this task in your notebook.

Portfolio task 10.1

Look at this column graph.

Write down three different sets of data that the graph could be illustrating.

You can define for yourself what the numbers 1–6 along the x-axis (the horizontal axis) stand for.

If you work with friends on this describe how you decided on your answers.

This may seem like starting at the end but the key reason for 'handling data' is to be able to come to decisions about what the data represents. Often learners do not know how to interpret data; they learn how to collect and organise data but do not realise that there may well be alternative interpretations that could be drawn from the data. It is important that our pupils see the big picture from the beginning and understand that interpretation is just as important as collection and representation of data.

The data handling cycle is shown below:

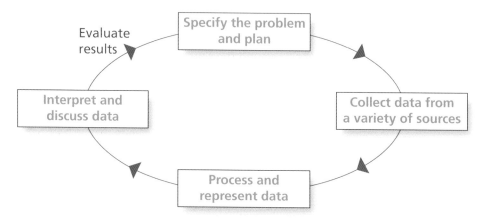

This diagram emphasises the importance of both problem posing and interpretation and is the key 'big idea' for this chapter. So skills in these areas are just as important as understanding how to collect data and the different ways you can represent it.

Progression in statistics and handling data

This section illustrates the progression for teaching handling data. The terms in red are defined and explained for you in the glossary.

Foundations for understanding statistics and handling data

At the early stages you will work with your learners, sorting familiar objects to identify their similarities and differences and counting how many objects share a particular property. You will support the children in presenting their results using pictures, drawings or numerals.

Beginning to understand statistics and handling data

At this stage children will be able to ask and research questions by recording information in lists and tables and present outcomes to data handling activities using practical resources, pictures, **block graphs** or **pictograms**. They will also use diagrams, including Venn diagrams and Carroll diagrams, to sort objects into groups according to a given criterion and suggest a different criterion for grouping the same objects. Later they will start to both collect and record data which they will represent as block graphs or pictograms to show the results. They will begin to use ICT to organise and present data and will use lists, tables and diagrams to sort objects. They will be able to explain the choices they are making.

Becoming confident in statistics and handling data

These children will use a wider range of diagrams to record data including **tally charts**, **frequency tables**, pictograms and bar charts to represent results and illustrate observations. They will use ICT to create a simple bar chart and use Venn diagrams or Carroll diagrams to sort data and objects using more than one criterion. They will be able to answer a question by identifying what data to collect and how best to organise, present, analyse and interpret the data using tables, diagrams, tally charts, pictograms and bar charts, and using ICT where appropriate. They will also be able to compare the impact of representations using different scales. They will understand the difference between **discrete** and **continuous data**.

Pupils will progress to be able to interpret data through constructing frequency tables, pictograms and bar and line graphs to show the **frequency** of events and changes over time. At this stage they will also understand how we use the **mean**, **median** and **mode** of a set of data.

Pupils should be introduced to the language of probability and the occurrence of familiar events using the language of chance or likelihood. The pupils should understand and use the **probability scale** from 0 to 1 and find and justify probabilities based on equally likely outcomes in simple contexts.

Extending learning in statistics and handling data

At this stage you can teach your pupils how to describe and predict outcomes and to solve problems by collecting, selecting, processing, presenting and interpreting data drawing conclusions in order to identify further questions to ask. They could construct and interpret frequency tables, bar charts with grouped discrete data, line graphs and interpret pie charts. They will explore hypotheses by planning surveys or experiments to collect small sets of discrete or continuous data, selecting, processing, presenting and interpreting the data in order to identify ways to extend the survey or experiment.

My aim is that this section illustrates to you the progression in the ideas that help us collect and interpret data. In the early years children are sorting objects and talking about the decisions being made in order to sort according to particular criteria. Then, as pupils progress, they are introduced to an increasing range of charts and diagrams that can be used to represent data until they are able to write a short report detailing the results of a survey they have carried out and justifying their choices of methods and representation.

Big ideas

The data handling cycle introduced earlier is the 'Big idea' when working with children on developing their understanding of this strand. Collecting, organising and interpreting data is at the heart of the mathematical ideas here.

Another important way to understand and interpret data is through the key ideas underpinning probability and chance so these concepts are explored in this section.

Collecting data

Before we begin to collect data we need a question we are trying to answer. It is important that learners are exploring data to answer questions that they want to know the answer to – and that they are supported to explore new questions that are raised by the data they have collected.

A question that has interested groups of children I have worked with is:

What is the ratio of the circumference of your head to your height?

We begin by estimating answers, usually guesses from '4 times' upwards. We then start measuring and plot the measurements on a scatter diagram. This means using one axis for 'height' and one axis for 'distance round head'.

Each child finds the point on the chart where they would place their data, marks a cross and initials it. By plotting boys and girls in different colours, and pupils and adults in different colours, the children notice that although the ratio is about 3:1 it may be slightly different for boys and girls, and for adults and children. One group decided that they would go into a foundation class and see if the ratio was different for very young children. Even though scatter graphs may not traditionally be introduced until secondary school, the children were fascinated to see this way of illustrating data.

Organising data

One of the important skills in handling data is deciding what the most appropriate way to organise the data is once it has been collected. This depends on the sort of data you are collecting and the questions you want to answer.

Discrete and continuous data

Discrete data can be counted – examples would be the ways that children travel to school (five pupils travel by bus) or children's birthdays (three children have birthdays in May). Continuous data are measured – examples would be heights, and weights and time. Continuous data has to be grouped in order to represent and interpret it. So, for example, if the children wanted to find out how fit their class was compared to other classes, they could devise an activity timing how long it takes individuals to run 25m. In order to represent the data the times would have to be grouped – perhaps into 2-second intervals. The children would need to decide the most appropriate interval after collecting the data. It is worth organising the data using a range of intervals – the children can then decide which is the most useful.

Pictograms, bar charts, line graphs and pie charts

Initially you will encourage young children to create pictograms through a practical activity. For example the children could explore a shop in the role-play area and draw pictures to record their favourite purchases. Using questions such as

What can you tell about what people in your class like to buy?

would encourage more in-depth interpretation of the data. You could also introduce different roles into the role play – the children could be teachers out shopping, or people who work on a building site. They could create different pictograms for these different groups of people.

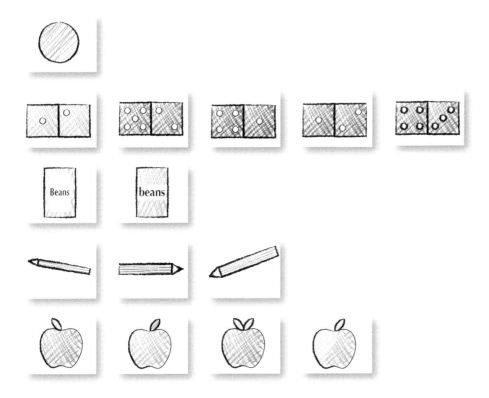

The activity on page 222 asks pupils to compare representations of data using a bar chart and a line chart.

BAR AND LINE CHARTS

In this activity you can see in the bar chart and line chart (below) two representations of data on the same page that encourage the children to explore which representation they think shows the data most usefully.

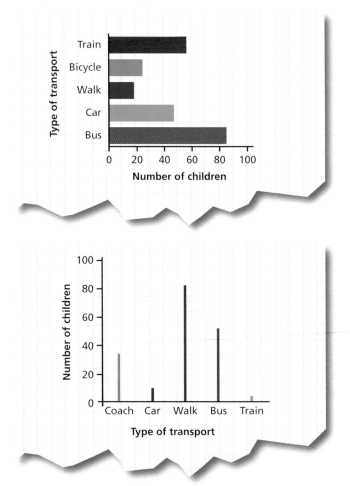

Your role when working with data represented in this way is to use the page for discussion. Ask questions such as:

- Which representation is most useful?
- What does the data show – about the children?
- Where do you think this school is?

As a follow up to this activity, which focuses on interpreting data, you could collect similar data from your class, or from the school, and then compare the data for your class with the data for 'Bancroft School' and 'Parson's School'.

Line graphs are used to look at trends over time. You will often see these types of graphs on the news. You can collect and interpret data using line graphs to answer questions like, 'Is it too hot/cold in our classroom?'

Does the classroom take a long time to warm up in the morning? What happens on particularly sunny or very cold days?

This data can be graphed on the same set of axes to allow for comparisons. The figure below shows the type of axes you would use to record temperature change in the classroom.

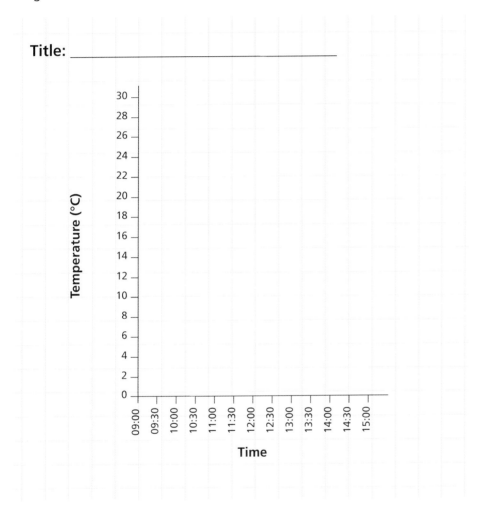

Children are also expected to be able to interpret pie charts. Pie charts show the proportions of data. Work on the task below and add it to your portfolio.

Portfolio task 10.2

Examine this pie chart. Write down three different sets of data that it could represent. Choose one of your sets of data and write a short paragraph analysing the data. This question is deliberately open as it exemplifies how data can be interpreted in many different ways.

Pie chart of countries

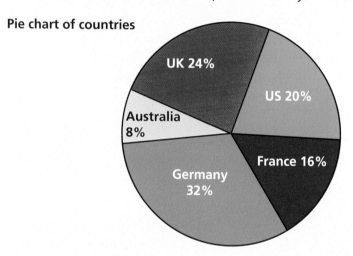

Venn and Carroll diagrams

Venn diagrams and Carroll diagrams are used to sort objects. Carroll diagrams are actually named after the author Lewis Carroll, who wrote *Alice in Wonderland* and was fascinated by mathematics. People have explored *Alice in Wonderland* for the mathematics it contains and Lewis Carroll also wrote academic books on geometry. Venn diagrams were introduced by a mathematician called John Venn in 1880.

The task below illustrates the different uses of Carroll and Venn diagrams. In fact, you have already used Carroll diagrams for sorting in Chapter 5.

Portfolio task 10.3

Look at the shape sorting task below and the number sorting activity which follows. Carry out the tasks and then find ways of sorting the shapes using Venn diagrams. What are the advantages of using a Carroll diagram for sorting? What are the advantages of using a Venn diagram for sorting?

CARROLL AND VENN DIAGRAMS

Carroll diagram

Sort the shapes and write the letters in a Carroll diagram like the one below.

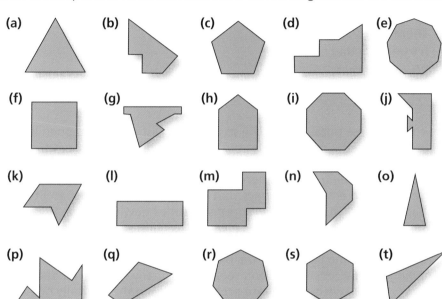

	Symmetrical	Not symmetrical
More than four sides		
Four sides or fewer		

Venn diagram

Write the multiples of 6 and 7 on this Venn diagram. The intersection should show the numbers which are in both the 6 and 7 times-table.

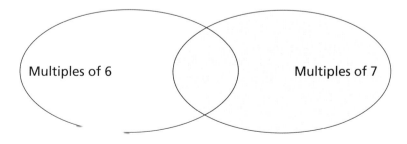

Chance and probability

Children have intuitive ideas about probability through the language that they use. Look at the phrases below and complete each sentence:

It is very likely that…
Once in a blue moon…
There's a 50/50 chance that…
It's unlikely that…
It's certain that…
It's impossible for…

Now organise these phrases on a line so that the least likely to happen is at the left-hand end and the most likely at the right-hand end. You have just created a probability scale. All probability is measured on a scale of 0 to 1 with 0 being impossible and 1 being certain; percentages are sometimes used, with 100% being certain. There are three ways that we can assess the probability of an event happening. First, we draw on prior scientific knowledge – an example of this would be predicting a 70% probability of rain given current weather patterns. Another way of assessing probability is to carry out an experiment – we could work out the likelihood of a piece of toast landing 'butter side down' by dropping 100 pieces of toast and seeing how many actually landed 'butter face down'. Finally, we can calculate probability based theoretically on equally likely outcomes. The way we calculate the probability of throwing a 5 on a six-sided dice is by listing the six equally likely outcomes 1, 2, 3, 4, 5 or 6; throwing a 5 is one of these outcomes, so the probability of throwing a 5 is 1/6 (1 out of 6). More formally we write this as p(5) = 1/6.

Teaching points

Teaching point 1: Making data meaningful

I was observing a first-year student teacher recently who was introducing a data handling session with her class. She had been asked to 'teach tally charts and bar charts' and advised to 'stick to shoe sizes because it is easy'. She let the group decide how to organise the collection of data, which was pleasing, so the children arranged themselves in groups of the same shoe size. This, however, removed the need for tallying as the children could simply count how many children had each shoe size and so wrote down the frequency, or how many children wore a particular shoe size, and then represented this as a tally, for example 4 = IIII.

They then drew the bar chart without noticing that the total number of children represented by the chart was more than the number in the class. The class did not engage with the data collection in any meaningful way as they weren't really interested in the outcome. This is in contrast to the activity with which I opened the chapter. Another area which children have been interested in has been linked to the environment – one class became very engaged in finding out which class in their school was the 'greenest'.

TAKING IT FURTHER: **FROM THE CLASSROOM**

In their article 'Curricular opportunity and the statistics of lines', Paul Andrews and Heather Massey suggest that 'data, unless collected within a meaningful context and then analysed purposefully, is not worth collecting. No-one in the real world collects data for the sake of collecting data.' They also suggest that learners often carry out data handling and statistical enquiries in subjects other than mathematics to a much more sophisticated level than we expect in mathematics sessions.

The lesson they describe appears very simple on the surface – they ask pupils to estimate the length of five pre-drawn straight lines. The pupils complete a table which asks for their estimate, the actual length, the error and the percentage error. However, they then ask the class to explore some complex questions:

- Are humans more accurate when estimating long or short lengths?
- Does relative error increase or decrease with length?
- How much do humans vary in their estimations of length?
- Do humans tend to overestimate or underestimate lengths?

These questions can also be asked of curved lines and angles, which allows the teacher to explore and develop skills in handling data while drawing on other areas of the mathematics curriculum.

Teaching point 2: Making sensible observations from data

This teaching point follows directly from the point made above. If learners do not see the data as meaningful, or have not been involved in formulating the questions which they are trying to respond to through collecting and analysing data, they may well only see simplistic, closed interpretations of data.

The interpretation of data should take place alongside the representation of data. In this way children are always making decisions about the most appropriate form of representation. Children should also be encouraged to come up with alternative interpretations of data so that they become used to being critical about the way that data is represented and interpreted.

TAKING IT FURTHER: **FROM THE RESEARCH**

In the paper 'Exploring the complexity of the interpretation of media graphs', published in *Research in Mathematics Education* (Volume 6, 2004), Carlos Monteiro and Janet Ainley describe the way they used graphs from the media to develop a 'critical sense' in learners' interpretation of data. They suggest that there are three main types of graph reading:

1   Reading the data: lifting information from the data to answer specific questions.
2   Reading between the data: finding relationships and patterns within the data.
3   Reading beyond the data: using the data to predict future patterns or to ask new questions.

The example used earlier in the chapter exploring the relationship between a person's height and the circumference of their head showed learners carrying out all three processes.

  The researchers used graphs and charts from the media to explore the ways in which student teachers interpreted data, encouraging them to read the data in the three ways described above. They found that the student teachers drew on four aspects of prior knowledge to interpret the graphs:

1   Mathematical knowledge to describe the quantitative relationships they observed (that is, relationships based on numbers).
2   Personal opinions to make generalisations based on the data.
3   Personal experience to make generalisations based on the data.
4   Feelings and emotions to describe how the data made them 'feel'.

Thinking again about the data handling activity which opened the chapter, you can see an 'emotional' response to the data as it is related to a real, lived experience.

Portfolio task 10.4

Find a chart or graph from a newspaper or magazine which illustrates data that you are interested in.

Write down your own analysis of the data. Try to decide when you are 'reading the data', 'reading between the data' and 'reading beyond the data'.

Teaching point 3: Using mean, median, mode appropriately

For many people the word 'average' is used interchangeably with 'mean'. There are, in fact, three different sorts of 'average': the mean, the median and the mode.

The mean is the 'average' that is most commonly used. You calculate the mean by adding up all the different items of data and dividing by the total number of items. So, if you are finding the mean height of all the children in your class, and you had 28 children, you would find the total height by adding all the individual measurements together and then dividing by 28.

The median is the middle value when all the data is arranged in order. This is a measure of 'central tendency' in the same way as the mean, but is helpful if there are extremes in the data, or 'outliers'. So if we have a list of house prices in a particular area, say

£78 000, £150 000, £175 000, £180 000, £200 000,
£210 000 and £750 000

the mean works out as £249 000, which isn't a useful measure if you are trying to decide whether you can afford a house in the area. The median is £180 000, which is more informative in this case. If there is an even number of values the median value is exactly half way between the two central values.

The mode is the value that occurs most frequently – this time shoe sizes are a good example. You could ask the children in your class to decide how many of each shoe size they would stock if they were to set up a shoe shop for children their age. This is the data for a mixed group of boys and girls age 11:

Shoe size	Frequency
2	2
3	4
4	5
5	5
6	9
7	6
8	3
9	0
10	1

The mode is size 6, so they would stock more of this shoe size. To make it more challenging you may describe the size of the population that may visit the shop. If there are two values which are most popular, the data is said to be **bi-modal**.

A final measure which is used is the range. This measures the spread of the set of data. So, in the example of house prices above the range is £672 000 (78 000–750 000).

When you are exploring and interpreting data with your class it is worth asking them to find all three measures of average and the range, and then decide which is the most useful measure to answer the question you have asked of the data.

Portfolio task 10.5

Try to find:

1 six numbers with a mean of 6

2 eight numbers with a median of 4

3 ten numbers with a mode of 7.2.

Teaching point 4: Probability – equally likely outcomes

A boy once gave me the best explanation of probability and equally likely outcomes I have ever heard. He was carrying out an experiment tossing a coin and had tossed three 'heads' in a row. His friend said, 'The next one is bound to be a "tail".' The first boy responded, 'Don't be silly, the coin hasn't got a memory.' And he was right – the probability of tossing a 'tail' is always 1/2; or 50% or 50/50 whatever you have just tossed. Similarly, lots of children seem to think that it is harder to get a 6 when throwing a dice than any other number. This isn't the case – the chance is 1/6, the same as the chance of getting a 1, or a 2, or any other number. I wonder if children just remember times when they couldn't get a 6, to start or finish a board game, and so think this is more difficult.

The outcomes of an experiment are equally likely to occur when the probability of each outcome is equal. Tossing a head or a tail on a coin, or throwing a 1, 2, 3, 4, 5, 6 on a six-sided dice, are called equally likely outcomes. To find the probability of an event happening you need to decide which equally likely outcomes are acceptable and divide that by how many equally likely outcomes there are. So for example

**The probability of throwing an even number
on a six-sided dice = 3/6 or 1/2**

There are three possible outcomes that are acceptable – throwing a 2, 4 or 6 – and there are six possible outcomes altogether.

You can explore theoretical probabilities when events are not equally likely by carrying out a range of experiments. For example, tossing a match box – you can get the whole class tossing (empty) match boxes. If you were to toss it a total of 100 times and it landed on the end 22 times, the side 4 times and the faces 74 times, the probabilities would be 22%, 4% and 74% respectively. You could also explore how the judicious placing of sticky tack changes the probabilities. You could set a challenge to try to reach 50% probability of landing on one end by 'weighting' the box.

In practice

The following lesson plan and evaluation describe a lesson taught to a group of 10- and 11-year-old pupils who had been working on handling data with a particular focus on using data to explore real-life questions. I wanted to work on an extended activity with the group so that they could see the data handling cycle as a continuous process. I also wanted the group to see that often a data handling investigation throws up new questions for us to consider.

Objectives:	• To solve problems by collecting, processing, presenting and interpreting data • To draw conclusions and identify further questions to ask • To suggest, plan and develop lines of enquiry

Note: I will use a whole morning for this activity rather than try to fit it into a single hour, or run over several lessons, as I feel this will lose continuity

Key vocabulary	Survey, data, frequency table, hypothesis
Resources: Mini- whiteboards	**Starter activity:** Write on the whiteboard, 'The children in this class enjoy reading.' Ask the class to vote on this. Choose one of the group who voted for the statement – ask them to describe in detail what they mean when they say, 'The children in this class enjoy reading'. Do the same with someone who disagreed. Ask the children to work in pairs for five minutes and come up with several statements about the class which may or may not be true. They should write these on mini-whiteboards. Take feedback from the groups and agree which are the six most interesting questions to ask about the class. Phrase these as hypotheses and tell the class they are going either to prove or disprove these hypotheses. The children will choose which group to work in depending on the question they are most interested in
Main activity:	Each group should spend ten minutes deciding how they will test their hypothesis. For example, the group exploring 'We think this class enjoy reading' might decide that someone who reads ten books a month and likes at least three different genres enjoys reading. The whole class should comment on each group's criteria
	Once each group has amended their criteria based on the feedback they have been given, they should develop a questionnaire – this time I will ask them to get feedback from me
	Finally, the group collect the data. They complete frequency tables and use the program data charts to display their data. Each group will prepare a short PowerPoint presentation to present their findings

Plenary: Each group present their findings – I will ask for feedback from all the other children using the two stars and a wish system. (That is, each group assess each other's presentation giving them two positive features – 'stars' – and one way of improving it – a 'wish')

Rationale and evaluation

I was pleased that I planned to run this over a morning rather than trying to work in blocks of an hour. I needed the flexibility to manage the time differently and the session didn't fit naturally into my normal structure for the numeracy sessions. In the end the groups didn't get to present their ideas at the end of the morning – in fact I had to build in some flexible time during the week for groups to finish their presentations as they took very different time scales. I should have expected this, but it was important that the groups could take the time they needed over preparing their presentations as it allowed them to draft and redraft. I asked each group to show me their data as pie charts, bar charts and line graphs if they could. I then asked them to make the decision about which was the most useful representation. I think this is the first time that they have thought carefully about how pie charts are better at representing 'proportion' than bar charts. Jan said, 'I'm going to use a bar chart for the information that has lots of numbers that are important but the pie chart when I just need to show where the "most" is.' I thought this showed a good understanding of the alternative representations.

All the groups found the hardest part deciding on the initial criteria – I needed to support them carefully initially as all the groups wanted to use just one criterion. So for example they asked, 'Do you like to read?' rather than 'Do you read action stories, or poetry books, or science books?' In the end I had to structure the learning by asking for three criteria they could explore. However, when we revisited the criteria at the end and started thinking of new questions to ask, they could see how they might devise criteria. There has been some impact I think as yesterday I said, 'Well done Class 6, you've worked very hard today.' Graeme chirped up, 'What do you mean exactly by we've worked hard?'

All the attainment groups were effective; this allowed people like Shauna, who are normally very quiet, to take a lead. She became very animated as she worked on the question 'Children in this class are good at looking after animals' as that is her passion. Similarly, Lauren and Westley became the IT experts for their groups and showed them all sorts of techniques for using PowerPoint.

The groups' skills in peer assessment were also developed – they are becoming much more sophisticated in using the two stars and a wish feedback system. Earlier in the year the responses would have been along the lines of 'it was very colourful' or 'it could have been neater'. This time there were comments such as 'I think a pie chart would have been a better way of showing the data because you could very quickly see the different fractions.'

Observing the teaching of statistics and handling data

There are two examples of how to explore the data handling cycle holistically on the companion website.

In the first clip the teacher takes a holistic view of the data handling cycle, collecting, recording and analysing data about school meals. He sets this as a genuine question, suggesting that the new school cook wants some feedback. He chooses to use human charts as one way of representing the data. Watch the clip and then think about the following questions:

- What are the advantages of using the pupils to create human bar charts?
- Can you think of other ways of involving learners so directly in representing data?

Watch the second lesson in the clip which links the data handling cycle to athletic achievements. Here the children actively engage in 'athletic' type activities and record the results. After watching the clip think about these questions.

- How would you safeguard children's self-esteem if using this activity?
- How would you make sure that pupils who are less confident in their athletic ability were involved in the activities?

Focus on the use of cameras and video to help in assessing these activities and the range of activities which require the use of different units in measurement. This activity shows how data handling can be used as a part of a cross-curricular project.

Assessing knowledge of statistics and handling data

It is important that the activities you use to assess data handling treat the data handling cycle holistically whilst allowing you to assess the component parts. Many of the activities that you have been introduced to in this chapter can be used as assessment activities. For example the activity presented earlier in the chapter can be used to assess children's abilities in classifying data and explaining the different choices available to them when sorting data. Most importantly it allows you to assess your pupils' ability to explain the choices they are making.

Similarly, the activity presented in the bar and line charts activity, if extended into an activity which compares this data with data collected about your class, allows you to assess learners' abilities across the data handling cycle.

Cross-curricular teaching of statistics and handling data

One of the most effective mathematics project I have worked on was setting up a healthy tuck shop for the school. In order to get the project off the ground we had to carry out a large-scale data handling activity. I asked the class to decide what information they would need to find out if we were setting up a healthy tuck shop. This included:

- What do we mean by a 'healthy' food?
- What healthy foods would you buy?
- How much would the children in school spend at a healthy tuck shop?
- Where would the best site for the healthy tuck shop be?
- When would be the best time to run the tuck shop?
- How much would it cost to buy the stock?

The children opted to join a group they were interested in and then carried out the research necessary to answer the question. They then had to present their findings to the school council as it had the final decision about funding the tuck shop. The research was a success – the tuck shop was funded and ran successfully for several years.

Summary

The main focus of this chapter has been the data handling cycle reproduced here:

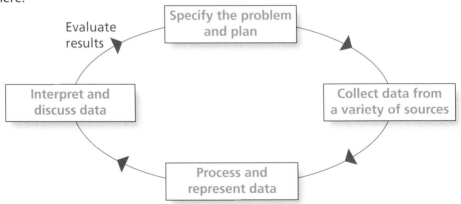

You should have a clearer understanding of each part of the cycle and how important it is to see the cycle as a whole, and that working with children to see the cycle as a whole is central to learning how to handle and interpret data.

You have seen the range of ways in which data can be represented, and been reminded of the ways in which the spread of data can be measured, such as mean, median, mode and range.

Reflections on this chapter

Statistics and data handling can be an exciting and motivating area to explore with the children you teach. It is also, arguably, one of the most important areas of mathematics in which to develop skills in order to be able to make sense of and understand the world around us as presented through the media.

I would hope that by gaining confidence in seeing the data handling as a process of posing questions, gathering data, which is then interpreted to answer those questions, and finally using this process to ask new questions, you will have become excited at the prospect of working through this cycle with your learners.

It is possibly the only area of mathematics that can be taught through a totally cross-curricular approach; indeed it can possibly only be taught in this way. Similarly, it is an area of mathematics that can be taught by drawing on the children's interests as a starting point.

Several years ago I was having a drink with a cousin of mine whom I don't see very often – out of the blue she asked me if she should stop taking the contraceptive pill. I was taken aback and asked why she wanted to know. She told me that she had read in the paper that being on the pill doubled her chance of getting thrombosis in her legs. I asked her to show me the article and was able to explain to her that even doubling the risk still meant that the risk of thrombosis was very small. I realised she had asked me because I was 'good at maths', in her words. She didn't feel confident in making important decisions based on her data handling skills. So, I would argue that teaching statistics and data handling is very important – enjoy it!

Going further

If the World Were a Village

DAVID SMITH AND SHELAGH ARMSTRONG

This invaluable resource allows you to work with your pupils on issues of global importance whilst introducing them to ways of representing and interpreting data. The book uses the construct of imagining the world was a village of 100 people to present data around issues such as access to electricity, the number of languages spoken globally and poverty.

Smith, D. and Armstrong, S. (2004) *If the World Were a Village: Imagine 100 people live in a village*. London: A & C Black.

Bad Science

BEN GOLDACRE

This is a great book to share with your older learners as it exposes how statistics can be used to make mistaken observations about science. It is based on Goldacre's *Guardian* column and is written in an entertaining and witty style.

Goldacre, B. (2009) *Bad Science*. London: Harper Perennial.

Data Handling

J MICHAEL SHAUGNESSY, JOAN GARFIELD and BRIAN GREER

These authors have contributed a chapter on data handling in the most recent *International Handbook of Mathematics Education*. This explores the historical role of data handling in mathematics curricula around the world and pays particular attention to the way in which ICT can support the learning and teaching of data handling.

Shaughnessy, J.M., Garfield, J. and Greer, B. (1996) in Bishop, A. (ed.) *The International Handbook of Mathematics Education*. Dordrecht: Kluwer Academic Publishers.

Self-audit

Gather some achievement data that you have on a class that you are teaching. This may be previous achievement on optional SATs, it may be results on reading ages – it can be any quantitative data. Decide what you want to find out from the data, such as comparing boys' and girls' achievements, or a particular subject area you have been focusing on, and write a list of questions. Use the data handling techniques you have met in this chapter to analyse the data. Make sure you use range, mean, median and mode, and comment on which of these measures is the most useful. Also use a range of ways of representing the data. Use your analysis to write a short report on the achievements of your class. Include this report in your portfolio.

CHAPTER 11

TEACHING AND LEARNING MATHEMATICS IN THE EARLY YEARS

Introduction

Millie came home from school the other night and sat at the kitchen table whilst I made a cup of tea. She fetched herself a pencil and a piece of paper and said to me, 'I'm just going to do my work.' After a couple of minutes I asked her what she was doing. 'I've got to finish off my sums,' she said. I looked at the paper and she was writing numbers and the equals, plus and minus signs randomly across the paper.

I was interested that at age five, Millie was describing this as 'doing work' rather than learning, and described anything to do with numbers as 'sums'. This chapter offers a broader view of mathematics in the early years and aims to illustrate how, by planning a wide range of mathematical experiences for your young learners, they will come to see how mathematics is embedded in many aspects of their day-to-day experience.

Starting point

Portfolio task 11.1

Explore this with a group of friends. One of you should read out this list of numbers one at a time. After each number is read out draw the images that you see or associate with the number.

8; 25; 6; 13; 100; 1 000 000

You will draw a range of images – discuss the reasons that lay behind your choice of image. These are often influenced by life experiences. So for example, people may see boxes of eggs for 6:

An egg box is a useful image. It means that as well as seeing 6 we see 6 as 2 × 3 or 3 × 2; we may also see 5 as an egg box with one missing, so we know that 6 − 1 = 5. I have seen schools beginning to use egg boxes with 10 'holes' to model counting to 10. Of course, two of these boxes takes us up to 20.

As the numbers get bigger we may have more abstract images, or images that don't help us relate to the size of a number. I often hear children referring to any big numbers as 'millions and trillions and millions' – this just really means 'big'. So children's early mathematical experiences are very important in providing them with images that they will carry with them as they grow.

When Harry was three we were sharing a book called *Window* by Jeannie Baker (available from Walker Books). This is a beautiful book consisting of drawings of the view through a window on each birthday of a child from age 1 to 20. In each picture the birthday card is displayed so that the numeral can be seen. As we flicked through the book Harry made no comment until we reached the child's 15th birthday. Harry looked at the card and said, 'I know that one – that's 15. Sam is 15.' Sam, my eldest, and at that time a hero of Harry's, had just had his 15th birthday. I remembered that he had asked me to show him 'how to write 15' when I told him that Sam was 15 years old. So even though Harry was not writing numbers in order he was recognising numbers that were important to him – and beginning to order and describe his world using numbers.

Similarly, my two sons were out with their grandad when they were very small and walking down our road. One of them started chanting 2, 4, 6, 8, 10, 12 until he reached our door and said, 'we live at 14'. We had, of course, at an early age made sure the boys knew their address in case they got lost. The other one picked up the chant using the houses on the other side of the road, counting 1, 3, 5, 7, 9, 11. Here we can use evidence of young children noticing pattern in number and using these patterns to describe and navigate their world. There has been some discussion in England about the readiness of young children to count to 20. We must be careful not to limit children to numbers that we feel are within their understanding. Many children live at house numbers larger than 20, have seen three-digit numbers on the fronts of buses and on car registration plates, may have a birthday on the 31st! They will see and use numbers larger than 10 in their everyday experience. We must make sure that we draw on this everyday experience rather than make a false dichotomy between 'school mathematics' and the kind of mathematics that all learners use to understand and interpret their everyday worlds.

Children know bus numbers, know how many brothers and sisters they have, know about sharing, may have a sense of money, a sense of size from very young. We cannot and should not assume that we are working with blank slates when we start exploring number or shape, or handling data with our young learners. They have been using mathematics since they were born – an exciting task is to discover how they are using their mathematics to understand and describe their world.

This chapter will explore how every child brings with them their own mathematical understanding and is capable of developing this understanding, with a 'teacher', who may be an early years practitioner, another adult, a parent or a friend.

The early years foundation stage

I think it is also worth reminding us all of the overarching principles on which the statutory framework for the early years foundation stage in England is based. These are principles which apply well to education at any age. And we should ask ourselves how we model these principles in the teaching of mathematics.

- Every child is a **unique child**, who is constantly learning and can be resilient, capable, confident and self-assured.

- Children learn to be strong and independent through positive relationships.
- Children learn and develop well in enabling environments, in which their experiences respond to their individual needs and there is a strong partnership between practitioners and parents and/or carers.
- Children develop and learn in different ways and at different rates.

TAKING IT FURTHER: **FROM THE RESEARCH**

In her article 'Handing control to 5-year-olds' published in September 2003, Cynthia Collins describes how she allowed her group of young learners to create their own rules for playing together when engaged in mathematical activities. The activity she describes allows her to explore children's personal, social and emotional development, as they negotiate their ways of playing and learning together, and at the same time support them in developing their mathematical understanding. She gave her group a box of felt tip pens and a pile of square pieces of card. She told the group she needed a new set of number cards for the number washing line in the classroom. One of the group decided to take charge and gave each of the group some cards – they then had to decide who would write which number. At first everyone started writing 1, 2 before realising this would mean they ran out of cards. Immediately one boy changed his cards to 11 and 12. The group then decided they had finished and laid the cards out in order. When they looked at the number line they had left a long gap between 7 and 11 and they realised there were numerals missing. They completed the task and called the teacher back over, satisfied that they had solved the problem. By leaving the children to the task they had drawn on their understandings and had engaged in the activity over an extended period. They had also very carefully and thoughtfully negotiated their roles within the group.

Problem solving, reasoning and numeracy

Early years practitioners and teachers of young children will develop young learners' mathematics through playful activities in a broad range of contexts to allow learners to explore, enjoy, learn, practise and talk about their developing understanding of mathematics. Young children's mathematical development occurs as they seek patterns, make connections and recognise relationships through finding out about and working with numbers and counting, with sorting and matching, and with shape, space and measures.

Another important role that a teacher plays is to support children in talking about the activities they are engaged in, allowing them to describe how they are solving problems and encouraging them to ask new questions about the areas they are exploring. A word that I often hear being used when teachers are talking about effective lessons is 'pace'. They will tell me that they were pleased with the pace of the lesson – they felt as though they covered a lot of ground. Early years practitioners may hold different view of effective mathematics teaching. They should aim to allow children sufficient time, space and encouragement to discover and use new words and mathematical ideas, concepts and language during child-initiated activities in their own play. So, don't be afraid to let children explore mathematics over extended periods of time – and try not to interrupt too early.

The sense of allowing children to explore and develop also applies to their jottings and notes. It is important to allow children to explore their own ways of recording their thinking. The opening of the chapter outlined the importance of the environment in supporting children's mathematical activity. Through carefully planning the environment, both indoor and outdoor, you can encourage the children to see and explore mathematics that is all around them. Using stories, games, songs and role play to develop young children's mathematical understanding is vital. So keep a lookout for as many books as you can which can support mathematical understanding.

Portfolio task 11.2

Choose one of the books that you enjoy sharing with young learners. Jot down some notes for your portfolio about the way you can use this book to develop children's mathematical skills and understanding.

Numbers as labels for counting

When we use the term 'numbers as labels for counting' we mean the cardinal numbers 1, 2, 3, 4, 5 and so on, rather than 'labels' such as bus numbers or house numbers.

Early skills in number that we would aim to teach at this stage are:

- saying and using number names in order in familiar contexts
- counting reliably up to 20 everyday objects
- recognising numbers 1 to 20.

Effective practice which would contribute towards children achieving these objectives would include encouraging children to create their own displays to record choices that the group makes – for example, preferences for school lunch, ways of travelling to school, birthdays. As mentioned earlier, you will bring counting into everyday practice through the books you are sharing and use a wide range of nursery rhymes and songs every day. These will include songs that involve counting back – for example,

Five green and speckled frogs,
Sat on a speckled log.

Eating the most delicious worms
YUM, YUM.
One jumped into the pool,
Where it was nice and cool.
Then there were four green speckled frogs
GLUG, GLUG.
Four green and speckled frogs…

Or

Ten fat sausages, sizzling in the pan,
Ten fat sausages, sizzling in the pan,
And if one went POP!
and the other went BANG!
There'll be eight fat sausages,
sizzling in the pan,
Eight fat sausages, sizzling in the pan.
And if one went POP!
and the other went BANG!…

If you are lucky enough to be working in a multicultural classroom make sure you ask the parents for counting songs and rhymes from their cultures to enrich your collection. It is worth spending more time on counting back than on counting on in planned activities. I would aim for a ratio of 2:1. That is twice as many counting-back activities as counting-on activities.

You will also make sure that you have number lines, number washing lines and 100 squares on display and number games available for children to play when they are able to choose their own activities. Chapter 4 expands these ideas in much more detail and should be read in conjunction with this section.

Calculating

The foundations for calculating will be laid if your young learners can:

- begin to use the language of addition and subtraction in practical activities and discussion
- use language such as 'more' and 'less' to compare numbers
- find one more or one less than a number
- use objects to add or subtract small quantities seeing additions as combining groups and subtractions as 'taking away'
- begin to use the language of doubling and halving and sharing using objects which they can split into equal groups.

Effective practice in developing calculating skills would involve posing questions as you read stories – 'How many friends will be left when one gets off the bus?', as well as using everyday events in the setting to pose questions – 'How many girls are here today?' Encourage children to record what they are telling you, allowing them to record in their own way and talking about the choices they are making. Use number lines and make use of number lines physically, allowing children actually to jump forward and backwards on a number line.

Chapter 4 details the progression in 'counting' as children move through the early years into the primary. If you work through this chapter it will help you understand how counting skills develop as children move through the primary years.

TAKING IT FURTHER: **FROM THE RESEARCH**

Ian Thompson, currently a visiting professor at Edge Hill University, has edited one of the most useful books about teaching early number. Published by the Open University Press and now in its third edition, *Teaching and Learning Early Number* is an accessible guide to recent research exploring how young children begin to make sense of counting and the number system. The book explores developing mathematics through play, assessment of early mathematical knowledge through interviewing children, children's early recording of number activities as well as detailing recent research on the complex process of learning how to count. For example the different ways in which children make errors in counting out loud are examined. These include continuing with a count in order but omitting numbers, or repeating numbers and then recounting from that number. The authors show how using puppets to count with the children can encourage children to recognize and correct their mistakes.

Shape, space and measures

In the early years you will develop children's understanding of shape, space and measure if your learners are able to:

- use language such as 'greater', 'smaller', 'heavier' or 'lighter' to compare quantities
- talk about, recognise and re-create simple number patterns
- explore the characteristics of everyday objects and shapes and use mathematical vocabulary to talk about them
- use everyday words to describe position such as 'in front of' and 'behind' or 'above' and 'below'.

You can achieve this through practical activity. Make sure that the children have access to a range of 2D and 3D shapes. Try to avoid the commercially produced sets that only include regular shapes. If the only triangle a child ever sees is equilateral they will notice the regularity rather than the fact that a shape with three straight sides and three corners is a triangle. Don't forget that all these shapes are triangles (see overleaf).

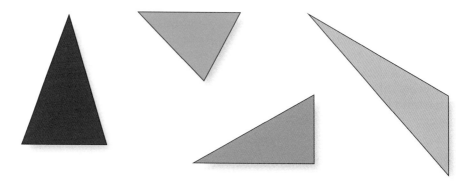

Use building blocks and large boxes and cartons and whilst they are engaged in building and making you can introduce names of the shapes and model the language of comparison by asking which is the biggest cuboid or the smallest cube. Bring a range of shapes and solids into the role-play areas that you construct, talking with the children about the shapes as you construct the role-play areas and as you join in the children's role-play. Observe the use of the role-play areas carefully to see how children use the resources you have provided; this will help you decide which role-play settings are richest for mathematical activity. When you go out for walks, or are playing outside, use positional language: Who is at the end of the line? Who is behind Tony? Who is in front of Emma? Who is next to Tom?

One way that you can support your young learners in becoming mathematical is by developing a more mathematical view of the world yourself. Go for a walk around the school – notice all the different shapes that you can see. You will come across shapes that you don't know the name off. Take a photograph or sketch the shape and find out what it is called when you get back to your computer.

TAKING IT FURTHER: **FROM THE RESEARCH**

The book *Mathematics with Reason* edited by Sue Atkinson is subtitled *The emergent approach to primary maths*. This is a book which, although research based, is structured around teachers and early years practitioners, describing the ways that young children learn in their classrooms and settings. You'll read about children planning a picnic, making maps and designing natural wildlife areas. The PROBLEMS acronym, first introduced by the Open University, is widely used to analyse the process through which these young learners are encouraged to solve problems:

- Pose the problem.
- Refine the problem into areas for investigation.
- Outline the questions we need to ask.
- Bring the data home.
- Look for solutions.
- Establish recommendations.

- Make it happen – put the solution into action and test it out.
- So what next? Start the process again.

Sue Atkinson also describes the importance of supporting young learners in developing their own, intuitive methods for solving problems. The following extract shows the joy that working to support children in developing their own understandings can bring:

> *Unlocking children's own intuitive methods is one of the most thrilling things in teaching. It's like that magic moment when a small child rushes up to you, her face glowing with pleasure and tells you she can read. When those special moments come you can stand back and watch the child race off, powered with her own understanding.*

I hope this section has offered a clear view of the sorts of mathematical activity which may be seen in an early years setting. The most important point to emphasise is that this should all be taking place through talk and activity. The subject knowledge that you need here is the ability to find the mathematics in the everyday – and the confidence to draw out the mathematics all day, every day.

Assessment in the early years

Effective assessment in the early years is an analysis and review of children's learning in order to make informed decisions about what you will plan to meet their next learning needs. This is the basis of assessment for learning: you are not assessing simply to find out what a young learner can do, you are observing their skills and understandings so that you can decide what you do next. There is a range of things you might look out for. Some practitioners choose to keep notes in a journalists' notebook during the day; you will see some practitioners using sticky notes and photographs so that they can reflect at the end of the day on children's individual progress and the next steps in learning they should provide. The following sections provide you areas to focus on when you are assessing your learners' current understandings in order to plan for their next stage of development.

Numbers as labels for counting

As you sing number songs and rhymes with actions with the children make a note of their responses. Observe how confident the children are with their actions. Do they initiate the actions or are they following their friends without understanding what the meanings of the actions are?

When you count with children using displays observe whether the children point at the numbers on the display and name them accurately and see what range of numbers they refer to.

You will be estimating small numbers of objects and should note down how accurate their estimates of numbers of things are. Similarly, when you use the language of comparison on a day-to-day basis you can note when children begin to use the language of first, second, and third. You could also make a note of how the children refer to numbers they use in everyday life – house number, number of brothers, and so on.

When carrying out counting activities with the children you can take note of their developing skills in this area. At what stage do they understand the one-to-one principle; the stable order principle; when do they realise that the last number in a count always gives the total? (See Chapter 4.)

Calculating

As you observe and engage the children in activities involving calculating you can look for how accurately children share things out between them. See if the children share accurately and make a note of how they go about sharing.

Observe the children to see if they know whether or not the sharing has been fair by noticing that groups of objects have the same number or different numbers of objects in them.

You can pose questions whenever you have planned a 'sorting' activity. See if the children work out how many more or less there are in some groups and notice how the children respond if you combine two groups and ask them how many altogether. Alternatively, if you remove objects from a group, what forms of records are they developing to record your actions?

Shape, space and measure

At an early stage you will be noticing how the children respond to shape sorting games and the language they use to describe shapes. Listen to their vocabulary when describing the properties of shapes. You will want to listen out for language such as 'bigger' and 'smaller' or 'heavier' and 'lighter', or 'in front' and 'behind', as well as simple shape properties and names.

Make a note when children start noticing shapes in the environment or responding to you, pointing out shapes around the classroom. You can also observe the children working on practical activities such as modelling or wrapping presents, to see if they are estimating sensible amounts of materials.

You can talk about where the children live, in order to see if the children can describe the routes they have taken to and from school, getting them to draw very simple maps.

Don't see any of the questions above as 'testing' the children – you can pose these questions, engage the children in the activities I have described and observe how they respond. As children become more familiar with the activities and as they hear their teachers and friends model more complex mathematical vocabulary, you will notice the children develop their understandings.

These are examples of activities which are rich in assessment opportunities – the first will help you explore children's understanding of counting.

- Create a set of 'lily pads', numbered 1–20, that the children can stand on.
- Then ask the children to put them in order so that you can 'play a game'.

It is very often mathematically worthwhile for the children to help you prepare for an activity. You can notice how the children order the lily pads:

- Who takes control?
- Who decides on the correct order?

Then ask the children to start on 1 and hop on the lily pads until they reach 15 or start on 12 and hop back to 2. For some children you could ask them to hop in 2s and others could count out loud the numbers they land on. You can also create 'number frogs' – these are frogs with numbers on them that children have to match to the correct lily pad. Alternatively, children can make their own number frogs.

This activity allows you to assess children's developing understanding of shape, space and measure. Provide the children with a large collection of newspapers, sticky tape, paper, modelling straws, pipe cleaners – the wider the range of resources, the better. Initially, talk about all the different sorts of houses the children can think of. Ask the children which houses are 'big', 'small' and 'medium sized'. Try to get children to explain how they are making the decisions about which category to place a house in. Give the group three different animals. Their task is to make a house for each of the animals. This assessment task relies on the teacher observing the process very carefully. It may be appropriate to use a digital camera to record the activities the children are involved in. Make sure you ask probing questions like:

How do you know that will be big enough?

How could you check the animal will fit?

How big is that house?

Which house is the biggest?

Observing teaching in the early years

The video clip available on the companion website describes how a school in Birmingham introduced personalised learning programmes for their learners in the early years in order to transform the view of mathematics for all learners in the primary school. As well as offering lots of starting points for teaching this extended clip gives you a clear sense of what effective mathematics teaching in the early years might look like. The reflective discussions between the practitioners will help you understand the reasons for the developments they are making.

Watch the clip and then make notes in your portfolio about the following questions:

- What are the implications for your teaching in the later years?
- What are the key things that primary classrooms should learn from early years practice?

Summary

This chapter has outlined how problem solving and reasoning underpins numeracy learning in the early years. It has also emphasised how your teaching should engage the young learners in games, songs and active learning through which their understandings of number and shape and space will emerge. The importance of playful activity for mathematics learning is revisited on several occasions.

There are suggestions for the early and developing skills that you should focus on at this stage and a range of foci for assessment are offered. There is a clear emphasis on assessment for learning; that is your assessment is made to inform your plans for the next stages in learning for individual learners.

Reflections on this chapter

I hope that the chapter has shown how mathematics in an early years setting can appear as natural and everyday as all the other activities across the other areas of learning for the children. The curriculum and activities that you can plan and provide should engage and challenge the children – and hopefully you will enjoy engaging with the children. Children are developing their sense of identity as they work with you – if part of that identity can be that they see themselves as successful in mathematics and able to tackle mathematical problems, you will have succeeded as their first mathematics teacher.

Going further

Mathematics Through Play in the Early Years

KATE TUCKER

This book offers lots of advice and practical activities for those of you working in early years settings. It is really helpful for all teachers as the activities are easily adapted for learners at all stages and learning through play is important across the primary school. There are chapters which explore creative ways of recording children's learning, suggestions of how to involve parents and case studies which will support you in developing your own individualised approach to mathematics teaching.

Tucker, K. (2010) *Mathematics through Play in the Early Years*. London: Sage.

Thinking and Learning about Mathematics in the Early Years

LINDA POUND

This draws on the research about young children's mathematics development to support teachers in finding ways to plan for playful and engaging mathematics. There is particularly useful advice on ways to link mathematics to everyday situations and ways to plan for cross-curricular activity.

Pound, L. (2008) *Thinking and Learning about Mathematics in the Early Years*. London: Routledge.

The Little Book of Maths Outdoors

TERRY GOULD

This very practical book supports all early years practitioners in developing their ideas for mathematics in the outdoors. It is vital that children see mathematics all around them and that they are not limited to learning mathematics on a mathematics table, or in a numeracy corner. This book has been well received by early years practitioners and will be helpful for all of you wanting to plan activities for your learners in outdoor spaces.

Gould, T. (2011) *The Little Book of Maths Outdoors*. London: Featherstone.

CHAPTER 12
ISSUES OF INCLUSION

Introduction

During the year that I was working on the third edition of this book I was also supporting the son of a friend of mine with his GCSE mathematics. He has Asperger's syndrome and this has led to him missing large parts of his schooling and being placed in special units for substantial amounts of his time at school. Unsurprisingly, his mock examination results suggested that he was unlikely to gain the 'C' that is necessary to progress into higher education as many colleges and universities now require grade 'C' or equivalent for a place on any course.

After a short intensive period of tutoring John achieved a grade 'D' – a great achievement as he gained 'just about zero' in his mock examination. However Leeds College of Music who had offered him a place on a music production course withdrew the offer, which was a huge disappointment. I know that together we will work so that he will achieve the 'C' – I also know that he will be incredibly successful in his music career. The whole episode has reminded me though of the huge influence that learning and teaching mathematics has and the particular struggles that young people with special learning needs face.

Understanding and becoming successful in mathematics can have a huge influence on individual life chances. None of you would have been able to gain places on teacher education courses without achieving a 'C' in GCSE mathematics.

In 2014 the think tank Demos showed that whilst 64.8% of pupils not on school meals achieved five A*–C grades in their GCSEs including maths and English, this percentage for pupils on free school meals shrank to 38.1%. They have coined the term 'achievement gap' for this difference.

The 'Ambitious about autism' webpage suggests that the equivalent statistic for students with autism is 26%. So the achievement gap here is even wider. This shows that success in mathematics, and the access to improved life chances that this success offers, is not equally distributed.

This chapter explores issues of inclusion – it aims to offer you support in helping all your learners to achieve their potential in mathematics.

Starting point

In 1997 Mike Askew, Margaret Brown, Dylan William and colleagues from King's College in London explored the links between teachers' practices, beliefs and knowledge and pupil learning outcomes in mathematics. They interviewed and observed 90 teachers and 2000 pupils. The full results are available in the book *Effective Teachers of Numeracy: Report of a study carried out for the Teacher Training Agency* (King's College).

In this book the authors identified three sets of beliefs which they suggested were important when understanding the impact of teacher beliefs on effective teaching of numeracy. These were:

1 Connectionist: a connectionist teacher values pupils' methods and teaching strategies with an emphasis on establishing connections within mathematics. This means that learners are able to see the links between the different areas of mathematics they are engaged with and can see the 'big picture' rather than view mathematics as a set of separate skills to be learnt in isolation from each other.

2 Transmission: a teacher with these beliefs sees mathematics as a collection of separate routines and procedures to be taught to pupils.

3 Discovery: these teachers see themselves as facilitators of learning and see mathematics as an area to be discovered by pupils.

You will recognise these terms from the audit questionnaire you completed in Chapter 2. The research showed that teachers with a strong connectionist view were most effective in terms of pupils making progress in their learning of mathematics.

A key belief for connectionist teachers is that 'most pupils are able to become numerate'. This means that they believe that all pupils are able to move forward in their mathematics learning. The challenge for teachers is to find the most effective ways for pupils to learn mathematics.

This chapter explores the ways in which you can adapt and develop your practice to include all children in your class, whatever their learning needs are.

Chapter 3 opened with this number square:

1	3	5	7	...
2	6	10	14	...
4	12	20	28	...
8	24	40	56	...
...	....	...	... ...	

I posed the questions 'What patterns can you see?' and 'Will 1000 appear?' I have used this activity with learners aged 10–70, with primary school pupils, secondary school pupils and degree-level mathematicians. Some groups of pupils focus on exploring patterns; the simplest patterns here are odd and even numbers, series of numbers that increase by 2, by 4, by 8, and so on. Another group noticed that the numbers in the first column are powers of 2 ($2^2 = 4$, $2^3 = 8$, and so on). Older learners used algebra to explore the patterns in the square and academic mathematicians came up with a proof that showed all numbers would appear once and only once.

As a teacher exploring ways of teaching for inclusion through mathematics, a key skill you will need to develop is the ability to plan activities that are accessible to the range of learners in your class. However, as well as offering accessibility, these activities need to offer challenge too.

Another activity I have introduced you to previously in Chapter 10 has engaged a wide range of pupils. If you remember I asked the children to try to think about the relationship between the distance around their head and their height and come up with some conjectures. I always ask learners to work in all attainment groups for this activity and I will explore the outcomes in a little more detail here. The children measure each other's height and the circumference of their heads to create a scatter graph using initials rather than dots so that each child can see themselves in the data. A scatter graph is a graph of plotted points which shows the relationship between two sets of data. For this activity, distance round head was measured on one axis and height on the other.

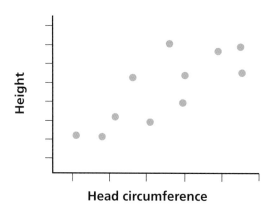

Head circumference

Different groups will interpret the graph in different ways. Some find the 'line of best fit'. The line of best fit is the line that can be drawn on a scatter graph which is the best approximate to all the points on the graph. If you have drawn it accurately the total distance of all the points from the line should be the same for points on each side of the line.

Some children used calculators and individual measurements to see if there was a pattern; some looked at boys and girls in the data to see if there were generalisations that could be made. But the whole class was engaged in exploring the data. At the end of the activity the teacher turned to me and said, 'That was interesting. The weaker mathematicians were the most successful.' In this class the teacher usually grouped her children by prior achievement in mathematics tests. These tests were usually number based. The teacher had noticed that for this activity prior achievement in a 'number' test did not predict how well an individual would engage with ideas if data handling and problem solving.

In an inclusive classroom all learners will be achieving to the best of their ability; and different learners may well excel in different areas of mathematics rather than individuals attaching labels of 'good at mathematics' to themselves. A key lesson for me here was how important it is to vary the groupings we operate with in schools. When I visit my students in schools many still operate with fixed groups for mathematics sessions. They may start a session by asking children to get into their 'numeracy groups'. If we never vary the groups that our children learn mathematics in we limit the range of their peers that they can learn from, and we also limit the possibility for children to excel in different areas of mathematics as they quickly come to understand they are in the 'bottom group' for mathematics and put limits on their own understanding.

This became clear one day when I was sitting with a group in a Year 2 classroom. One boy in the group said to me, 'Can you do all of your times-tables?' I told him I could, so he said, 'You need to go and sit with the blue group – they're the cleverest and we won't know our tables until next year.'

TAKING IT FURTHER: **FROM THE RESEARCH**

Professor Jo Boaler, whom you have met in previous chapters, has researched the impact of setting by ability (actually setting by prior attainment) in English schools for many years. She suggests that this practice means that many learners spend much of their time in school being given low-level and uninteresting activities. Many of these children are capable of achieving more if they were given appropriate learning activities.

In interviews she carried out she was moved by the pleas of learners in low groups who said that they just wanted to learn but were constantly given activities that they did not feel stretched them. She notes that some people believe the practice is right because it keeps the high achievers away from low achievers. However, her research shows that high achievers do not do any better in high sets than in mixed ability groups, and for some students, being in a high set is a source of considerable anxiety. She also shows us that comparisons of test performance in different countries always show that countries that set students the least and latest have the highest performance.

The reasons for this are obvious: once students are told that they are low achieving and given low-level work, their learning diminishes.

Her conclusion is that a mixed ability, multi-dimensional approach means that success is an option for all learners.

Jo has launched the organisation 'youcubed' as a result of this research and her work in the US. You can find this at the website www.youcubed.org. Their mission states that,

> All students can learn mathematics to high levels and teaching that is based upon this principle dramatically increases students' mathematics achievement. The need to make research widely available is particularly pressing now as new science on the brain and learning is giving important insights into mathematics learning.

If you follow this belief you will be working to close the achievement gap.

The rest of this chapter focuses on ways in which teachers can meet the specific needs of particular groups of learners who may currently be under-achieving in mathematics.

Children with special educational needs

It is important to remember that there will not necessarily be a correlation between children you teach who are identified as having a special educational need and their ability at mathematics. For example, a child in your class who is dyslexic may be a high achiever in mathematics or may achieve less well. There is often no direct correlation between a special educational need and attainment in mathematics. However, there are steps you can take that ensure you are giving all children the best possible chance to achieve their potential. It is vital that you become aware of the impact of an individual child's specific need and use this to support your planning.

The main implications for your planning are ensuring that activities are accessible for all learners so they can find a way to get into the activity, whilst ensuring the activities offer sufficient challenge for all pupils.

This might mean that you have to adapt resources that have previously been used to teach a particular idea.

For example, I have seen a group of children who are learning about 'adding money to 10p' set the following set of questions:

Copy and complete these number sentences

$2p + \_\_ = 10p$ $9p + \_\_ = 10p$

$4p + \_\_ = 10p$ $5p + \_\_ = 10p$

$7p + \_\_ = 10p$ $1p + \_\_ = 10p$

This very closed activity was accessible to children who already had the necessary skills but several of the children in the class found it hard to make a start on the activity. Similarly, those children who understood the task found it very easy and completed the activity without being challenged. An alternative to this is for the teacher to ask, 'How many different ways can you make 10p?', providing learners with 1p, 2p, 5p and 10p coins. Try this activity for yourself and you will see that it offers accessibility and flexibility.

If you plan the structure of your lessons carefully you can maximise the possibility of all your learners progressing in their learning. For example, in the sections of the lesson which focus on discussion led by the teacher it will help to plan questions specifically for pupils achieving below expected levels. By careful targeting of questions rather than asking for 'hands up' you can draw all pupils into the activity. This also allows you to focus on and develop key vocabulary. You may choose to sit these children close to you, or to use teaching assistants to work with them in oral sessions. Another good way to involve all pupils in oral sessions is through 'talk partners'. You can set up 'talk partners' and place those children who are achieving below expected levels with peers who are achieving well. Using paired discussions will support both sets of learners.

Careful thought about the resources you can use will also support your learners with specific learning needs. Flash cards and illustrated wall displays will support all learners in developing appropriate vocabulary. The use of number lines, 100 squares and other number apparatus will also support children in developing mental images of the ways in which the number system works.

There will be children you will meet in your career who have been identified as having specific learning needs. There are suggestions below as to how you may support these particular groups of learners. Don't forget, however, that most of these ideas will improve the learning experience for all your learners.

Children with emotional and behavioural difficulties

'EBD' stands for emotional behavioural disorder (often referred to as 'emotional and behavioural difficulties') and refers to a condition in which the behaviour or the emotional response of children is so different from the rest of your class that it impacts on the child's learning. This may take the form of disruptive, antisocial or aggressive behaviour; poor peer relationships; or hyperactivity, attention and concentration problems.

You may find that unstructured, open-ended tasks can exacerbate behavioural difficulties. If children are uncertain how to start an activity, or are unclear what your expectations of success are, they may avoid starting the activity in case they 'go wrong'. It may help to provide a clear structure and set time-specific targets. Try to be consistent in your routines, in particular the cycle of demonstration, modelling and summarising is very important for this group of learners. Giving children responsibility and involving them in demonstrations by bringing them to the front can support them in developing positive behaviour patterns. Also aim to avoid interrogational questioning as this may lead the learners to feel humiliated and this is a common cause of inappropriate behaviour; this is where using talk partners can help. Make sure you offer this group of learners challenge – they will soon realise if you are offering them low-level tasks, and this can lead to inappropriate behaviour too.

Children with autism

The National Autistic Society, on its website **www.nas.org.uk/autism**, describe autism as follows:

> *Autism is a lifelong developmental disability. It is part of the autism spectrum and is sometimes referred to as an autism spectrum disorder, or an ASD. The word 'spectrum' is used because, while all people with autism share three main areas of difficulty, their condition will affect them in very different ways. Some are able to live relatively 'everyday' lives; others will require a lifetime of specialist support.*

The three main areas of difficulty which all people with autism share are sometimes known as the 'triad of impairments'. They are:

- difficulty with social communication
- difficulty with social interaction
- difficulty with social imagination.

These are described in more detail below.

It can be hard to create awareness of autism as people with the condition do not 'look' disabled: parents of children with autism often say that other people simply think their child is naughty; while adults find that they are misunderstood. All people with autism can benefit from a timely diagnosis and access to appropriate services and support. (Visit **www.autism.org.uk** for further information.)

You need to be careful when setting up group or pair work as this can be problematic for some children on the autistic spectrum. It is important not to avoid group and pair work but you need to make sure that routines are followed consistently, in particular routines for moving into groups or pairs. For example, always sitting in the same pair on the carpet will help. Classroom transitions are another point of the lesson that can cause difficulties for children with autism. Plan for these transitions carefully, be very clear about how the transition will be managed and keep them calm and orderly – if you just send groups back to their tables without instructions this will prove difficult for children with autism. If they become overwhelmed by noise and movement they should be allowed to go to a quiet, calm place for a while. (So, it is important to have such a space in your classroom.)

Using familiar equipment also supports these children in their learning as novelty has little appeal. Extensive use of metaphor can also cause difficulty as children with autism are likely to interpret what you say literally. Making time to observe the children to check their understanding is important. Using picture sequences to break down activities into manageable tasks can also support progression. Finally, allowing a child to 'fiddle' with their fingers or small objects can help with concentration and focus.

Recent films and stories in the media seem to suggest that many people on the autistic spectrum can calculate huge numbers in their heads and have photographic memories. Unfortunately such stories give the false impression that all children with autism have these special skills. Most people on the spectrum do not have any special talents for mathematics. However it can be true that children on the autistic spectrum will exhibit keen interests in particular subjects, and so may know a great deal about very specific areas.

The following suggestions for children with dyspraxia will also prove helpful for children on the autistic spectrum.

Children with dyspraxia

Dyspraxia is thought to affect up to 10% of the population. It is an impairment in a child's development in terms of the way the brain processes information to help us organise our movements. It affects the way that we plan what we are going to do and how we do it. Dyspraxia can lead to difficulties in terms of perception, language and thought.

Avoid giving a series of instructions for a task as this may well confuse a child with dyspraxia. This will mean that you may have to differentiate, giving some groups more complex instructions whilst breaking the instructions down for others. Giving 'thinking time' is useful for children with dyspraxia – saying, 'In 30 seconds I will ask you to tell me three number pairs that sum to 100' for example. Using individual whiteboards to rehearse answers will also support these children.

Children with dyslexia

Dyslexia is a specific learning difficulty that mainly affects reading and spelling. Dyslexia is characterised by difficulties in processing word sounds and by weaknesses in short-term verbal memory and its effects may be seen in spoken language as well as written language. The current evidence suggests that these difficulties arise from inefficiencies in language processing areas in the left hemisphere of the brain which, in turn, appear to be linked to genetic differences.

You should avoid asking a child with dyslexia to read questions aloud unless you are sure they will be comfortable doing this. By checking individual needs you will know what specific support your dyslexic learners may need. It may be that coloured filters will support them in reading text, or printing on a particular colour of paper. Being able to use highlighters to pick out key words is an important skill for all pupils and will support dyslexic learners across all subjects.

Providing visualisation activities will help dyslexic learners – indeed they may excel in this area and be able to support other children in becoming more skilled at visualisation.

Children with dyscalculia

Dyscalculia describes children who have specific difficulties in carrying out calculations as a result of damage to specific regions of the brain. Recent research suggests that dyscalculia can also occur developmentally, as a genetically linked learning disability which affects a person's ability to understand, remember or manipulate numbers or number facts. The term is often used to refer specifically to the inability to perform arithmetic operations, but it is also seen as leading to a specific difficulty in conceptualising numbers as abstract concepts. This may be described as having 'number sense'.

Ways that you can support learners with dyscalculia include providing a wide range of concrete manipulatives to help understanding to develop before moving into the abstract concepts. This will also assist in providing learners with strategies to visualise. When working on problem solving or word problems, try to provide opportunities to use real-life situations or items to assist with visualisation.

It can also help to provide opportunities to use 'pictures, words or graphs' to help with understanding. Make sure you promote a 'can do' attitude as much as possible; praise and a positive outlook can start to overcome the fear of mathematics that learners with dyscalculia may have developed.

Children who are gifted and talented

Identifying a learner who is gifted and talented in terms of mathematics does not mean identifying those learners who are achieving very highly in tests. Gifted and talented learners may often be those children who take on leadership roles in group work, who show high-level practical skills or can see creative solutions to complex problems. The following are characteristics that gifted and talented children may exhibit. They may

- be very articulate
- offer quick verbal responses
- communicate well with adults
- show unusual responses to problem-solving activities
- be able to work things out in their head quickly
- have a good memory
- be easily bored
- show a strong sense of leadership.

So it is important in planning your lessons that you work to the strengths of these learners. Create opportunities for them to articulate their thoughts; this may be best in small-group work so they don't dominate whole class sessions. You may occasionally want to work in 'achievement' groups so that these learners can challenge each other, but it is also important that these learners articulate their thoughts with a wide range of pupils. Through describing their own thinking to their peers they will come to understand their thinking processes better.

Similarly, plan activities which demand quick verbal responses and offer leadership roles to this group of learners. Most importantly, watch out for signs of boredom and always have open, extension activities ready.

One website which will help you add stretch and challenge to your classroom is the NRICH site: **http://nrich.maths.org**. This site is coordinated by Cambridge University and offers a wide range of activities and free resources for teachers. For example, in October 2012 the theme for the month was 'Playing with numbers' and the site offered activities such as this one:

Zios and Zepts
On the planet Vuv there are two sorts of creatures.
The Zios have 3 legs and the Zepts have 7 legs.
The great planetary explorer Nico counted 52 legs.
How many Zios and how many Zepts were there?

These activities can be carried out interactively on-screen too.

TAKING IT FURTHER: **FROM THE RESEARCH**

In 1999, Keith Jones and Hannah Simons from Southampton University carried out an independent evaluation of the use of the online NRICH materials. They discovered that over two-thirds of the users of the site were boys and that a large number used the site at home.

This suggests that teachers were not using the site regularly as a part of their own teaching and were not making sure that girls had access to the materials.

The main impact on pupils of using the site was that they gained a wider appreciation of mathematics and began to view mathematics as an interesting subject which they might enjoy studying outside the classroom.

The interactive nature of the site was seen as a particular advantage. This research is available from the University of Southampton in a booklet entitled *Online mathematics enrichment: An evaluation of the NRICH project*.

Here is another NRICH problem to have a go at.

I am decorating 20 biscuits for my daughter's party. I line them up and put:

- icing on every second biscuit
- a cherry on every third biscuit
- chocolate on every fourth biscuit.

How many biscuits have no decoration on them? How many have icing, a cherry and chocolate?

If I ice 50 biscuits how many will have all three decorations on them?

Make notes in your portfolio about your thinking whilst you solved this problem. How do you think it would 'stretch' your high-attaining learners?

Multicultural and anti-racist approaches

The mathematics that we teach in schools is not value or culture free. Multicultural and anti-racist practice does not assume that any other practice is overtly racist, rather it acknowledges that the historical and social context in which our current system of schooling has developed may advantage some groups over others. It also takes the view that these systems can be challenged in order to ensure access to mathematics learning for all learners.

Values and cultural beliefs are embedded in:

- the content of the curriculum that we offer to pupils
- the ways in which we teach that content
- the environment in which children learn mathematics
- the view of mathematics we bring to the classroom as teachers
- the ways that we measure success in our mathematics classrooms.

So a multicultural and anti-racist approach to mathematics teaching would:

- Include content that develops pupils' understanding of cultures other than their own through reflecting on cultural and linguistic diversity.
- Use resources that draw on pupils' cultural heritage, counter or challenge bias in materials such as textbooks or draw on pupils' own experience.
- Present positive images of learners as mathematicians and use familiar contexts as starting points, as well as illustrating the diverse cultural heritage of the discipline of mathematics. This may include photographs of your

current learners being successful in mathematics, or may be people from the communities you draw your pupils from who are successful in mathematics.

- Use teaching strategies that both develop pupil confidence with mathematical language and develop positive attitudes towards linguistic diversity. Children here will see linguistic diversity as a benefit to the classroom and would expect to hear a range of languages in the classroom.
- Encourage collaborative teaching and learning which offers challenge to the pupils, encourage learners to express and examine their own views, encourage learners to become involved in their own learning, encourage learners to pose their own problems.
- Develop anti-racist attitudes through mathematics by using data that critiques stereotyped views of particular groups of people. So for example looking at images in newspapers and carrying out a data handling activity may well show the images that newspapers present of minority ethnic groups in a small number of roles, as sportspeople, or as underprivileged. It is interesting to contrast these images with those found in newspapers such as *The Voice* or *The Asian Times*.
- Monitor achievement and grouping by ethnicity to ensure equal access to the curriculum.

This set of bullet points can be seen as a series of prompts for planning. It accepts the need for the numeracy strategy to form the basis for planning but offers a way in which key questions can inform the planning so that values of multiculturalism and anti-racism pervade the planning.

An activity which would support this view of teaching and learning uses a 100 square in a range of scripts or languages to develop children's understanding of place value and the Hindu–Arabic number system. (The Hindu–Arabic number system is the system widely used in European schools; it is also called the decimal number system or sometimes the European system. This system has developed from combining the Hindu and Arabic representations of number.)

In this activity give groups of children 100 squares in a range of scripts which you have previously cut up to form a jigsaw. They have to reconstruct the 100 square – this will draw on and develop their understanding of the 100 square they are used to working with as they explore it with a new set of eyes.

১	২	৩	৪	৫	৬	৭	৮	৯	১০
১১	১২	১৩	১৪	১৫	১৬	১৭	১৮	১৯	২০
২১	২২	২৩	২৪	২৫	২৬	২৭	২৮	২৯	৩০
৩১	৩২	৩৩	৩৪	৩৫	৩৬	৩৭	৩৮	৩৯	৪০
৪১	৪২	৪৩	৪৪	৪৫	৪৬	৪৭	৪৮	৪৯	৫০
৫১	৫২	৫৩	৫৪	৫৫	৫৬	৫৭	৫৮	৫৯	৬০
৬১	৬২	৬৩	৬৪	৬৫	৬৬	৬৭	৬৮	৬৯	৭০
৭১	৭২	৭৩	৭৪	৭৫	৭৬	৭৭	৭৮	৭৯	৮০
৮১	৮২	৮৩	৮৪	৮৫	৮৬	৮৭	৮৮	৮৯	৯০
৯১	৯২	৯৩	৯৪	৯৫	৯৬	৯৭	৯৮	৯৯	১০০

Children with English as an Additional Language (EAL)

In January 2004, 21 local authorities piloted a programme designed by the Department for Education (then the Department for Education and Science) aimed at raising the achievement of bilingual learners in primary schools as this group of learners were not achieving as well as the rest of the population. The project involved each authority receiving the funding to appoint an EAL consultant to work in participating primary schools to support them in developing the curriculum better to support bilingual learners. Whilst this project resulted in improving the achievement in English there were no significant gains in mathematics or science. In an evaluation reported by Tom Benton and Kerensa White in 2007, 'Raising achievement of bilingual learners in schools', it was suggested that this may have been because initial interventions were not as consistent in mathematics lessons as in English lessons. This means that teachers may not support EAL learners in developing their linguistic skills in mathematics sessions as much as they would in English sessions.

Schools which are effective in supporting bilingual learners realise that these learners enhance our classrooms. The pupils bring a wealth of experience to the classroom which offers a wide range of starting points for exploring mathematics. As I have mentioned for other groups with particular needs, the advice on how best to support bilingual learners will also benefit all the learners in your class.

Try to encourage learners in your class to use mathematical language in a wide range of different contexts: some familiar, such as counting up the school dinners, talking about how many children are away; and some new, so whenever you introduce new ideas in any subject try to explore these ideas mathematically. Bilingual learners may need to listen to mathematical language to allow both mathematical and language development. This means that discussion becomes very important. This allows learners both to hear and use mathematical language. To support this discussion use visual resources and engage in practical activities too. Bilingual learners should also be encouraged to develop fluency in their home language through mathematics by engaging in discussions with teaching assistants or peers who share their language.

Observing inclusive mathematics teaching

The video clip available at **www.teachfind.com/teachers-tv/special-needs-inclusion** and on the companion website shows how a piece of IT called a visualiser is used to support deaf children in a mathematics lesson. This allows a teacher to film their demonstration and record or add text to the piece of video. This particular clip shows the equipment being used in a secondary school to demonstrate the construction of bisectors of angles. Watch the clip and then reflect on the following question in your portfolio.

What could you use the 'visualisor' for in your classroom? Can you think of a lesson you have taught recently which would have been enhanced by the use of a visualisor?

Summary

This chapter took as its starting point the importance of supporting all learners in becoming as good at mathematics as possible. This is vital in order to maximise their life choices. Through drawing on a range of research studies and advice from organisations with the interests of children with specific learning needs at heart, you have learnt about a wide range of strategies you can use to support the learners in your class. The key areas I have focused on have been children with specific learning needs, children who have particular gifts in mathematics and children from minority ethnic groups, all of whom may not reach their potential if we do not adapt the way that we plan and teach.

Reflections on this chapter

As you read this chapter you may well have realised that most of the suggestions for changes and adaptations to mathematics teaching would benefit all learners in your classroom. By focusing on the needs of specific groups of children that you teach, you begin to plan for individual needs. And by doing this all learners will become more engaged in the mathematics you are teaching.

Going further

Mathematics for Dyslexics (including Dyscalculia)

STEVE CHINN

Now in its third edition, as well as outlining the difficulties that learners with dyslexia or dyscalculia may have in the classroom it offers suggestions for you to support these pupils in overcoming these difficulties. The mixture of theory in the first part of the book together with practical examples in the second half of the book should help you in developing your practice to be more inclusive.

Chinn, S. and Ashcroft, R. (eds) (2006) *Mathematics for Dyslexics (including Dyscalculia)*. London: Wiley-Blackwell.

Overcoming Difficulties with Number: Supporting dyscalculia and students who struggle with maths

RONIT BIRD

This practical book offers teaching plans for pupils aged 9–16 who have dyscalculia. The focus is on practical activities, visualisation and building self-esteem. A resource bank including games and other activities is provided on an accompanying CD.

Bird, R. (2009) *Overcoming Difficulties with Number: Supporting dyscalculia and students who struggle with maths.* London: Sage Publishing.

Inclusive Mathematics 11–18 (special needs in ordinary schools)

MIKE OLLERTON AND ANNE WATSON

This book is written by two innovative and very experienced teachers and shares the approaches that they have used to raise student achievement and opportunity with a specific focus on learners with special educational needs.

Ollerton, M. and Watson, A. (2005) *Inclusive Mathematics 11–18.* London: Continuum Press.

CHAPTER 13

ICT AND THE USE OF CALCULATORS IN TEACHING AND LEARNING MATHEMATICS

Introduction

As a teacher in the twenty-first century it is vital that you can use your skills in ICT to support your teaching and that you are able to design opportunities for learners to develop their own ICT skills. It is an area that I have seen many students excel in. It is also an area in which you will notice your own learning progress, from the first time you try to write on an interactive whiteboard and can't make anything legible, to gaining confidence in working with a range of technologies.

This chapter takes an overview of ICT describing how we can best select from the wealth of software available to make sure we are genuinely designing opportunities for learners to develop their skills rather than just filling time working at a computer. The chapter also discusses how you can use calculators to support children's learning, drawing on the research around the use of calculators in primary schools. The view that I take towards calculator use is described in more detail below.

Starting point

Many years ago I was asked to write a 'comment' piece for *Micromath*, the journal of the Association of Teachers of Mathematics, which focuses on the use of technology to support the teaching and learning of mathematics. As

I was writing the article David Blunkett, the then Minister for Education, had made a statement that suggested children should not be 'encouraged' to use calculators until they were eight years old. But after another change in minister for education it was seen as important that children in foundation stage had calculators available to support their role-play areas, especially if these are shops or cafés and such like.

However, the worry that calculators somehow 'inhibit' the learning of mathematics persists to the extent that the current programmes of study in England contain the following sentences.

> *Calculators should not be used as a substitute for good written and mental arithmetic. They should therefore only be introduced near the end of key stage 2 to support pupils' conceptual understanding and exploration of more complex number problems, if written and mental arithmetic are secure.*

Interestingly this is the only part of the programmes of study which offer pedagogical advice. Whilst we would all agree that calculators should not be used as a substitute for good written and mental arithmetic it does not follow that they should not be introduced until key stage 2. In fact the research evidence – particularly that associated with the Calculator Aware Number (CAN) project – shows that pupils who have had free access to calculators from Year 1 and have followed a calculator aware curriculum are 'more liable to compute mentally and adopt powerful mental strategies' than pupils who have not had access to calculators until key stage 2. This research is discussed in more detail later in the chapter.

As a result of this evidence I would argue that teachers in primary schools and early years settings should have calculators available all the time for the children they teach, whatever their age. A teacher's role is to teach their learners how to use calculators effectively, and to notice when they are useful. For example, if you are teaching multiplication by 10 you can give children a range of numbers and ask them to multiply these by 10 using a calculator and write down what they notice. Try it for yourself with these numbers:

14
157
13.8
2051
18.7
483.1
15.85
72.876
95 231

By exploring multiplication by 10 in this way the learners themselves will realise that you don't 'add a nought' when multiplying by 10. This is a commonly held misconception.

Suggesting that calculators should not be available is a bit like suggesting that children shouldn't be able to use a ruler as it might stop them estimating lengths. Calculators are just one of the tools of the trade for mathematicians – our job is to teach children how to use them well.

Fortunately the use of computers to support learning has not been seen in the same way. Teachers I speak to, although some may lack confidence in their own technical abilities, usually speak positively about the impact that interactive computer software can have on supporting children's learning. In fact, on occasions, I think that computers are overused in the classroom. This chapter explores the use of calculators and computers to support the teaching and learning of mathematics. In both cases the focus is on the effective, efficient and appropriate use of these powerful tools.

Progression in using calculators

The role for a teacher in developing effective and efficient use of calculators in their classroom would include:

- Teach children how to use the calculator effectively so they can decide when it is appropriate to use a calculator and when mental methods would be quicker and more efficient.
- Use calculators when the focus is on solving a problem rather than the process of calculation.
- Use the calculator as a tool to support children in exploring number patterns.
- Consolidate children's learning of number facts and calculation strategies.

This can be developed into the following progression sequence for developing children's calculator use:

Foundations in using calculators

Initially children may well see calculators at home or in out-of-school contexts. It is important that these are replicated in school. Provide a calculator in any role-play environment where it is sensible or realistic to have one. This allows young learners to use calculators to support their creative play and to begin to explore how the keys on a calculator operate. Young children also enjoy using calculators to display numbers that are familiar to them, such as their age, or their house number.

Beginning to use calculators

When children are learning to read and write numbers up to 20 they can use calculators to illustrate two-digit numbers – and keying in these numbers can support them in their early understanding of place value. A six-year-old child wanted to use a calculator to show me 17 (their brother's age) and asked me how to 'spell seventeen'. We looked at the possibilities – 17 or 71 – and then by looking at a number line agreed it should be 17. I have also worked with six- and seven-year-old children to explore adding and subtracting 10 using a calculator. So for example I would write

19

13

18

11

16

and ask the children to use a calculator to subtract 10 from each number and ask them to tell me what they notice.

As children are asked to learn the 2, 5 and 10 times-tables it is useful to show children how to use the constant function on a calculator to notice the patterns that are formed in the times-tables. (If you don't know how the constant function on your calculator works, read the handbook – if you haven't got a calculator, buy one!)

An activity that uses a calculator to support the development of mental skills is shown below:

5	9	3	8	2	12	9	19	15	5

Draw the number track on your whiteboard and ask your pupils to work in pairs with one calculator between them. The aim is to move from one box to the next using a calculator so that the calculator display shows the appropriate number after an operation and a number have been keyed in. The pupils take it in turns and in this way will keep a check on each other.

Developing the use of calculators

As pupils come to understand partitioning a calculator game that can support them is to ask one pupil to write a three- or four-digit number on a piece of scrap paper, say 3582. Their partner then has to remove the digits from the display one at a time using the calculator. So one way to do this would be

$$3582 \ - \ 3000 \ = \ 582$$
$$582 \ - \ 500 \ = \ 82$$
$$82 \ - \ 80 \ = \ 2$$
$$2 \ - \ 2 \ = \ 0$$

You can add challenges to this game. Change the order in which the digits must be eliminated, ban the use of particular keys, try to eliminate two numbers at once. I promise you that the children in your class will very quickly come up with interesting and challenging rules for the game.

At this stage children can be introduced to the following calculator skills and learn how to:

- clear the display before starting a calculation
- correct mistakes using the clear entry (CE) key
- carry out one- and two-step calculations involving all four operations
- interpret the display correctly, particularly in the context of money
- recognise negative numbers on the display.

The most appropriate way to focus on these skills is to provide problem-solving situations which will require children to develop these skills. Some teachers use self-assessment such as 'I can' statements so that their learners can notice for themselves when they develop these core skills.

As learners become more confident in their mathematics I would be expecting them to use the calculator for the following:

- Estimating the likely size of answers and checking calculations. I often stop children pressing the = button on the calculator and ask them to estimate the answer – they are then very excited if they are proved correct by the calculator.
- Carrying out measurement calculations and interpreting the answer. For example, if I add 1m 35cm to 2m 15cm I will get 2m 50cm, but the calculator will show 2.5 rather than 2.50.
- Solving problems involving fractions – to do this pupils will need to recognise decimal equivalents of fractions. This in itself is a useful exercise to carry out using a calculator.

Portfolio task 13.1

Write the following fractions as decimals by using a calculator.

3/4   1/2   4/5   1/4   1/5   2/10   7/10

For example, if you want to find 3/5 as a decimal you key in 3 ÷ 5 = .

You should see 0.6.

Convert 1/5, 2/5, 3/5, 4/5, 5/5 to decimals.

Do the same with

1/4, 2/2, 3/5, 4/4, 5/5, 6/10, 7/10, 8/10, 9/10, 10/10

What do you notice about your answers to 'fifths' and tenths'?

Now explore all the other fractions from 1/3s to 1/12s.

Describe the patterns you are seeing.

Can you see how this activity helped develop a sense of the value of fractions, and would have been impossible without the use of calculators?

Extending the use of calculators

Your most confident pupils should be able to use a calculator to:

- solve multi-step problems.
- recognise recurring decimals. If you try to change 1/3 into a decimal using a calculator you will get 0.33333333; similarly, sevenths and ninths give recurring decimals.

TAKING IT FURTHER: **FROM THE CLASSROOM**

A calculator-aware curriculum

Between 1986 and 1989 a research project called the Calculator Aware Number (CAN) project took place. Initially the project was based in 15 schools but by the end of the process hundreds of schools had enrolled. Perhaps more importantly, all the schools which started the project, led by Hilary Shuard from Homerton College, Cambridge University, remained with it to the end.

The philosophy of CAN was that 'Children should be allowed to use calculators in the same way that adults use them: at their own choice, whenever they wish to do so.' The key principles that underpinned this philosophy were:

- Children should always have a calculator available and the choice to use it should be the child's not the teacher's.
- Traditional paper and pencil methods for the four operations will not be taught.
- There should be a teacher emphasis on practical investigational and cross-curricular mathematics.
- Children should engage in mathematical activities which involve a range of apparatus.
- Teachers should support learners in developing confidence in talking about numbers using precise mathematical language.

- Mental methods should be emphasised and sharing children's mental methods encouraged.
- Teaching and learning 'number' should occupy less than 50% of the time spent teaching and learning mathematics.

Research carried out into the long-term impact of the CAN project was reported by Kenneth Ruthven in *Research Papers in Education* 12 (3), 1997, in the paper 'The long term influence of a calculator aware number curriculum on pupils' attitudes and attainments in the primary phase'. This study compared the attitude and attainment of pupils in post-project schools matched with non-project schools. This used national tests at ages 7 and 11 to compare attainments. The study found that more pupils attained at high levels in post-project schools than in non-project schools at age seven, but this was also the case for low attainment. This suggests that there had been a greater differentiation of attainment in post-project schools than non-project schools. Teachers in post-project schools thought that this may be the result of their not offering enough support and structure to lower attaining pupils carrying out open, unstructured activities.

Interestingly, by age 11 there were no differences in post-project and non-project schools in terms of either attainment or enjoyment. That's to say, both groups of pupils did equally well in tests and when asked if they enjoyed mathematics the responses were the same whichever group the pupils belonged to.

The appropriate use of computers

When I visit schools I am excited by the number of schools which have facilities for using interactive software to support the teaching and learning of mathematics. However, I am also concerned sometimes when I see how the technology is used and find myself asking the question: 'Is this software enhancing the learning of mathematics or is it simply replacing practices that might be more appropriately carried out by teachers?'

I had been observing an engaging lesson exploring a group of Year 2 children's understanding of time. They had been discussing times that they knew – the time they got up, the time they left for school, the time they went to bed, the time their mum got in from work, and so on. They had recorded these times on clocks, both analogue and digital, and this had led to some complex discussions about how to record times and why the big hand tends not to be where you would expect it to be. The lesson continued as we moved into the IT suite: the children all showed considerable skill in quickly logging on and finding the appropriate program. This asked multiple choice questions requiring them to attach the correct written time to the time on the clock. The room fell silent as the children took it in turns to answer the questions. I noticed two strategies to get the correct answer: try each answer in turn until you got affirmation from the machine, or ask your friend. All discussion had stopped and as I asked children how they were applying their prior knowledge they suggested that wasn't the point. The idea was to get as many answers correct as they could in as short a time as possible. For me, what had been a lesson which drew the children into exploring and developing their own understandings of telling the time had become a very traditional mathematics lesson focused around routine and practice and for which the main motivation was not learning mathematics but finishing the exercise.

So, how can we measure the effectiveness of a piece of software? There are some key criteria I use with my teacher education students to analyse the effectiveness of a range of resources from number lines to coat hangers. You may find it useful to apply these criteria to any ICT you use as a learning and teaching resource.

The first question I ask is: 'To what extent does the resource provide an image or a representation of the mathematical idea you wish to teach?' In other words, does it model the mathematics that you are asking the children to engage with?

An example of this that is seen in classrooms around the country would be the number line. This models the 'big idea' of place value as well as supporting children in developing mental strategies for carrying out calculations. One example would be a zoom number line. Here the traditional number line has been developed to create a zoom number line. This number line allows the teacher to define the central number of the line and to alter the scale.

This capability of zooming in and out of a number line offers a view of the number system that is only available using ICT. It also meets the criteria of representing the number system and modelling the mathematics of place value. More than this, it allows us to begin discussions about such ideas as rational and irrational numbers. A rational number is one that can be placed exactly on a number line, an irrational number, such as pi, is a recurring decimal and we do not know exactly where it is on the number line. We can also see that no matter how far we zoom in on the number line, there will always be another 'zoom' to be made. We can talk about infinity with primary mathematicians – and they love it.

The second question is: 'To what extent does the resource encourage learners to describe what they are doing?'

An example of this in everyday classroom practice is the teacher asking children 'how have you worked that out?' as a normal part of their teaching. Of course, a resource cannot force learners to describe what they are thinking, only good teaching can do this – however, a program which can be used to support learners thinking 'out loud' is a good place to start. There are many pieces of software often called 'number boards' which randomly generate boards of numbers according to criteria set by the teacher.

Once the class have explored one 'number board' the software can then immediately create another grid which allows children to repeat processes in a way which is not available without using ICT. Learners can be encouraged by the teacher to describe why they are making decisions at each step, or other learners can be asked to give instructions to the learner at the interactive whiteboard – of course justifying why they are asking them to make a particular move.

The final question I ask is: 'To what extent is the resource able to offer a range of representations of the same mathematical idea?'

Those of you that use Excel or similar programs to support the study of statistics and data handling know that these programs can enhance the learning by allowing teacher and learner to move between different representations of the same data. They also allow pupils to compare quickly the representations and decide which they think most effectively represents the data. They have not had to invest time and effort on drawing the different representations and so will be happy to decide that a bar chart is more useful than a pie chart. If they had spent time drawing a pie chart it would have been difficult to motivate the same children to draw a bar chart in order to decide which is the most appropriate representation.

It is always exciting to see young learners motivated and excited by their developing understandings of mathematics. ICT has a vital role to play in supporting their learning and showing them that mathematics is something they can do and something that has an internal logic which they can explore and ask questions of. My aim here is to suggest that an important role for the teacher is to ensure that the software we use when working with our learners genuinely enhances their learning. Who knows? You may even find yourself waking up in the middle of the night with some mathematical questions.

Summary

This chapter has illustrated how calculators and computers can be effective tools for teaching and learning mathematics. I have aimed to give you the confidence to encourage children to use calculators at all stages of their learning. Using the guidance from the National Strategy I have illustrated how calculators can be used progressively to develop mathematical skills appropriate to the age of learners so that they can develop both appropriate mathematical skills and appropriate calculator skills. In this way you have seen how the calculator is both a tool for learning mathematics and a tool for carrying out mathematics. Finally, by drawing on a radical piece of curriculum development, I hope I have convinced you that using calculators in the classroom is not harmful to children's mathematical development.

To support you in using appropriate software to support your teaching and to enhance your pupils' learning I raised questions which aim to help you in deciding which particular pieces of software will be useful.

Reflections on this chapter

Mark kept coming up to my desk and swapping a ruler that he was using for a new one. After he had repeated this four or five times – I was an over-patient teacher sometimes – I asked him what he was doing. He told me that he was trying to find a ruler that worked. I was confused so I asked him what he meant.

He said that he was measuring a line and he knew the answer was 8cm but all of these rulers kept giving him '8 and a bit'. When I went over to see what he was doing, he was using the end of the ruler as his starting point rather than the '0'. Once I had shown him this he didn't see the need to keep changing rulers!

It strikes me that those who suggest that calculators might inhibit children's learning of mental methods or slow down their learning of written calculation are trying to solve Mark's problem by taking away the ruler rather than showing him how to use it. A calculator cannot inhibit children's learning – the way that we teach children how to use it can, but then that is within our control. I hope that this chapter has offered you a way to view calculators and computers as powerful mathematical tools that we are in control of and maybe even encouraged you to get your old calculator out of your bag and explore how you can best use it both to teach your learners and to carry out mathematics yourself.

Going further

ICT and Primary Mathematics

JENNI WAY and TONI BEARDON

The arguments made in this chapter about the value of using calculators in the primary classroom are expanded in this book. The chapters are written as case studies which describe how teachers have developed powerful learning experiences for their learners through the imaginative use of a range of digital technologies. There are lots of practical ideas for you to try out in your classrooms.

Way, J. and Beardon, T. (2003) *ICT and Primary Mathematics*. London: Open University Press.

ICT and Primary Mathematics (A Teacher's Guide)

NICK EASINGWOOD and JOHN WILLIAMS

This covers similar ground. It is more practically focused with sections covering the use of databases and spreadsheets. It includes teaching using LOGO and the floor turtle and advice on using an interactive whiteboard.

Easingwood, N. and Williams, J. (2004) *ICT and Primary Mathematics: A teacher's guide*. London: Routledge.

GLOSSARY

2D: Two-dimensional. Describes a shape that has length and width, but not depth. 2D shapes move so that we can see them in any orientation.

3D: Three-dimensional. Describes a shape that has length, width and depth. 3D shapes can roll, slide, build and balance.

acute angle: An angle less than 90°.

algorithm: Finite sequence of instructions. An explicit, step-by-step procedure for solving a problem, often used for calculation.

area: The amount of space a shape takes up. Measured in units such as square millimetres, square centimetres or square kilometres, written mm², cm² or km².

array: A set of numbers or objects arranged in order, often in rows and columns.

axes: Reference lines that cross at right angles; used to locate points by their coordinates.

bar chart: Diagram that uses bars or rectangles to represent discrete data.

bi-modal: Data that contains two values that are equally common.

block graph: Diagram similar to a bar chart, in which each block represents one item of data.

cardinal number: Whole number that tells us how many there are in a set of objects. Cardinal numbers can be written as words (one, two, three…) or using numerical symbols (1, 2, 3…).

Carroll diagram: Diagram used to represent data in a tabular, yes/no format.

centre of rotation: Point about which an object rotates.

closed shape: Shape whose sides all join together.

common multiple: Multiple that is shared by two or more numbers. So a common multiple of 3 and 6 is 12, as 3 and 6 are both factors of 12.

concave shape: Shape that has at least one interior angle greater than 180°.

congruent shapes: Two shapes that will fit perfectly on top of each other.

continuous data: Data that has an infinite number of possible values, such as heights, weights and time.

convex shape: Shape whose interior angles are all less than 180°.

coordinates: Pair of numbers such as (2, 3) or (21, 4), used to define or locate a point by reference to a pair of axes.

counting on: Technique for performing simple calculations (addition, subtraction) by reference to a number line.

cube: A 3D shape with all its faces squares.

cuboid: A 3D shape with all its faces rectangles.

decimal notation: System used to express numbers and parts of numbers as multiples and sub-multiples of 10.

degree of rotational symmetry: The amount by which a shape with rotational symmetry must be turned for it to look the same as before.

denominator: The lower part of a fraction, representing the number of parts into which the whole has been divided. For example, the denominator of 5/7 is 7.

directed number: Number with a plus or minus sign attached, to show whether it is a positive or negative number. So +7 means 'positive' 7 and −3 means 'negative' 3.

discrete data: Data that can be counted.

edge: The boundary line of a 2D shape, or the straight line where two faces of a 3D shape meet.

equivalent fractions: Fractions with the same value, such as 6/8 and 3/4, or 70/100 and 7/10.

faces: The flat regions of a 3D shape.

factors: The various numbers that divide exactly into a given number. For example, the factors of 12 are 1, 2, 3, 4, 6 and 12.

frequency: The number of times a particular value occurs.

frequency table: Used to record observations of frequencies.

generalise: To make a statement that is true about a wide range of cases.

improper fraction: Fraction with its numerator larger than or equal to its denominator, such as 7/4 or 4/3.

inequality: Statement showing which number is greater or less than another.

integer: Number that has no decimal or fractional part; sometimes called a whole number. Can be either positive or negative. Integers should not be confused with natural numbers.

inverse operations: Arithmetical operations that are the opposite of each other, such as multiplication and division.

irregular shape: Shape with sides and angles that are different lengths and sizes.

line graph: Diagram used to represent continuous data.

line of symmetry: Line about which a shape with reflective symmetry can be folded so that the two halves fit exactly on top of each other.

mass: The amount of substance in an object. Not to be confused with its weight, which is the strength of the gravitational pull on the object – that is, how heavy it is.

mean: Average value, calculated by adding up all the different items of data and dividing by the total number of items.

median: The middle value of a set of data when all the data is arranged in order.

mirror lines: When an image is reflected in a mirror line each point in the image is exactly the same distance from the mirror line as the corresponding point on the original object.

mixed number: A number that contains both a whole number and a fraction, such as 3 3/4.

mode: The value that occurs most frequently in a set of data.

multiples: Numbers that can be divided by another number without any remainder. For example 24 is a multiple of 6 and 21 is a multiple of 3.

natural number: A positive integer, such as 1, 2, 3, 4.

net: Two-dimensional shape that can be folded to make a three-dimensional shape.

numerator: The upper part of a fraction, representing the number of parts of the whole that have been taken.

oblong: A rectangle that isn't a square.

obtuse angle: An angle between 90° and 180°.

open shape: Shape that has a gap between two corners.

operation: The four operations are addition, subtraction, multiplication and division.

order of rotational symmetry: The number of times a shape with rotational symmetry is repeated before it makes a complete 360° turn.

ordinal number: Number used to indicate position, such as 1st, 2nd, 3rd.

origin: Point at which coordinate axes cross.

parallel lines: Two lines that are always the same distance apart and will never meet, no matter how far you extend them.

parallelogram: Quadrilateral with opposite sides parallel.

partitioning: Splitting a number to enable you to carry out a calculation mentally: so, for example, 24 = 2 tens and 4 ones = 20 + 4.

perfect square: The square of a whole number. For example, 36 is a perfect square as it is 6×6 or 6^2.

perimeter: The distance all the way round the outside edge of a shape; measured in mm, cm or km, for example.

perpendicular: Describes the relationship between two objects – such as lines or surface – that meet at right angles (90°) to each other.

perpendicular lines: Two lines at 90° to each other.

pictogram: Diagram that uses pictures of objects to represent discrete data.

polygon: Any shape with straight edges.

prime factor: Factor of a number that is also a prime number

prime number: Number with only two factors: itself and 1.

prism: Solid object with two identical ends and all flat sides.

probability: The likelihood of an event occurring.

probability scale: Numerical scale from 0 to 1, or from 0% to 100%, used to measure probability.

proportion: Proportion compares a part to the whole. For example there are 10 boys in a class of 25, so 10/25 or, by cancelling, 2/5 of the class are boys. We would say that 2 out of 5 of the people on the trip were boys.

pyramid: Solid object with a base that is a polygon, and with sides that meet at the top.

quadrant: Any one of the four equal areas created by dividing a 2D area up using two perpendicular axes.

range: A measure of the spread of a set of data.

ratio: A ratio compares part to part. We use a phrase like 'to every' or 'for every'. So for example there are 10 boys to 15 girls, so the ratio is 10:15.

ratio notation: Used to express the proportional relationship of one value to another as two numbers: for example, 30:100.

rectangle: Any quadrilateral with four sides.

rectilinear shape: Shape that can be split up into a series of rectangles.

reflection: Transformation of a shape about a mirror line.

reflective symmetry: The property of a shape that can be folded in half so that the two halves fit exactly on top of each other.

reflex angle: Angle greater than 180°.

regular polygon: Polygon with all sides the same length and all angles between the sides the same; any other sort of polygon is irregular.

regular shape: Shape with all sides the same length and all interior angles the same size.

rhombus: Quadrilateral with four equal sides.

right-angled triangle: Triangle in which two of the sides join at a right angle.

rotation: Transformation of a shape about a centre of rotation.

rotational symmetry: Property of a shape that looks the same after it has been rotated through less than 360°.

rounding: Reducing the number of digits in a number but keeping its value roughly the same.

similar shapes: Shapes that are not congruent, but whose sides are all in the same ratio.

specialising: Looking at specific examples in order to get started on a problem.

square: Quadrilateral with four equal sides and four right angles.

square number: The result of multiplying (squaring) a number by itself.

square root: Number that produces a required number when multiplied by itself (squared).

standard units: Units that are in common usage, such as metres, litres or kilograms, and all the derived (related) units.

surface area: Total area of all faces of a 3D shape.

symmetry: The property of a shape that is made up of identical parts facing each other or when rotated round an axis.

tally chart: Diagram that uses sets of ticks of hash marks to represent discrete data.

transformation: Process of moving a shape on a grid, by translation, reflection or rotation.

translation: Transformation of a shape that alters its position, but leaves its dimensions and orientation unchanged.

uniform non-standard units:
Quantities that are uniform in size
(e.g. multilink cubes or wooden
blocks), and are used to measure
something, but are not part of a
standard system such as the metric
system of units.

Venn diagram: Diagram that uses
overlapping shapes (usually circles or
ellipses) to show the relationships
between groups of things that share
something in common.

vertex: Point at which two or more
edges meet.

vertically opposite angles: Angles
made where two lines cross. They
have the same value.

INDEX

Also available:

Teaching for Mathematical Understanding

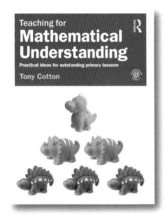

Teaching for Mathematical Understanding develops the subject knowledge support and practical ideas from Tony Cotton's *Understanding and Teaching Primary Mathematics* into resources for full lessons. With an emphasis on developing outstanding lessons using a problem-solving approach, this highly practical guide is packed with activities that all trainee and practising teachers can use in the primary classroom.

Covering each area of mathematics, every activity offers helpful step-by-step guidance, including teaching and learning objectives; resources; lesson outlines; ideas for differentiation; assessment for learning and key probing questions. Also featured in this text are call-outs to the information contained on the book's companion website, a shared site with a range of relevant resources to support and consolidate your learning.

Teaching for Mathematical Understanding is an essential text for all trainee and practising teachers looking for inspiration and guidance towards outstanding mathematics teaching.

What the experts are saying about the book:

Teaching for Mathematical Understanding *uses a consistent approach to all mathematics teaching, and is not simply offering 'problem-solving lessons'. Teachers, both serving and training, can use the tasks and adapt them for a broad range of learners. I recommend this volume as the tasks cover all aspects of the mathematics curriculum.*

> **Ray Huntley**, Lecturer in Primary Education, Brunel University London, UK

This book has an emphasis on developing deep subject knowledge through a range of creative ways with problem solving being at the heart of its approach. Trainee and practising teachers will be able to use this book as a guide to secure their understanding of key mathematical concepts and teach them to their pupils in a creative way.

> **Nasreen Majid**, Lecturer in Primary Mathematics, University of Reading, UK

PB ISBN: 978-1-138-90634-1
HB ISBN: 978-1-138-90633-4
eISBN: 978-1-315-69555-6